FEMINISM AND METHODOLOGY

FEMINISM
AND
METHODOLOGY

Social Science Issues

EDITED WITH AN INTRODUCTION BY
SANDRA HARDING

INDIANA UNIVERSITY PRESS
Bloomington and Indianapolis

 OPEN UNIVERSITY PRESS
Milton Keynes

Published jointly by

Indiana University Press
Tenth and Morton Streets
Bloomington, Indiana 47405

and

Open University Press
Open University Educational Enterprises Limited
12 Cofferidge Close
Stony Stratford
Milton Keynes MKll lBY

Manufactured in the United States of America

Library of Congress Cataloging-in-Publication Data
Feminism and methodology.
Includes bibliographical references and index.
1. Social sciences. 2. Feminism. 3. Women social
scientists. I. Harding, Sandra G.
H61.F38   1987   300   86–43050
ISBN   0–253–32243–X
ISBN   0–253–20444–5 (pbk.)
6 7 8 9   96 95 94 93

British Library Cataloguing-in-Publication Data
Feminism and methodology: social science issues.
1. Social sciences—Methodology
I. Harding, Sandra, 1935–
300'.1'8   H61
ISBN   0–335–15561–8
ISBN   0–335–15560–X Pbk

CONTENTS

PREFACE

Is there a unique feminist method of inquiry? If so, what is it? If not, how should one describe what it is that is responsible for the many startling challenges to established beliefs in psychology, sociology, economics, political science, anthropology, and history? New students find these issues perplexing. For seasoned scholars, much that we learned as graduate students about the history of scientific method and about how to pursue knowledge appears to be thrown into doubt by the new research on women and gender. This volume is intended to provide an introduction to the methodological issues but also to contribute to the discussions among seasoned researchers.[1]

My approach to this project is to invite the reader to consider just what has been responsible for producing the most widely acclaimed feminist social analyses. While several of the essays reprinted here do focus on methodological issues, that was not one of the requirements the essays had to meet in order to be included. Many discussions of feminist research methods do not provide good introductions to these issues. Some are too abstract; others assume a familiarity with the depth and breadth of the new research which is inappropriate for introducing these topics. More importantly, these discussions tend to represent only one type of feminist approach to research methods and issues of methodology: researchers who do not think their methods unusual do not bother to draw the reader's attention to them (beyond the usual brief report of what they actually did). The explicit discussions tend to focus only on what the author takes to be an alternative to familiar methods of research.

A closer examination of the full range of feminist social analyses reveals that often it is not exactly alternative methods that are responsible for what is significant about this research. Instead, we can see in this work alternative origins of problematics, explanatory hypotheses and evidence, alternative purposes of inquiry, and a new prescription for the appropriate relationship between the inquirer and her/his subject of inquiry. One can think of these as part of the "method of feminist inquiry," but to do so conflates research methods, methodologies, and epistemologies, as I shall point out in the introductory essay. The corollary to this point is that, as I hinted above, these essays on novel methods also draw our attention away from the fact that by any sense of method which would be uncontroversial in a social science "methods course," it is familiar and uncontroversial research methods that have been used to produce some of the most important of the new feminist analyses. Thus I intend that the papers in this collection demonstrate a wide range of feminist theoretical approaches and research methods—a range that can serve as a test case for any claim to have identified *the* feminist research method (or methods). The introduction discusses what *is* unusual about these analyses, and the concluding essay provides an overview of the epistemological issues that are often intertwined with methodological ones.

No doubt every social scientist will think of a favorite analysis that is missing from this collection. Each paper was selected because it fulfilled several requirements. Each was responsible for creating an important new feminist understanding about social science and social life. Each has stood the test of time—it is still cited as an up-to-date and first-rate analysis of the problem it addresses.[2] In each case, the paper's argument is interesting and understandable to young students. (Of course, some are more accessible than others.) Additionally, in the ten essays collectively I have tried to include as broad a representation as possible along several dimensions. The social science disciplines represented here include psychology, sociology, economics, history, political theory, and jurisprudence—and in some cases, several subfields of each. Moreover, in selecting from each discipline I have made sure to include only essays in which the author's point has implications for the ways issues about women and gender are addressed in several social sciences. Thus, the arguments in the essays reprinted here also have important implications for the many fields and subfields of social science not represented by selections. Diverse feminist theoretical and methodological approaches are represented: the reader will find liberal feminists, Marxist feminists, socialist feminists, radical feminists, black feminists, and various combinations and permutations of these.[3] A variety of modes of evidence gathering are also represented.

A number of friends have provided me with helpful critical comments on either the entire project or on the editorial essays. I thank especially Margaret Andersen, Donna Haraway, Nancy Hartsock, Barrie Thorne, Gerald Turkel, and Kathleen Turkel.

NOTES

1. Of course feminists have also raised methodological and epistemological issues about the natural sciences. A number of monographs and collections take up the issues there. See, for instance, my *The Science Question in Feminism* (Ithaca, N. Y.: Cornell University Press, 1986); Sandra Harding and Merrill Hintikka, eds., *Discovering Reality: Feminist Perspectives on Epistemology, Metaphysics, Methodology and Philosophy of Science* (Dordrecht, Holland: D. Reidel Publishing Co., 1983); and Jean O'Barr and Sandra Harding, eds., *Sex and Scientific Inquiry* (Chicago: University of Chicago Press, 1987).

2. It seems odd to speak of passing the test of time for such recent analyses as these: the earliest was published in 1971 and three appeared in the early 1980s. However, the shape of new research fields tends to be set relatively quickly, and feminist research on women and gender has proved to be no exception to this rule—at least *in the respects represented in this collection.*

3. For discussion of the differences between these, see Alison Jaggar and Paula Rothenberg, eds., *Feminist Frameworks: Alternative Theoretical Accounts of the Relations between Women and Men*, 2nd ed. (New York: McGraw-Hill, 1984); and Alison Jaggar's more extended analysis in *Feminist Politics and Human Nature*, (Totowa, N.J.: Rowman & Allenheld, 1983).

ACKNOWLEDGMENTS

Sandra Harding, "Introduction: Is There a Feminist Method?" and "Conclusion: Epistemological Questions." © 1987 by Sandra Harding.

Joan Kelly-Gadol, "The Social Relation of the Sexes: Methodological Implications of Women's History," is reprinted from *Signs: Journal of Women in Culture and Society*, vol. 1, no. 4, 1976, by permission of University of Chicago Press. © 1976 by The University of Chicago. All rights reserved.

Marcia Millman and Rosabeth Moss Kanter, "Introduction," is reprinted from *Another Voice: Feminist Perspectives on Social Life and Social Science*, published by Doubleday Anchor Books. Copyright © 1975 by *Sociological Inquiry*.

Carolyn Wood Sherif, "Bias in Psychology," is reprinted from Julia A. Sherman and Evelyn Torton Beck, eds. *The Prism of Sex: Essays in the Sociology of Knowledge* (Madison: University of Wisconsin Press, 1979). Copyright © 1979, The Board of Regents of the University of Wisconsin System.

Carol Gilligan, "Woman's Place in Man's Life Cycle," is reprinted from the *Harvard Educational Review*, 1979, 49:4, 431–46. Copyright © 1979 by President and Fellows of Harvard College. All rights reserved.

Joyce A. Ladner, introduction to *Tomorrow's Tomorrow: The Black Woman*, is reprinted by permission of Doubleday & Company, Inc. Copyright © 1971 by Joyce A. Ladner.

Dorothy E. Smith, "Women's Perspective as a Radical Critique of Sociology," is reprinted from *Sociological Inquiry*, vol. 44, no. 1, 1974, pp. 7–13, by permission of the author and the University of Texas Press.

Bonnie Thornton Dill, "The Dialectics of Black Womanhood," is reprinted from *Signs: Journal of Women in Culture and Society*, vol. 4, no. 3, 1979, by permission of author and publisher. © 1979 by The University of Chicago.

Heidi I. Hartmann, "The Family as the Locus of Gender, Class, and Political Struggle: The Example of Housework," is reprinted from *Signs: Journal of Women in Culture and Society*, vol. 6, no. 3, 1981, by permission of author and publisher. © 1981 by The University of Chicago.

Catharine A. MacKinnon, "Feminism, Marxism, Method, and the State: Toward Feminist Jurisprudence," is reprinted from *Signs: Journal of Women in Culture and Society*, vol. 8, no. 4, 1983, by permission of author and publisher. © 1983 by The University of Chicago.

Nancy C. M. Hartsock, "The Feminist Standpoint: Developing the Ground for a Specifically Feminist Historical Materialism," is reprinted from *Discovering Reality: Feminist Perspectives on Epistemology, Metaphysics, Methodology and Philosophy of Science*, ed. Sandra Harding and Merrill B. Hintikka (Dordrecht, Holland: D. Reidel Publishing Co., 1983) by permission of author and publisher. © 1983 by D. Reidel Publishing Company.

FEMINISM AND METHODOLOGY

I.

INTRODUCTION
IS THERE A FEMINIST METHOD?

Sandra Harding

Over the last two decades feminist inquirers have raised fundamental challenges to the ways social science has analyzed women, men, and social life. From the beginning, issues about method, methodology, and epistemology have been intertwined with discussions of how best to correct the partial and distorted accounts in the traditional analyses. Is there a distinctive feminist method of inquiry? How does feminist methodology challenge—or complement—traditional methodologies? On what grounds would one defend the assumptions and procedures of feminist researchers? Questions such as these have generated important controversies within feminist theory and politics, as well as curiosity and anticipation in the traditional discourses.

The most frequently asked question has been the first one: is there a distinctive feminist method of inquiry? However, it has been hard to get a clear focus on the kind of answer to this question that we should seek. My point here is to argue against the idea of a distinctive feminist method of research. I do so on the grounds that preoccupation with method mystifies what have been the most interesting aspects of feminist research processes. Moreover, I think that it is really a different concern that motivates and is expressed through most formulations of the method question: what is it that makes some of the most influential feminist-inspired biological and social science research of recent years so powerful? I shall first try to disentangle some of the issues about method, methodology, and epistemology. Then I turn to review briefly (or to introduce, depending on the reader) the problems with thinking that attempting to "add women" to existing social science analyses does all that should be done in response to feminist criticisms. Finally, I shall draw attention to three distinctive characteristics of those feminist analyses that go beyond the additive approaches. I shall try to show why we should not choose to think of these as methods of research, though they clearly have significant implications for our evaluations of research methods.

Method, Methodology, Epistemology

One reason it is difficult to find a satisfactory answer to questions about a distinctive feminist method is that discussions of method (techniques for gathering evidence) and methodology (a theory and analysis of how research should proceed) have been intertwined with each other and with epistemological issues (issues about an adequate theory of knowledge or justificatory strategy) in both the traditional and feminist discourses. This claim is a complex one and we shall sort out its components. But the point here is simply that "method" is often used to refer to all three aspects of research. Consequently, it is not at all clear what one is supposed to be looking for when trying to identify a distinctive "feminist method of research." This lack of clarity permits critics to avoid facing up to what *is* distinctive about the best feminist social inquiry. It also makes it difficult to recognize what one must do to advance feminist inquiry.

A research *method* is a technique for (or way of proceeding in) gathering evidence. One could reasonably argue that all evidence-gathering techniques fall into one of the following three categories: listening to (or interrogating) informants, observing behavior, or examining historical traces and records. In this sense, there are only three methods of social inquiry. As the essays in this collection show, feminist researchers use just about any and all of the methods, in this concrete sense of the term, that traditional androcentric researchers have used. Of course, precisely how they carry out these methods of evidence gathering is often strikingly different. For example, they listen carefully to how women informants think about their lives and men's lives, and critically to how traditional social scientists conceptualize women's and men's lives. They observe behaviors of women and men that traditional social scientists have not thought significant. They seek examples of newly recognized patterns in historical data.

There is both less and more going on in these cases than new methods of research. The "less" is that it seems to introduce a false sense of unity to all the different "little things" feminist researchers do with familiar methods to conceptualize these as "new feminist research methods." However, the "more" is that it is new methodologies and new epistemologies that are requiring these new uses of familiar research techniques. If what is meant by a "method of research" is just this most concrete sense of the term, it would undervalue the transformations feminist analyses require to characterize these in terms only of the discovery of distinctive methods of research.

That social scientists tend to think about methodological issues primarily in terms of methods of inquiry (for example, in "methods courses" in psychology, sociology, etc.) is a problem. That is, it is primarily when they are talking about concrete techniques of evidence gathering that they raise methodological issues. No doubt it is this habit that tempts social scientists to seek a unique method of inquiry as the explanation for what is unusual about feminist analyses. On the other hand, it is also a problem that philosophers use such terms as "scientific method" and "the method of science" when they are really referring to issues of methodology and epistemology. They, too, are tempted to seek whatever is unique about feminist research in a new "method of inquiry."

A *methodology* is a theory and analysis of how research does or should proceed; it includes accounts of how "the general structure of theory finds its application in particular scientific disciplines."[1] For example, discussions of how functionalism (or Marxist political economy, or phenomenology) should be or is applied in particular research areas are methodological analyses.[2] Feminist researchers have argued that traditional theories have been applied in ways that make it difficult to understand women's participation in social life, or to understand men's activities as gendered (vs. as representing "the human"). They have produced feminist versions of traditional theories. Thus we can find examples of feminist methodologies in discussions of how phenomenological approaches can be used to begin to understand women's worlds, or of how Marxist political economy can be used to explain the causes of women's continuing exploitation in the household or in wage labor.[3] But these sometimes heroic efforts raise questions about whether even feminist applications of these theories can succeed in producing complete and undistorted accounts of gender and of women's activities. And they also raise epistemological issues.

An *epistemology* is a theory of knowledge. It answers questions about who can be a "knower" (can women?); what tests beliefs must pass in order to be legitimated as knowledge (only tests against men's experiences and observations?); what kinds of things can be known (can "subjective truths" count as knowledge?), and so forth. Sociologists of knowledge characterize epistemologies as strategies for justifying beliefs: appeals to the authority of God, of custom and tradition, of "common sense," of observation, of reason, and of masculine authority are examples of familiar justificatory strategies. Feminists have argued that traditional epistemologies, whether intentionally or unintentionally, systematically exclude the possibility that women could be "knowers" or *agents of knowledge;* they claim that the voice of science is a masculine one; that history is written from only the point of view of men (of the dominant class and race); that the subject of a traditional sociological sentence is always assumed to be a man. They have proposed alternative theories of knowledge that legitimate women as knowers.[4] Examples of these feminist epistemological claims and discussions can be found in the essays that follow. These issues, too, are often referred to as issues about method. Epistemological issues certainly have crucial implications for how general theoretical structures can and should be applied in particular disciplines and for the choice of methods of research. But I think that it is misleading and confusing to refer to these, too, as issues about method.[5]

In summary, there are important connections between epistemologies, methodologies, and research methods. But I am arguing that it is *not* by looking at research methods that one will be able to identify the distinctive features of the best of feminist research. We shall next see that this distinctiveness is also not to be found in attempts to "add women" to traditional analyses.

Problems with "Adding Women"

In order to grasp the depth and extent of the transformation of the social sciences required in order to understand gender and women's activities, one needs to recognize the limitations of the most obvious ways one could try to rectify the androcentrism of traditional analyses. Feminist researchers first tried to "add women" to these analyses. There were three kinds of women who appeared as obvious candidates for this process: women social scientists, women who contributed to the public life social scientists already were studying, and women who had been victims of the most egregious forms of male dominance.

In the first of these projects, scholars have begun to recover and to reappreciate the work of women researchers and theorists. Women's research and scholarship often has been ignored, trivialized, or appropriated without the credit which would have been given to a man's work. One of the notorious examples of this kind of sexist devaluation in the natural sciences is the treatment of Rosalind Franklin's work on DNA by her Nobel prize-winning colleagues.[6] How many other outstanding women social and natural scientists will we never have the chance to appreciate because they, unlike Franklin, had no close friend capable of setting the record straight?

However, there are severe problems with imagining that this is the only or most important way to eliminate sexism and androcentrism from social science. Obviously, one should not expect to understand gender and women's roles in social life merely through learning about the work of women social scientists in the past. Insightful as these "lost women" were, their work could not benefit from the many feminist theoretical break-throughs of the last two decades. Moreover, these women succeeded in entering a world which largely excluded women from the education and credentialling necessary to become social scientists. Thus their work was constrained by the immense pressures on them to make their research conform to what the men of their times thought about social life. Such pressures are still very great, as we will see all of the essayists in this volume argue. Fortunately they often succeeded in resisting these pressures. Nevertheless, we should not expect their research projects to produce the kinds of powerful analyses that can emerge when women's and men's thinking is part of a broad social revolution such as the women's movement has created. What remains amazing is the intellectual courage and frequent flashes of brilliance exhibited in the thinking of these social scientists in spite of the social, professional, and political constraints they faced.[7]

A different concern of feminist social research has been to examine women's contributions to activities in the public world which were already the focus of social science analysis. We now can see that women, too, have been the originators of distinctively human culture, deviants, voters, revolutionaries, social reformers, high achievers, wage workers, and so forth. Important studies have expanded our understanding of women's roles in public life both historically and in other cultures today.

This focus still leaves some powerfully androcentric standards firmly in place, thereby insuring only partial and distorted analyses of gender and women's social activities. It falsely suggests that only those activities that men have found it important to study are the ones which constitute and shape social life. This leads us to ignore such crucial issues as how changes in the social practices of reproduction, sexuality, and mothering have shaped the state, the economy, and the other public institutions. Futhermore, this research focus does not encourage us to ask what have been the *meanings* of women's contributions to public life *for women*. For instance, Margaret Sanger's birth control movement played an important and unfortunate role in eugenics policy. But it also signified to women that they could plan their reproductive lives and in that sense systematically and effectively control the consequences of their sexual activities. This second meaning is not likely to be noticed when the focus is on only women's contributions to "men's world." To take another example, both white and black women worked courageously in the antislavery, black suffrage, and antilynching movements. But what did it mean for their lives *as women* to work in these movements? (They learned public speaking, political organizing, and the virulence of white men's hositility to women learning how to speak and organize, among other things!)[8]

A third kind of new focus of research on women can be found in the study of women as victims of male dominance. Male dominance takes many forms. Researchers have provided path-breaking studies of the "crimes against women"—especially rape, incest, pornography, and wife beating. They have examined the broader patterns of institutionalized economic exploitation and political discrimination against women. And they have looked at the forms of white male domination which have particularly victimized women of color—in slavery, in state reproductive and welfare policies, in "protective" legislation, in union practices, and in other circumstances.[9] The emergence to public consciousness of this ugly underside of women's condition has made it impossible for serious thinkers to continue to believe in the reality of unmitigated social progress in this culture or most others. One might reasonably find contemporary cultures to be among the most barbaric from the perspective of the statistics on the victimization of women.

Victimologies have their limitations too. They tend to create the false impression that women have *only* been victims, that they have never successfully fought back, that women cannot be effective social agents on behalf of themselves or others. But the work of other feminist scholars and researchers tells us otherwise. Women have always resisted male domination.

I have pointed out problems with three basic approaches to the study of women and gender which initially looked promising. While each is valuable in its own right, the most widely acclaimed examples of the new feminist scholarship include analyses of these "kinds of women," but also move far beyond these projects.[10] Let us turn to look at just what it is that characterizes the best of this research, for these characteristics should offer more promising criteria than research methods for what is distinctive in feminist analyses.

What's New in Feminist Analyses?

Let us ask about the history of feminist inquiry the kind of question Thomas Kuhn posed about the history of science.[11] He asked what the point would be of a philosophy of science for which the history of science failed to provide supporting evidence. We can ask what the point would be of elaborating a theory of the distinctive nature of feminist inquiry that excluded the best feminist social science research from satisfying its criteria. Some of the proposals for a feminist method have this unfortunate consequence. Formulating this question directs one to attempt to identify the characteristics that distinguish the most illuminating examples of feminist research.

I shall suggest three such features. By no means do I intend for this list to be exhaustive. We are able to recognize these features only after examples of them have been produced and found fruitful. As research continues, we will surely identify additional characteristics that expand our understandings of what makes feminist accounts explanatorily so powerful. No doubt we will also revise our understandings of the significance of the three to which I draw attention. My point is not to provide a definitive *answer* to the title question of this section, but to show that this historical approach is the best strategy if we wish to account for the distinctive power of feminist research. While these features have consequences for the selection of research methods, there is no good reason to call them methods.

New Empirical and Theoretical Resources: Women's Experiences

Critics argue that traditional social science has begun its analyses only in men's experiences. That is, it has asked only the questions about social life that appear problematic from within the social experiences that are characteristic for men (white, Western, bourgeois men, that is). It has unconsciously followed a "logic of discovery" which we could formulate in the following way: Ask only those questions about nature and social life which (white, Western, bourgeois) men want answered. How can "we humans" achieve greater autonomy? What is the appropriate legal policy toward rapists and raped women which leaves intact the normal standards of masculine sexual behavior?[12] On the one hand, many phenomena which appear problematic from the perspective of men's characteristic experiences do not appear problematic at all from the perspective of women's experiences. (The above two issues, for example, do not characteristically arise from women's experiences.) On the other hand, women experience many phenomena which they think *do* need explanation. Why do men find child care and housework so distasteful? Why do women's life opportunities tend to be constricted exactly at the moments traditional history marks as the most progressive? Why is it hard to detect black women's ideals of womanhood in studies of black families? Why is men's sexuality so "driven," so defined in terms of power? Why is risking death said to represent the distinctively human act but giving birth regarded as merely natural?[13] Reflection on how social phenomena get defined as problems in need of explanation in the first place quickly reveals that there is no such thing as a problem without a person (or groups of them) who have this problem: a problem is always a problem *for* someone or other. Recognition of this fact, and its implications for the structure of the scientific enterprise, quickly brings feminist approaches to inquiry into conflict with traditional understandings in many ways.

The traditional philosophy of science argues that the origin of scientific problems or hypotheses is irrelevant to the "goodness" of the results of research. It doesn't matter where one's problems or hypotheses come from—from gazing into crystal balls, from sun worshipping, from observing the world around us, or from critical discussion with the most brilliant thinkers. There is no logic for these "contexts of discovery," though many have tried to find one. Instead, it is in the "context of justification," where hypotheses are tested, that we should seek the "logic of scientific inquiry." It is in this testing process that we should look for science's distinctive virtues (for its "method"). But the feminist challenges reveal that the questions that are asked—and, even more significantly, those that are not asked—are at least as determinative of the adequacy of our total picture as are any answers that we can discover. Defining what is in need of scientific explanation only from the perspective of bourgeois, white men's experiences leads to partial and even perverse understandings of social life. One distinctive feature of feminist research is that it generates its problematics from the perspective of women's experiences. It also uses these experiences as a significant indicator of the "reality" against which hypotheses are tested.

Recognition of the importance of using women's experiences as resources for social analysis obviously has implications for the social structures of education, laboratories, journals, learned societies, funding agencies—indeed, for social life in general. And it needs to be stressed that it is *women* who should be expected to be able to reveal *for the first time* what women's experiences are. Women should have an equal say in the design and administration of the institutions where knowledge is produced and distributed for reasons of social justice: it is not fair to exclude women from gaining the benefits of participating in these enterprises that men get. But they should also share in these projects because only partial and distorted understandings of ourselves and the world around us can be produced in a culture which systematically silences and devalues the voices of women.

Notice that it is "women's experiences" *in the plural* which provide the new resources for research. This formulation stresses several ways in which the best feminist analyses differ from traditional ones. For one thing, once we realized that there is no universal *man*, but only culturally different men and women, then "man's" eternal companion— "woman"—also disappeared. That is, women come only in different classes, races, and cultures: there is no "woman" and no "woman's experience." Masculine and feminine are always categories within every class, race, and culture in the sense that women's and men's experiences, desires, and interests differ within every class, race, and culture. But so, too, are class, race, and culture always categories within gender, since women's and men's experiences, desires, and interests differ according to class, race, and culture.[14] This leads some theorists to propose that we should talk about our "feminisms" only in the plural, since there is no one set of feminist principles or understandings beyond the very, very general ones to which feminists in every race, class, and culture will assent. Why should we have expected it to be any different? There are very few principles or understandings to which sexists in every race, class, and culture will assent!

Not only do our gender experiences vary across the cultural categories; they also are often in conflict in any one individual's experience. My experiences as a mother and a professor are often contradictory. Women scientists often talk about the contradictions in identity between what they experience as women and scientists. Dorothy Smith writes of the "fault line" between women sociologists' experience as sociologists and as women.[15] The hyphenated state of many self-chosen labels of identity—black feminist, socialist feminist, Asian-American feminist, lesbian feminist—reflects this challenge to the "identity politics" which has grounded Western thought and public life. These fragmented identities are a rich source of feminist insight.[16]

Finally, the questions an oppressed group wants answered are rarely requests for so-called pure truth. Instead, they are queries about how to change its conditions; how its world is shaped by forces beyond it; how to win over, defeat, or neutralize those forces arrayed against its emancipation, growth, or development; and so forth. Consequently, feminist research projects originate primarily not in any old "women's experiences," but in women's experiences in political struggles. (Kate Millett and others remind us that the bedroom and the kitchen are as much the site of political struggle as are the board room or the polling place.[17]) It may be that it is only through such struggles that one can come to understand oneself and the social world.

New Purposes of Social Science: For Women

If one begins inquiry with what appears problematic from the perspective of women's experiences, one is led to design research *for* women, as a number of the authors in this volume point out. That is, the goal of this inquiry is to provide for women explanations of social phenomena that they want and need, rather than providing for welfare departments, manufacturers, advertisers, psychiatrists, the medical establishment, or the judicial system answers to questions that they have. The questions about women that men have wanted answered have all too often arisen from desires to pacify, control, exploit, or manipulate women. Traditional social research has been *for men*. In the best of feminist research, the purposes of research and analysis are not separable from the origins of research problems.

New Subject Matter of Inquiry: Locating the Researcher in the Same Critical Plane as the Overt Subject Matter

There are a number of ways we could characterize the distinctive subject matter of feminist social analysis. While studying women is not new, studying them from the perspective of their own experiences so that women can understand themselves and the world can claim virtually no history at all. It is also novel to study gender. The idea of a systematic social construction of masculinity and femininity that is little, if at all, constrained by biology, is very recent. Moreover, feminist inquiry joins other "underclass" approaches in insisting on the importance of studying ourselves and "studying up," instead of "studying down." While employers have often commissioned studies of how to make workers happy with less power and pay, workers have rarely been in a position to undertake or commission studies of anything at all, let alone how to make employers happy with less power and profit. Similarly, psychiatrists have endlessly studied what they regard as women's peculiar mental and behavioral characteristics, but women have only recently begun to study the bizarre mental and behavioral characteristics of psychiatrists. If we want to understand how our daily experience arrives in the forms it does, it makes sense to examine critically the sources of social power.

The best feminist analysis goes beyond these innovations in subject matter in a crucial way: it insists that the inquirer her/himself be placed in the same critical plane as the overt subject matter, thereby recovering the entire research process for scrutiny in the results of research. That is, the class, race, culture, and gender assumptions, beliefs, and behaviors of the researcher her/himself must be placed within the frame of the picture that she/he attempts to paint. This does not mean that the first half of a research report should engage in soul searching (though a little soul searching by researchers now and then can't be all bad!). Instead, as we will see, we are often explicitly told by the researcher what her/his gender, race, class, culture is, and sometimes how she/he suspects this has shaped the research project—though of course we are free to arrive at contrary hypotheses about the influence of the researcher's presence on her/his analysis. Thus the researcher appears to us not as an invisible, anonymous voice of authority, but as a real, historical individual with concrete, specific desires and interests.

This requirement is no idle attempt to "do good" by the standards of imagined critics in classes, races, cultures (or of a gender) other than that of the researcher. Instead, it is a response to the recognition that the cultural beliefs and behaviors of feminist researchers shape the results of their analyses no less than do those of sexist and androcentric researchers. We need to avoid the "objectivist" stance that attempts to make the researcher's cultural beliefs and practices invisible while simultaneously skewering the research objects beliefs and practices to the display board. Only in this way can we hope to produce understandings and explanations which are free (or, at least, more free) of distortion from the unexamined beliefs and behaviors of social scientists themselves. Another way to put this point is that the beliefs and behaviors of the researcher are part of the empirical evidence for (or against) the claims advanced in the results of research. *This* evidence too must be open to critical scrutiny no less than what is traditionally defined as relevant evidence. Introducing this "subjective" element into the analysis in fact increases the objectivity of the research and decreases the "objectivism" which hides this kind of evidence from the public. This kind of relationship between the researcher and the object of research is usually discussed under the heading of the "reflexivity of social science." I refer to it here as a new subject matter of inquiry to emphasize the unusual strength of this form of the reflexivity recommendation. The reader will want to ask if and how this strong form of the reflexivity recommendation can be found in the following analyses. How is it implicitly directing inquiry? How might it have shaped some of these research projects yet more strongly?

To summarize my argument, it is features such as these three—not a "feminist method"—which are responsible for producing the best of the new feminist research and scholarship. They can be thought of as methodological features because they show us how to apply the general structure of scientific theory to research on women and gender. They can also be thought of as epistemological ones because they imply theories of knowledge different from the traditional ones. Clearly the extraordinary explanatory power of the results of feminist research in the social sciences (such as that exhibited by the papers that follow) is due to feminist-inspired challenges to the grand theories and the background assumptions of traditional social inquiry.

Two Final Issues

Before concluding this essay, I want to warn the reader against two inferences one should resist drawing from the analysis above. It is sometimes falsely supposed that in using women's experiences rather than men's as an empirical and theoretical resource, feminism espouses a kind of relativism. It is sometimes also falsely imagined that men cannot make important contributions to feminist research and scholarship. The two issues are related to each other.

First, we should note that on the account I gave above, women's and men's experiences are not equally reliable guides to the production of complete and undistorted social research. Feminist inquirers are never saying that sexist and antisexist claims are equally plausible—for example, that it's equally plausible to regard women as incapable of the highest kind of moral judgment (as men have claimed) and as exercising a different but equally "high" kind of moral judgment (as Carol Gilligan argues). The reader can identify innumerable additional directly contradictory claims in the reports of feminist challenges to traditional social analyses which follow. Feminist researchers are arguing that women's and men's characteristic social experiences provide different but not equal grounds for reliable knowledge claims. In the concluding essay I shall explore the grounds that several contrasting feminist epistemologies advance for why we all—men as well as women—should prefer women's experiences to men's as reliable bases for knowledge claims. Here I can only relativize relativism itself; that is, I can point to the limited social contexts in which it appears to be a reasonable position to advance.

Historically, relativism appears as an intellectual possibility, and as a "problem," only for dominating groups at the point where the hegemony (the universality) of their views is being challenged. As a modern intellectual position, it emerged in the belated recognition by nineteenth-century Europeans that the apparently bizarre beliefs and behaviors of non-Europeans had a rationality or logic of their own. Perhaps the preferred Western beliefs might not be the only reasonable ones.[18] The point here is that relativism is not a problem originating in, or justifiable in terms of, women's experiences or feminist agendas. It is fundamentally a sexist response that attempts to preserve the legitimacy of androcentric claims in the face of contrary evidence. "Perhaps," the relativists argue, "men's views are not the *only* legitimate views. Women have their views of the matter and men have theirs. Who is to say objectively that one is better than the other?" The feminist epistemologies we shall examine later offer uncompromising rejections of this way of conceptualizing feminist understandings. I hope the reader can already glimpse why one should be skeptical of claims that the results of feminist social research rest on relativist grounds.

The second faulty inference one might be tempted to make is that men cannot make important contributions to feminist research and scholarship. If the problems feminist inquiry addresses must arise from women's experiences, if feminist social science is to be for women, and if the inquirer is to be in the same critical plane as subject matters (which are often about women and gender), how could men do feminist social science? This vexing question has gained increasing attention as more and more men are, in fact, teaching in women's studies programs and producing analyses of women and gender.

On the one hand, there are clearly important contributions to the history of feminist thought which have been made by men. John Stuart Mill, Karl Marx, and Friedrich Engels are just the most obvious of these thinkers. Their writings are certainly controversial and, at best, imperfect; but so, too, are the writings of the most insightful women thinkers of these periods or, for that matter, in the present day. Moreover, there have always been women willing and able to produce sexist and misogynistic thought—Marabel Morgan and Phyllis Schlafly are just two of such recent writers. Obviously, neither the ability nor the willingness to contribute to feminist understanding are sex-linked traits!

Moreover, significant contributions to *other* emancipation movements have been made by thinkers who were not themselves members of the group to be emancipated. Marx and Engels were not members of the proletariat. There are whites in our own nation as well as in South Africa and other racist regimes who have been willing and able to think in antiracist ways—indeed, they have been lynched, exiled, and banned for their antiracist writings. Gentiles in Europe and the United States have argued for and suffered because of their defenses of Jewish freedoms. So it would be historically unusual if the list of contributors to women's emancipation alone excluded by fiat all members of the "oppressor group" from its ranks.

On the other hand, surely women, like members of these other exploited groups, are wise to look especially critically at analyses produced by members of the oppressor group. Are women's experiences used as the test of adequacy of the problems, concepts, hypotheses, research design, collection, and interpretation of data? (Must the "women's experience" from which feminist problematics arise be the experience of the investigator her/himself?) Is the research project *for* women rather than for men and the institutions men control? Does the researcher or theorist place himself in the same class, race, culture, and gender-sensitive critical plane as his subjects of study?

Once we ask these questions, we can see many research projects which are particularly suitable for men sympathetic to feminism to conduct. These are the critical examination of the gendered dimensions of men's thoughts and behaviors historically and cross-culturally—what is referred to in literary criticism as the "phallic critique." The reader can examine for her/himself how this project appears to satisfy the requirements of the most successful feminist inquiries discussed above. (Note that the requirement to "study up" will direct these projects toward the beliefs and behaviors of men of the same or higher social classes as the investigator; neither men nor women should try to "blame" classes of people who are *not* responsible for designing and maintaining our social institutions for the sins of those institutions.) Moreover, there are some areas of masculine behavior and thought to which male researchers have easier and perhaps better access than do women researchers: primarily male settings and ones from which women are systematically excluded, such as board rooms, military settings, or locker rooms. They can bring a feminist perspective to bear on certain aspects of some relationships that is valuable in different ways from the perspective women would bring to such relationships. I am thinking here of the "phallic critique" men could provide of friendships between men, or of relationships between fathers and sons, or between male lovers. How do these feel lacking to their participants? How do they contrast with the characteristics of friendships between women, and so forth?[19]

In addition to the scholarly or scientific benefits which could accrue from such studies, this kind of self-critical research by men makes a kind of political contribution to the emancipation of women which inquires *by women* cannot achieve. Just as courageous whites can set an example for other whites, and can use for antiracist ends the great power institutional racism bestows on even the most antiracist of whites, so too can men make an important but different kind of contribution to women's emancipation. If men are trained by sexist institutions to value masculine authority more highly, then some courageous men can take advantage of that evil and use their masculine authority to resocialize men.

There are two final arguments to be made on behalf of the possibility of male feminist social scientists. I suggest that feminists should find it inappropriate both to criticize male scholars and researchers for ignoring women and gender and also to insist that they are incapable of conducting research which satisfies feminist requirements. Moreover, since feminists often insist (and correctly so, I would argue) that *every* issue is a feminist issue, it seems a bit odd, and at least a strategic error, to adopt a policy which in effect recommends that only women do social science at all.[20]

What is clear is that whether they are women or men, those who do not actively struggle against the exploitation of women in everyday life are unlikely to produce social science research about any subject at all that is undistorted by sexism and androcentrism. As Nancy Hartsock says, "the vision available to the oppressed group must be struggled for and represents an achievement which requires both science to see beneath the surface of the social relations in which all are forced to participate, and the education which can only grow from struggle to change those relations."

In spite of these arguments to the contrary, it is easy to understand why many feminists take a skeptical attitude toward a man's claim to be doing feminist research or providing an adequate account of gender or women's activities. Of course it is important to discourage men from thinking they can take over feminist research the way they do everything else which becomes significant in the public world—citing only other male researchers, doing little to alleviate the exploitation of their female colleagues or the women in their lives whose work makes their eminence possible, and so forth.

My own preference is to argue that the designation "feminist" can apply to men who satisfy whatever standards women must satisfy to earn the label. To maximally increase our understanding, research must satisfy the three criteria discussed earlier. The issue here is not so much one of the right to claim a label as it is of the prerequisites for producing less partial and distorted descriptions, explanations, and understandings.

It is time to turn to examine what has been responsible for generating some of the most widely acclaimed of the new feminist social analyses.

NOTES

1. Peter Caws, "Scientific Method," in *The Encyclopedia of Philosophy*, ed. Paul Edwards (New York: Macmillan, 1967), p. 339.

2. Feminist methodologists have even achieved the heroic in showing that through ingenious applications of what have been widely regarded as hopelessly sexist theories—such as sociobiology—we can increase our understandings of women and gender. See Donna Haraway's discussion of this issue in "Animal Sociology and a Natural Economy of the Body Politic," pt. 2, in *Signs: Journal of Women in Culture and Society* 4, no. 1 (1978).

3. Dorothy Smith, Heidi Hartmann and Nancy Hartsock explicitly provide such methodological discussions in their essays in this volume.

4. The concluding essay in this volume examines feminist epistemologies. For further discussion of the feminist science and epistemology critiques see my *The Science Question in Feminism* (Ithaca, N.Y.: Cornell University Press, 1986) and Jean O'Barr and Sandra Harding, eds., *Sex and Scientific Inquiry* (Chicago: University of Chicago Press, 1987).

5. I suggest that readers try to distinguish these three aspects of research in the papers that follow.

6. See James Watson, *The Double Helix* (New York: New American Library, 1969), and Anne Sayre, *Rosalind Franklin and DNA* (New York: Norton, 1975). Carolyn Wood Sherif discusses such practices in psychology in her essay in this volume.

7. See Margaret Rossiter, *Women Scientists in America: Struggles and Strategies to 1940* (Baltimore: Johns Hopkins University Press, 1982), for documentation of the efforts by women natural and social scientists in the 19th and early 20th centuries.

8. Bettina Aptheker, *Women's Legacy: Essays on Race, Sex and Class in American History* (Amherst: University of Massachusetts Press, 1982); and Angela Davis, *Women, Race and Class* (New York: Random House, 1983).

9. It needs to be said that white women, too, have participated in oppressing women of color in a variety of ways.

10. Peggy McIntosh provides an interestingly harsher judgment than I of these additive approaches to feminist scholarship in "Interactive Phases of Curricular Revision: A Feminist Perspective," working paper no. 124 (Wellesley, Mass.: Wellesley College Center for Research on Women, 1983).

11. Thomas S. Kuhn, *The Structure of Scientific Revolutions*, 2d. ed. (Chicago: University of Chicago Press, 1970).

12. Problems with these "men's problems" are discussed in the essays.

13. These "women's problems" generate analyses in the essays below.

14. In this collection, the essays by Joyce A. Ladner and Bonnie Thornton Dill make this point most clearly.

15. See Smith's essay in this volume.

16. We shall return to this issue in the concluding essay.

17. Kate Millett, *Sexual Politics* (New York: Doubleday & Co. 1969).

18. There are situations where relativism could be a reasonable epistemological stance: where two *equally powerful* and noncompetitive perspectives generate different understandings. For example, an artist and a geologist could have different and equally valid grounds on which to base their claims about a particular group of mountains. But precisely because these are noncompetitive grounds, the issue never comes up: no one imagines a geologist would have any reason to contradict an artist, or vice versa.

19. One such study is the chapter on friendships between men, "Man to Man," in Michael E. McGill, *The McGill Report on Male Intimacy* (New York: Harper & Row, 1986). Gerald Turkel brought this to my attention.

20. "So why, after all this impassioned argument, is there no essay by a man in this collection?" one might well ask. There were two essays by men on the original list from which the present set were winnowed. Both were dropped, along with essays by an anthropologist, a linguist, a feminist sociobiologist, women of color other than black Americans, a demographer, a phenomenological sociologist, a colonial historian, a statistician in psychology, etc. I chose to discuss the issue here, leaving space in the collection itself for essays which each had to satisfy a number of different criteria.

II.

THE SOCIAL RELATION OF THE SEXES
METHODOLOGICAL IMPLICATIONS
OF WOMEN'S HISTORY

Joan Kelly-Gadol

In this influential essay, Joan Kelly-Gadol begins by pointing to the inadequacy of the "add women and stir" approaches to which historians were tempted when they first recognized the need for the study of women and gender. She discusses the radical implications for professional history of assuming "that women are a part of humanity in the fullest sense." The reader will notice that it is familiar methods of historical research, such as reinterpreting existing legal records, that have been used in producing the new scholarship. But it is new problematics, concepts, hypotheses, and purposes of inquiry that have generated the new research. As her title indicates, it is at the level of methodological assumptions (not techniques of gathering evidence—"methods") that she sees traditional history most deeply challenged by the task of explaining and understanding a world that now must be perceived to include women as fully historical persons.

As one follows her argument, one can wonder if male historians would be likely to focus on the problems or to come up with the concepts and hypotheses that she reports. Would they be likely to do so in the absence of a women's movement? (Why didn't anyone produce these arguments earlier?) In either the androcentric or the new feminist histories, can research be separated from social values and interests? What should be the goals of historical inquiry in the kind of gender-stratified society in which we live? (In a culture which professes to value social justice for all, who should have the right to answer the last question?)

The challenges to traditional thinking that we can see in this essay will be of interest far beyond the borders of history departments. For one thing, every discipline *has* a history which is taught—formally or informally—to its students. What are the implications of Kelly-Gadol's arguments for the histories of literature, art, sociology, psychology, economics, philosophy, and even of the natural sciences? Moreover, history is part of the subject matter of the social sciences. Thus we have psychological studies of historical figures and epochs, and sociological, anthropological, linguistic, and economic studies of cultures of the past. What questions do these feminist critiques raise about this research? Finally, the reader will want to see how the three kinds of challenges to traditional history that Kelly-Gadol describes are echoed in the feminist criticisms of sociology, psychology, and the other social sciences which follow.[1]

Women's history has a dual goal: to restore women to history and to restore our history to women. In the past few years, it has stimulated a remarkable amount of research as well as a number of conferences and courses on the activities, status, and views of and about women. The interdisciplinary character of our concern with women has also newly enriched this vital historical work. But there is another aspect of women's history that needs to be considered: its theoretical significance, its implications for historical study in general.[1] In seeking to add women to the fund of historical knowledge, women's history has revitalized theory, for it has shaken the conceptual foundations of historical study. It has done this by making problematical three of the basic concerns of historical thought: (1) periodization, (2) the categories of social analysis, and (3) theories of social change.

Since all three issues are presently in ferment, I can at best suggest how they may be fruitfully posed. But in so doing, I should also like to show how the conception of these problems expresses a notion which is basic to feminist consciousness, namely, that the relation between the sexes is a social and not a natural one. This perception forms the core idea that upsets traditional thinking in all three cases.

Periodization

Once we look to history for an understanding of woman's situation, we are, of course, already assuming that woman's situation is a social matter. But history, as we first came to it, did not seem to confirm this awareness. Throughout historical time, women have been largely excluded from making war, wealth, laws, governments, art, and science. Men, functioning in their capacity as historians, considered exactly those activities constitutive of civilization: hence, diplomatic history, economic history, constitutional history, and political and cultural history. Women figured chiefly as exceptions, those who were said to be as ruthless as, or wrote like, or had the brains of men. In redressing this neglect, women's history recognized from the start that what we call compensatory history is not enough. This was not to be a history of exceptional women, although they too need to be restored to their rightful places. Nor could it be another subgroup of historical thought, a history of women to place alongside the list of diplomatic history, economic history, and so forth, for all these developments impinged upon the history of women. Hence feminist scholarship in history, as in anthropology, came to focus primarily on the issue of women's status. I use "status" here and throughout in an expanded sense, to refer to woman's place and power—that is, the roles and positions women hold in society by comparison with those of men.

In historical terms, this means to look at ages or movements of great social change in terms of their liberation or repression of woman's potential, their import for the advancement of her humanity as well as "his." The moment this is done—the moment one assumes that women are a part of humanity in the fullest sense—the period or set of events with which we deal takes on a wholly different character or meaning from the normally accepted one. Indeed, what emerges is a fairly regular pattern of relative loss of status for women precisely in those periods of so-called progressive change. Since the dramatic new perspectives that unfold from this shift of vantage point have already been discussed at several conferences, I shall be brief here.[2] Let me merely point out that if we apply Fourier's famous dictum—that the emancipation of women is an index of the general emancipation of an age—our notions of so-called progressive developments, such as classical Athenian civilization, the Renaissance, and the French Revolution, undergo a startling re-evaluation. For women, "progress" in Athens meant concubinage and confinement of citizen wives in the gynecaeum. In Renaissance Europe it meant domestication of the bourgeois wife and escalation of witchcraft persecution, which crossed class lines. And the Revolution expressly excluded women from its liberty, equality, and "fraternity." Suddenly we see these ages with a new, double vision—and each eye sees a different picture.

Only one of these views has been represented by history up to now. Regardless of how these periods have been assessed, they have been assessed from the vantage point of men. Liberal historiography in particular, which considers all three periods as stages in the progressive realization of an individualistic social and cultural order, expressly maintains—albeit without considering the evidence—that women shared these advances with men. In Renaissance scholarship, for example, almost all historians have been content to situate women exactly where Jacob Burckhardt placed them in 1890: "on a footing of perfect equality with men." For a period that rejected the hierarchy of social class and the hierarchy of religious values in its restoration of a classical, secular culture, there was also, they claim, "no question of 'woman's rights' or female emancipation, simply because the thing itself was a matter of course."[3] Now while it is true that a couple of dozen women can be assimilated to the humanistic standard of culture which the Renaissance imposed upon itself, what is remarkable is that *only* a couple of dozen women can. To pursue this problem is to become aware of the fact that there was no "renaissance" for women—at least not during the Renaissance. There was, on the contrary, a marked restriction of the scope and powers of women. Moreover, this restriction is a consequence of the very developments for which the age is noted.[4]

What feminist historiography has done is to unsettle such accepted evaluations of historical periods. It has disabused us of the notion that the history of women is the same as the history of men and that significant turning points in history have the same impact for one sex as for the other. Indeed, some historians now go so far as to maintain that, because of woman's particular connection with the function of reproduction, history could, and women's history should, be rewritten and periodized from this point of view, according to major turning points affecting childbirth, sexuality, family structure, and so forth.[5] In this regard, Juliet Mitchell refers to modern contraception as a "world-historic event"—although the logic of her thought, and my own, protests against a periodization that is primarily geared to changes in reproduction. Such criteria threaten to detach psychosexual development and family patterns from changes in the general social order, or to utterly reverse the causal sequence. Hence I see in them a potential isolation of women's history from what has hitherto been considered the mainstream of social change.

To my mind, what is more promising about the way periodization has begun to function in women's history is that it has become *relational*. It relates the history of women to that of men, as Engels did in *The Origin of the Family, Private Property and the State,* by seeing in common social developments institutional reasons for the advance of one sex and oppression of the other. Handled this way, traditional periodizing concepts may well be retained—and ought to be insofar as they refer to major structural changes in society. But in the evaluation of such changes we need to consider their effects upon women as distinct from men. We expect by now that those effects may be so different as to be opposed and that such opposition will be socially explicable. When women are excluded from the benefits of the economic, political, and cultural advances made in certain periods, a situation which gives women a different historical experience from men, it is to those "advances" we must look to find the reasons for that separation of the sexes.

Sex as a Social Category

Two convictions are implicit in this more complete and more complex sense of periodization: one, that women do form a distinctive social group and, second, that the invisibility of this group in traditional history is not to be ascribed to female nature. These notions, which clearly arise out of feminist consciousness, effect another, related change in the conceptual foundations of history by introducing sex as a category of social thought.

Feminism has made it evident that the mere fact of being a woman meant having a particular kind of social and hence historical experience, but the exact meaning of "woman" in this historical or social sense has not been so clear. What accounts for woman's situation as "other," and what perpetuates it historically? The "Redstockings Manifesto" of 1969 maintained that "women are an oppressed class" and suggested that the relations between men and women are class relations, that "sexual politics" are the politics of class domination. The most fruitful consequence of this conception of women as a social class has been the extension of class analysis to women by Marxist feminists such as Margaret Benston and Sheila Rowbotham.[6] They have traced the roots of woman's secondary status in history to economics inasmuch as women as a group have had a distinctive relation to production and property in almost all societies. The personal and psychological consequences of secondary status can be seen to flow from this special relation to work. As Rowbotham and Benston themselves make clear, however, it is one thing to extend the tools of class analysis to women and quite another to maintain that women *are* a class. Women belong to social classes, and the new women's history and histories of feminism have borne this out, demonstrating, for example, how class divisions disrupted and shattered the first wave of the feminist movement in nonsocialist countries, and how feminism has been expressly subordinated to the class struggle in socialist feminism.[7]

On the other hand, although women may adopt the interests and ideology of men of their class, women as a group cut through male class systems. Although I would quarrel with the notion that women of all classes, in all cultures, and at all times are accorded secondary status, there is certainly sufficient evidence that this is generally, if not universally, the case. From the advent of civilization, and hence of history proper as distinct from prehistorical societies, the social order has been patriarchal. Does that then make women a caste, a hereditary inferior order? This notion has its uses, too, as does the related one drawn chiefly from American black experience, which regards women as a minority group.[8] The sense of "otherness" which both these ideas convey is essential to our historical awareness of women as an oppressed social group. They help us appreciate the social formation of "femininity" as an internalization of ascribed inferiority which serves, at the same time, to manipulate those who have the authority women lack. As explanatory concepts, however, notions of caste and minority group are not productive when applied to women. *Why* should this majority be a minority? And why is it that the members of this particular caste, unlike all other castes, are not of the same rank throughout society? Clearly the minority psychology of women, like their caste status and quasi-class oppression, has to be traced to the universally distinguishing feature of all women, namely their sex. Any effort to understand women in terms of social categories that obscure this fundamental fact has to fail, only to make more appropriate concepts available. As Gerda Lerner put it, laying all such attempts to rest: "All analogies—class, minority group, caste—approximate the position of women, but fail to define it adequately. Women are a category unto themselves: an adequate analysis of their position in society demands new conceptual tools."[9] In short, women have to be defined as women. We are the social opposite, not of a class, a caste, or of a majority, since we are a majority, but of a sex: men. We are a sex, and categorization by gender no longer implies a mothering role and subordination to men, except as social role and relation recognized as such, as socially constructed and socially imposed.

A good part of the initial excitement in women's studies consisted of this discovery, that what had been taken as "natural" was in fact man-made, both as social order and as description of that order as natural and physically determined. Examples of such ideological reasoning go back to the story of Eve, but the social sciences have been functioning the same way, as myth reinforcing partriarchy. A feminist psychologist argues: "It is scientifically unacceptable to advocate the natural superiority of women as child-rearers and socializers of children when there have been so few studies of the effects of male-infant or father-infant interaction on the subsequent development of the child."[10] An anthropologist finds herself constrained to reject, and suspect, so-called scientific contentions that the monogamous family and male dominance belong to primates in general. In fact, she points out, "these features are *not* universal among non-human primates, including some of those most closely related to humans." And when male domination and male hierarchies do appear, they "seem to be adaptations to particular environments."[11]

Historians could not lay claim to special knowledge about the "natural" roles and relation of the sexes, but they knew what that order was, or ought to be. History simply tended to confirm it. *Bryan's Dictionary of Painters and Engravers* of 1904 says of the Renaissance artist, Propertia Rossi: "a lady of Bologna, best known as a sculptor and carver, but who also engraved upon copper, and learnt drawing and design from Marc Antonio. She is said to have been remarkable for her beauty, virtues, and talents, and to have died at an early age in 1530, in consequence of unrequited love. Her last work was a bas-relief of Joseph and Potiphar's wife!"[12] An exclamation mark ends the entry like a poke in the ribs, signifying that the "lady" (which is not a class designation here), who was beautiful and unhappy in love, was naturally absorbed by just that. Historians really *knew* why there were no great women artists. That is why it was not a historical problem until the feminist art historian, Linda Nochlin, posed it as such—by inquiring into the institutional factors, rather than the native gifts, that sustain artistic activity.[13]

When the issue of woman's place did appear openly, and male historians such as H. D. Kitto rose to defend "their" society, the Greek in his case, the natural order of things again came to the rescue.[14] If Athenian wives were not permitted to go about at will, weren't they too delicate for the strain that travel imposed in those days? If they played no role in political life—the activity that was the source of human dignity to the Greek—was it not because government covered "matters which, inescapably, only men could judge from their own experience and execute by their own exertions"? If girls were not being schooled, weren't they being instructed by mother in the arts of the female citizen? ("If we say 'housework,' " Kitto admits, "it sounds degrading, but if we say Domestic Science it sounds eminently respectable; and we have seen how varied and responsible it was.") But Kitto's major argument was reserved for the family: its religious and social importance in Athenian society. His reasoning on this point sounds to us like an incomplete sentence. He rightly points out that extinction of a family or dissipation of its property was regarded as a disaster. But for him, this fact is an argument, for his position is that it *is* woman's "natural" place to serve that family and continue it by raising legitimate heirs through whom to pass on its property and its rites. If, under the conditions of Greek society, that task should require confinement to the household and its rounds, that justifies the legal disabilities of wives. As for the other orders of women Athenian society demanded and regulated by law, concubines are not mentioned and hetaerae are "adventuresses who had said No to the serious business of life. Of course they amused men—'But, my dear fellow, one doesn't *marry* a woman like that.' "

Kitto wrote his history in 1951.

If our understanding of the Greek contribution to social life and consciousness now demands an adequate representation of the life experience of women, so too the sexual order, as shaped by the institutions of family and state, is a matter we now regard as not merely worthy of historical inquiry but central to it. This, I think, is a second major contribution women's history has made to the theory and practice of history in general. We have made of sex a category as fundamental to our analysis of the social order as other classifications, such as class and race. And we consider the relation of the sexes, as those of class and race, to be socially rather than naturally constituted, to have its own development, varying with changes in social organization. Embedded in and shaped by the social order, the relation of the sexes must be integral to any study of it. Our new sense of periodization reflects an assessment of historical change from the vantage point of women as well as men. Our use of sex as a social category means that our conception of historical change itself, as change in the social order, is broadened to include changes in the relation of the sexes.

I find the idea of the social relation of the sexes, which is at the core of this conceptual development, to be both novel and central in feminist scholarship and in works stimulated by it. An art historian, Carol Duncan, asks with respect to modern erotic art, "what are the male-female relations it implies," and finds those relations of domination and victimization becoming more pronounced precisely as women's claims for equality were winning recognition.[15] Michelle Zimbalist Rosaldo, coeditor of a collection of studies by feminist anthropologists, speaks of the need for anthropology to develop a theoretical context "within which the social relation of the sexes can be investigated and understood."[16] Indeed almost all the essays in this collective work are concerned with the structure of the sexual order—patriarchal, matrifocal, and otherwise—of the societies they treat. In art history, anthropology, sociology, and history, studies of the status of women necessarily tend to strengthen the social and relational character of the idea of sex. The activity, power, and cultural evaluation of women simply cannot be assessed except in relational terms: by comparison and contrast with the activity, power, and cultural evaluation of men, and in relation to the institutions and social developments that shape the sexual order. To conclude this point, let me quote Natalie Zemon Davis's address to the Second Berkshire Conference on the History of Women in October 1975:

> It seems to me that we should be interested in the history of both women and men, that we should not be working only on the subjected sex any more than an historian of class can focus exclusively on peasants. Our goal is to understand the significance of the *sexes*, of gender groups in the historical past. Our goal is to discover the range in sex roles and in sexual symbolism in different societies and periods, to find out what meaning they had and how they functioned to maintain the social order or to promote its change.[17]

Theories of Social Change

If the relationship of the sexes is as necessary to an understanding of human history as the social relationship of classes, what now needs to be worked out are the connections between changes in class and sex relations.[18] For this task, I suggest that we consider significant changes in the respective roles of men and women in the light of fundamental changes in the mode or production. I am not here proposing a simple socioeconomic scheme. A theory of social change that incorporates the relation of the sexes has to consider how general changes in production affect and shape production in the family and, thereby, the respective roles of men and women. And it has to consider, as well, the flow in the other direction: the impact of family life and the relation of the sexes upon psychic and social formations.

The study of changes in the social relation of the sexes is new, even if we trace it as far back as Bachhofen, Morgan, and Engels. Engels in particular solidly established the social character of woman's relation to man, although it was only one change in that relation— albeit the major one—that concerned him: the transition to patriarchy with the advance from kin society to civilization, and the overthrow of patriarchy with the advent of socialism. His analysis of the subordination of women in terms of the emergence of private property and class inequality is basic to much of feminist scholarship today. Engels had almost no effect upon historical scholarship, except for socialist theorists such as August Bebel, and historians of women such as Emily James Putnam and Simone de Beauvoir, but contemporary efforts to understand the social causes of patriarchy, and the reasons for the various forms it takes, tend to confirm his ideas on the social relation of the sexes. Certain conclusions, which in turn open new directions for historical and anthropological research, can already be drawn from this recent work. One is that "woman's social position has not always, everywhere, or in most respects been subordinate to that of men."[19] I am quoting here from an anthropologist because the historical case for anything other than a patriarchal sexual order is considerably weaker. The dominant causal feature that emerges from anthropological studies of the sexual order (in the Rosaldo and Lamphere collection I have mentioned) is whether, and to what extent, the domestic and the public spheres of activity are separated from each other. Although what constitutes "domestic" and what "public" varies from culture to culture, and the lines of demarcation are differently drawn, a consistent pattern emerges when societies are placed on a scale where, at one end, familial and public activities are fairly merged, and, at the other, domestic and public activities are sharply differentiated.

Where familial activities coincide with public or social ones, the status of women is comparable or even superior to that of men. This pattern is very much in agreement with Engels's ideas, because in such situations the means of subsistence and production are commonly held and a communal household is the focal point of both domestic and social life. Hence it is in societies where production for exchange is slight and where private property and class inequality are not developed that sex inequalities are least evident. Women's roles are as varied as men's, although there are sex-role differences; authority and power are shared by women and men rather than vested in a hierarchy of males; women are highly evaluated by the culture; and women and men have comparable sexual rights.

The most one can say about the sexual division of labor in societies at this end of the scale is that there is a tendency toward mother/child or women/children grouping and toward male hunting and warfare. This "natural" division of labor, if such it is, is not yet socially determined. That is, men as well as women care for children and perform household tasks, and women as well as men hunt. The social organization of work, and the rituals and values that grow out of it, do not serve to separate out the sexes and place one under the authority of the other. They do just that at the opposite end of the scale where the domestic and public orders are clearly distinguished from each other. Women continue to be active producers all the way up the scale (and must continue to be so until there is considerable wealth and class inequality), but they steadily lose control over property, products, and themselves as surplus increases, private property develops, and the communal household becomes a private economic unit, a family (extended or nuclear) represented by a man. The family itself, the sphere of women's activities, is in turn subordinated to a broader social or public order—governed by a state—which tends to be the domain of men. This is the general pattern presented by historical or civilized societies.[20]

As we move in this direction on the scale, it becomes evident that sexual inequalities are bound to the control of property. It is interesting to note in this regard that in several societies class inequalities are expressed in sexual terms. Women who have property, in livestock, for example, may use it for bridewealth to purchase "wives" who serve them.[21] This example, which seems to confound sex and class, actually indicates how sex and class relations differ. Although property establishes a class inequality among such women, it is nevertheless "wives," that is, women as a group, who constitute a propertyless serving order attached to a domestic kind of work, including horticulture.

How does this attachment of women to domestic work develop, and what forms does it take? This process is one of the central problems confronting feminist anthropology and history. By definition, this query rejects the traditional, simple biological "reasons" for the definition of woman-as-domestic. The privatizing of child rearing and domestic work and the sex typing of that work are social, not natural, matters. I suggest, therefore, that in treating this problem, we continue to look at *property relations* as the basic determinant of the sexual division of labor and of the sexual order. The more the domestic and the public domains are differentiated, the more work, and hence property, are of two clearly distinguishable kinds. There is production for subsistence and production for exchange. However the productive system of a society is organized, it operates, as Marx pointed out, as a continuous process which reproduces itself: that is, its material means and instruments, its people, and the social relations among them. Looked at as a continuous process (what Marx meant by reproduction), the productive work of society thus includes procreation and the socialization of children who must find their places within the social order.[22] I suggest that what shapes the relation of the sexes is the way this work of procreation and socialization is organized in relation to the organization of work that results in articles for subsistence and/or exchange. In sum, what patriarchy means as a general social order is that women function as the property of men in the maintenance and production of new members of the social order; that these relations of production are worked out in the organization of kin and family; and that other forms of work, such as production of goods and services for immediate use, are generally, although not always, attached to these procreative and socializing functions.[23]

Inequalities of sex as well as class are traced to property relations and forms of work in this scheme, but there are certain evident differences between the two. In the public domain, by which I mean the social order that springs from the organization of the general wealth and labor of society, class inequalities are paramount. For the relation of the sexes, control or lack of control of the property that separates people into owners and workers is not significant. What *is* significant is whether women *of either class* have equal relations to work or property with men of their class.

In the household or family, on the other hand, where ownership of all property resides in historic societies characterized by private property, sex inequalities are paramount and they cut through class lines. What is significant for the domestic relation is that women in the family, like serfs in feudal Europe, can both have and *be* property. To quote from an ancient description of early Roman law,

> a woman joined to her husband by a holy marriage, should share in all his possessions and sacred rites. . . . This law obliged both the married women, as having no other refuge, to conform themselves entirely to the temper of their husbands and the husbands to rule their wives as necessary and inseparable possessions. Accordingly, if a wife was virtuous and in all things obedient to her husband, she was mistress of the house to the same degree as her husband was master of it, and after the death of her husband she was heir to his property in the same manner as a daughter. . . . But if she did any wrong, the injured party was her judge, and determined the degree of her punishment. . . .[24]

Regardless of class, and regardless of ownership (although these modify the situation in interesting ways), women have generally functioned as the property of men in the procreative and socializing aspect of the productive work of their society. Women constitute part of the means of production of the private family's mode of work.

Patriarchy, in short, is at home at home. The private family is its proper domain. But the historic forms that patriarchy takes, like its very origin, are to be traced to the society's mode of production. The sexual order varies with the general organization of property and work because this shapes both family and public domains and determines how they approach or recede from each other.

These relations between the domestic and the public orders, in turn, account for many of the unexpected oppositions and juxtapositions expressed by our new sense of historical periods.[25] Blurring the lines between family and society diminished a number of sexual inequalities, including the double standard, for feudal noblewomen, for example, as well as for women in advanced capitalistic societies. The status of the feudal noblewoman was high before the rise of the state when the family order *was* the public order of her class; and the scope that familial political power gave women included the Church where aristocratic women also commanded a sphere of their own. Again today, the two domains approach each other as private household functions—child rearing, production of food and clothing, nursing, and so forth—become socially organized. Women can again work and associate with each other outside the household, and the sexual division of labor, although far from overcome, appears increasingly irrational.

Where domestic and public realms pulled apart, however, sexual inequalities became pronounced as did the simultaneous demand for female chastity and prostitution. This was the case with Athens of the classical period, where the private household economy was the basic form of production and the social or public order of the polis consisted of many such households which were subordinated to and governed by it. Wives of the citizenry were confined to the order of the household: to production of legitimate heirs and supervision of indoor slave production of goods and services for use. Although necessary to the public order, wives did not directly belong to or participate in it, and free women who fell outside the domestic order and its property arrangements fell outside the public order as well. The situation of women was much the same in the middle classes of modern Europe, although here capitalist commodity production moved out of the home and became socially organized. What capitalist production did was to turn the working-class family, too, after an initial, almost disastrous onslaught upon it, into a complement of social production. The family in modern society has served as the domain for the production and training of the working class. It has been the alleged reason for women having to function as underpaid, irregular laborers whose wages generally had to be supplemented by sexual attachment to a man, inside or outside family arrangements. And it has served to compensate the worker whose means of subsistence were alienated from him but who could have private property in his wife.

Such has been the institutionally determined role of the family under capitalism, and women of both the owning and the working classes, women both in and outside the family, have had their outer and inner lives shaped by the structure of its social relations.

Surely a dominant reason for studying the social relation of the sexes is political. To understand the interests, aside from the personal interests of individual men, that are served by the retention of an unequal sexual order is in itself liberating. It detaches an age-old injustice from the blind operation of social forces and places it in the realm of choice. This is why we look to the organization of the productive forces of society to understand the shape and structure of the domestic order to which women have been primarily attached.

But women's history also opens up the other half of history, viewing women as agents and the family as a productive and social force. The most novel and exciting task of the study of the social relation of the sexes is still before us: to appreciate how we are all, women and men, initially humanized, turned into social creatures by the work of that domestic order to which women have been primarily attached. Its character and the structure of its relations order our consciousness, and it is through this consciousness that we first view and construe our world.[26] To understand the historical impact of women, family, and the relation of the sexes upon society serves a less evident political end, but perhaps a more strictly feminist one. For if the historical conception of civilization can be shown to include the psychosocial functions of the family, then with that understanding we can insist that any reconstruction of society along just lines incorporate reconstruction of the family—all kinds of collective and private families, and all of them functioning, not as property relations, but as personal relations among freely associating people.

EDITOR'S NOTE

1. Kelly-Gadol's collected essays have been published posthumously as *Women, History and Theory: The Essays of Joan Kelly* (Chicago: University of Chicago Press, 1984).

NOTES

1. The central theme of this paper emerged from regular group discussions, from which I have benefited so much, with Marilyn Arthur, Blanche Cook, Pamela Farley, Mary Feldblum, Alice Kessler-Harris, Amy Swerdlow, and Carole Turbin. Many of the ideas were sharpened in talks with Gerda Lerner, Renate Bridenthal, Dick Vann, and Marilyn Arthur, with whom I served on several panels on women's history and its theoretical implications. My City College students in Marxism/feminism and in fear of women, witchcraft, and the family have stimulated my interests and enriched my understanding of many of the issues presented here. To Martin Fleisher and Nancy Miller I am indebted for valuable suggestions for improving an earlier version of this paper, which I delivered at the Barnard College Conference on the Scholar and the Feminist II: Toward New Criteria of Relevance, April 12, 1975.

2. Conference of New England Association of Women Historians, Yale University (October 1973): Marilyn Arthur, Renate Bridenthal, Joan Kelly-Gadol; Second Berkshire Conference on the History of Women, Radcliffe (October 1974): panel on "The Effects of Women's History upon Traditional Historiography," Renate Bridenthal, Joan Kelly-Gadol, Gerda Lerner, Richard Vann (papers deposited at Schlesinger Library); Sarah Lawrence symposium (March 1975): Marilyn Arthur, Renate Bridenthal, Gerda Lerner, Joan Kelly-Gadol (papers available as *Conceptual Frameworks in Women's History* [Bronxville, N.Y.: Sarah Lawrence Publications, 1976]). For some recent comments along some of these same lines, see Carl N. Degler, *Is There a History of Women?* (Oxford: Clarendon Press, 1975). As I edit this paper for printing, the present economic crisis is threatening the advances of feminist scholarship once again by forcing the recently arrived women educators out of their teaching positions and severing thereby the professional connections necessary to research and theory, such as the conferences mentioned above.

3. *The Civilization of the Renaissance in Italy* (London: Phaidon Press, 1950), p. 241. With the exception of Ruth Kelso, *Doctrine for the Lady of the Renaissance* (Urbana: University of Illinois Press, 1956), this view is shared by every work I know of on Renaissance women except for contemporary feminist historians. Even Simone de Beauvoir, and of course Mary Beard, regard the Renaissance as advancing the condition of women, although Burckhardt himself pointed out that the women of whom he wrote "had no thought of the public; their function was to influence distinguished men, and to moderate male impulse and caprice."

4. See the several contemporary studies recently or soon to be published on Renaissance women: Susan Bell, "Christine de Pizan," *Feminist Studies* (Winter 1975/76); Joan Kelly-Gadol, "Notes on Women in the Renaissance and Renaissance Historiography," in *Conceptual Frameworks in Women's History* (n. 2 above); Margaret Leah King, "The Religious Retreat of Isotta Nogarola, 1418–66," *Signs* 3:4 (1978); an article on women in the Renaissance by Kathleen Casey in *Liberating Women's History*, Berenice Carroll, ed. (Urbana: University of Illinois Press, 1976); Joan Kelly-Gadol, "Did Women Have a Renaissance?" in *Becoming Visible*, ed. R. Bridenthal and C. Koonz (Boston: Houghton Mifflin Co., 1976).

5. Vann (n. 2 above).

6. "Redstockings Manifesto," in *Sisterhood Is Powerful*, ed. Robin Morgan (New York: Random House, 1970), pp. 533–36. Margaret Benston, *The Political Economy of Women's Liberation* (New York: Monthly Review reprint, 1970). Sheila Rowbotham, *Woman's Consciousness, Man's World* (Middlesex: Pelican Books, 1973), with bibliography of the periodical literature. A number of significant articles applying Marxist analysis to the oppression of women have been appearing in issues of *Radical America* and *New Left Review*.

7. Eleanor Flexner, *Century of Struggle* (New York: Atheneum, 1970); Sheila Rowbotham, *Women, Resistance and Revolution* (New York: Random House, 1974); panel at the Second Berkshire Conference on the History of Women, Radcliffe (n. 2 above), on "Clara Zetkin and Adelheid Popp: The Development of Feminist Awareness in the Socialist Women's Movement—Germany and Austria, 1890—1914." with Karen Honeycutt, Ingurn LaFleur, and Jean Quataert. Karen Honeycutt's paper on Clara Zetkin is in *Feminist Studies* (Winter 1975/76).

8. Helen Mayer Hacker did interesting work along these lines in the 1950s, "Women as a Minority Group," *Social Forces* 30 (October 1951—May 1952): 60–69, and subsequently, "Women as a Minority Group: Twenty Years Later" (Pittsburgh: Know, Inc., 1972). Degler has recently taken up these classifications and also finds he must reject them (see n. 2 above).

9. "The Feminists: A Second Look," *Columbia Forum* 13 (Fall 1970): 24–30.

10. Rochelle Paul Wortis, "The Acceptance of the Concept of Maternal Role by Behavioral Scientists: Its Effects on Women," *American Journal of Orthopsychiatry* 41 (October 1971): 733–46.

11. Kathleen Gough, "The Origin of the Family," *Journal of Marriage and the Family* 33 (November 1971): 760–71.

12. *Bryan's Dictionary of Painters and Engravers* (London: Geo. Bell, 1904), 4:285.

13. "Why Have There Been No Great Women Artists?" *Art News* 69, no. 9 (January 1971): 22–39, 67–71.

14. H. D. Kitto, *The Greeks* (Baltimore: Penguin Books, 1962), pp. 219–36.

15. Unpublished paper on "The Esthetics of Power" to appear in *The New Eros*, ed. Joan Semmel (New York: Hacker Art Books, 1975). See also Carol Duncan, "Virility and Domination in Early 20th Century Vanguard Painting," *Artforum* 12 (December 1973): 30–39.

16. Michelle Zimbalist Rosaldo and Louise Lamphere, eds. *Women, Culture and Society*, (Stanford, Calif.: Stanford University Press, 1974), p. 17.

17. "Women's History in Transition: The European Case," *Feminist Studies* 3:3–4 (1976): 83–103.

18. See panel papers, *Conceptual Frameworks in Women's History* (n. 2 above).

19. Karen Sacks, "Engels Revisited," in Rosaldo and Lamphere, p. 207. See also Eleanor Leacock's introduction to Engels, *The Origin of the Family, Private Property and the State* (New York: International Publishers, 1972); also Leacock's paper delivered at Columbia University Seminar on Women in Society, April 1975.

20. On this point, one would like to see many more specific studies as in n. 19 above, which trace in detail the process of social change that fosters male control of the new means of production for exchange, and with the new wealth, control of the broader social or public order and of the family as well. Historical studies of civilized societies would be useful for examples of extended processes of social change, including those of our own society.

21. E.g., among the Ibo, Mbuti, and Lovedu (see Rosaldo and Lamphere, pp. 149, 216).

22. In *Woman's Estate* (New York: Random House, 1973), Juliet Mitchell (developing an earlier essay) offered the categories of reproduction/production within which to consider the history of women. This is roughly equivalent to the domestic/public categorization, except that she added sexuality and socialization as two further socially ordered functions which need not be attached to reproduction universally, although they have been under capitalism. I believe we must consider sexuality and socialization in any study of the sexual order: what are the relations among love, sex, and marriage in any society, for women and for men, heterosexual and homosexual, and who socializes which groups of children, by sex and by age, so that they find their places in the social order—including their sexual places. I also believe, as Juliet Mitchell does, that the evidence clearly warrants working out relations between the dominant mode of production in a society and the forms of reproduction, sexuality, and socialization. However, certain difficulties emerge, not in using this scheme so much as in using its terms—especially when we deal with precapitalist societies. Neither cultural nor political activities have a clearly definable place under the heading of production, as they do, e.g., when we use the terms domestic/public or, more simply, family and society. Another reason I prefer family/society or domestic/public, is that the terms production/reproduction tend to confound biological reproduction with social reproduction, and this obscures the essentially *productive* work of the family and the property relation between husband and wife. See my review of Rowbotham in *Science and Society* 39, no. 4 (Winter 1975/76): 471–74, and Lise Vogel's review essay on Juliet Mitchell, "The Earthly Family," *Radical America* 7 (Fall 1973): 9–50.

23. Ideas along these lines have been developed by Rowbotham, *Woman's Consciousness, Man's World*; Bridget O'Laughlin, "Mediation of Contradiction: Why Mbum Women Do Not Eat Chicken," in Rosaldo and Lamphere, pp. 301–20.

24. Dionysius of Halicarnassus, *The Roman Antiquities*, trans. E. Cary (Cambridge, Mass.: Harvard University Press), 1:381–82. Milton extended the property relationship between husband and wife to the Garden of Eden where Adam's possession of Eve constitutes the first example of private property: "Hail, wedded Love, mysterious law, true source/Of human offspring, sole propriety/In Paradise of all things common else!" (*Paradise Lost*, pt. 4, lines 750–51). Needless to say, where Eve serves Adam while he serves God, the "propriety" is not a mutual relation.

25. For examples given here, see the articles on the periods in question in Bridenthal and Koonz, *Becoming Visible*.

26. This is one of Rowbotham's points in *Woman's Consciousness, Man's World*. I believe it should lead to development of the genre of psychohistorical studies and studies in family history exemplified by Philippe Aries, *Centuries of Childhood: A Social History of Family Life* (New York: Alfred A. Knopf, 1965); Nancy Chodorow, "Family Structure and Feminine Personality," in Rosaldo and Lamphere, pp. 43–67; David Hunt, *Parents and Children in History* (New York: Harper & Row, 1972); the Frankfort school in *Autorität und Familie*, ed. Max Horkheimer (Paris: Alcan, 1936); Wilhelm Reich, *The Mass Psychology of Fascism* (New York: Farrar, Straus & Giroux, 1970); and Eli Zaretsky, "Capitalism, the Family and Personal Life," *Socialist Revolution* nos. 13, 14, 16 (1973). See the excellent article on this mode of historical inquiry by Lawrence Stone, in the *New York Review of Books* 21 (November 14, 1974): 25.

III.

INTRODUCTION TO *ANOTHER VOICE:*
FEMINIST PERSPECTIVES ON SOCIAL LIFE
AND SOCIAL SCIENCE

Marcia Millman and Rosabeth Moss Kanter

In their early 1970s introduction to the work of feminist sociologists, Marcia Millman and Rosabeth Moss Kanter identified six criticisms which have remained central preoccupations not only in sociology, but also in other social sciences. One of these criticisms focuses explicitly on problems with the methods favored by sociologists. However, eliminating the other flaws identified by Millman and Kanter has been at least as important in generating the best of the last decade's feminist sociology. The criticisms Millman and Kanter cite appear primarily to be objections to how sociological theory is applied and to assumptions that are central to some sociological theories. Once one begins to see the world through women's eyes, radically new sociological assumptions are called for.[1]

The essay also raises interesting epistemological issues. In their opening paragraphs, Millman and Kanter borrow the story of the Emperor's new clothes in order to explain how it is that the women's movement could produce empirically more accurate pictures of social reality. In this essay they provide a clear formulation of one of the feminist epistemologies that will be examined in chapter 12. But the reader can already detect some ways in which Millman and Kanter's explanation differs from traditional accounts of how to achieve greater objectivity in science. (Hint: Do traditional accounts recommend the formation of movements of social liberation as a scientific strategy?)

The reader will find the criticisms of sociology that Millman and Kanter present to be powerful ones. This is a good place to begin speculation about why the social sciences have not changed much as a result of such criticisms. One possibility is that in spite of the important contributions feminists have made to this field, "feminist perspectives have been contained in sociology by functionalist conceptualizations of gender, by the inclusion of gender as a variable rather than as a theoretical category, and by being ghettoized, especially in Marxist sociology."[2] Moreover, sociology's excessive adherence to remnants of positivist epistemologies and the low status that theory commands in the discipline also make it difficult for sociologists to appreciate the importance of the feminist analyses. One sociologist has suggested that it may be especially disconcerting to male researchers to be asked to examine critically gender relations in their own kinds of societies rather than only in the geographically or historically distant ones with which such disciplines as history and anthropology are concerned.[3] We will see thinkers in other social sciences also concerned to account for the resistances to undistorted understandings of women and gender relations created by the historical, sociological, and political preoccupations of their disciplines.[4]

Every one knows the story about the Emperor and his fine clothes: although the towns-people persuaded themselves that the Emperor was elegantly costumed, a child, pos-sessing an unspoiled vision, showed the citizenry that the Emperor was really naked. The story instructs us about one of our basic sociological premises: that reality is subjective, or rather, subject to social definition. The story also reminds us that collective delusions can be undone by introducing fresh perspectives.

Movements of social liberation are like the story in this respect: they make it possible for people to see the world in an enlarged perspective because they remove the covers and blinders that obscure knowledge and observation. In the last decade no social move-ment has had a more startling or consequential impact on the way people see and act in the world than the women's movement. Like the onlookers in the Emperor's parade, we can see and plainly speak about things that have always been there, but that formerly were unacknowledged. Indeed, today it is impossible to escape noticing features of social life that were invisible only ten years ago.

Changes in personal and social consciousness bring to mind some of the most funda-mental issues of sociology: questions of knowledge and how what people know and see in the world is affected by their particular location in the social structure. Although so-ciology often assumes a "single society" (albeit with class distinctions), in fact it is more likely that members of different social categories as men and women, located differentially in the social structure, both subjectively and literally inhabit different social worlds and realities. In keeping with the expansion of consciousness emerging from the women's movement, it is obvious that most of what we have formerly known as the study of society is only the male study of male society (to borrow a phrase from Jessie Bernard, 1973). Feminist critiques have shown us how social science has been defined by models repre-senting a world dominated by white males, and so our studies of the social world have been limited by the particular interests, perspectives, and experiences of that one group. As new groups challenge the structure of power and attain new roles and opportunities, new models of society arise.

This collection of essays was undertaken to examine sociology critically and to ask how our knowledge of the social world and social behavior could be expanded to consider a broader range of theories, perspectives, and social realities. Specifically, those realities previously invisible but now taking shape because of the women's movement would be examined. Our purpose was not primarily to see whether women are treated stereotypically in social science, although that might be an unavoidable feature of the analysis. Nor did we wish to restrict our exploration to examining women's neglected participation in the social world (several excellent collections, such as Huber's [1973], meet this need). Instead, we wished to reassess the basic theories, paradigms, substantive concerns, and methodolo-gies of sociology and the social sciences to see what changes are needed to make social theory and research reflect the multitude of both female and male realities and interests. We also wanted to provide critical bibliographic reviews of existing studies about women to help orient those readers who wish to do further reading and research.

Therefore, we invited a number of authors known for their interest in such questions to critically review significant works in their own subfields and to suggest changes needed to understand the social realities and perspectives which have been previously overlooked. All of the authors came to the conclusion that the vision of social life embedded in conventional social science has been limited. Among the themes that emerge from their collective work, we may note six important types of critiques:

1. *Important areas of social inquiry have been overlooked because of the use of certain conventional field-defining models; alternative models can open new areas for examination, about both women and men.*

Because sociologists have relied extensively upon certain models of social structure and action, there has been a systematic blindness to crucial elements of social reality. Most of the models that dominate sociology focus upon traditionally masculine concerns and male settings. Hochschild argues that the sociological emphasis upon Weberian rationality in explaining human action and social organization defines out of existence, from the start, the equally important element of emotion in social life and structure. She suggests an original sociological framework for examining emotions in the study of social structure. Lofland argues that the unchallenged reliance by urban researchers upon the "community model" precludes notice of other important forms of social organization in the city— particularly those settings and patterns of urban life that women populate and dominate. Millman argues that the dramaturgical analysis of deviance and social control may mask the authentic suffering that people experience in such settings.

These themes emerge in more general discussions as several of the authors question the wisdom of many sociological models that do not use the person and her/his subjective experiences as the proper unit of analysis. This questioning is reminiscent of the comments by Jessie Bernard (1973) and Rae Carlson (1972) on David Bakan's distinction between two kinds of research approaches characterized by "agency" or "communion." Agency focuses upon variables and communion upon human beings:

> Agency operates by way of mastery and control; communion with naturalistic observation, sensitivity to qualitative patterning, and greater personal participation by the investigator (Carlson, 1972). Nothing in this polarity is fundamentally new. For almost 50 years I have watched one or another version of it in sociology (for example, statistical vs. case method, quantitative vs. qualitative, knowledge vs. understanding or *verstehen* . . .).
>
> What is new and illuminating, however, is the recognition of a *machismo* element in research. The specific processes involved in agentic research are typically male preoccupations; agency is identified with a masculine principle, the Protestant ethic, a Faustian pursuit of knowledge—as with all forces toward mastery, separation, and ego enhancement (Carlson, 1972). The scientist using this approach creates his own controlled reality. He can manipulate it. He is master. He

has power. He can add or subtract or combine variables. He can play with a simulated reality like an Olympian god. He can remain at a distance, safely behind his shield, uninvolved. The communal approach is much humbler. It disavows control, for control spoils the results. [Bernard, 1973]

Several of the authors in this collection demonstrate how research characterized by the "agentic," quantitative approach fails to capture the most important features of the social world.

2. *Sociology has focused on public, official, visible, and/or dramatic role players and definitions of the situation; yet unofficial, supportive, less dramatic, private, and invisible spheres of social life and organization may be equally important.*

Just as sociology has overlooked important social realities through the use of certain restrictive field-defining *models*, so has it ignored large chunks of social life by using restrictive notions of the *field* of social action. When focusing only on "official" actors and actions, sociology has set aside the equally important locations of private, supportive, informal, local social structures in which women participate most frequently. In consequence, not only do we underexamine and distort women's activities in social science, but we also fail to understand how social systems actually function because we do not take into account one of their most basic processes: the interplay between informal, interpersonal networks and the formal, official social structures. It can be argued that sociologists have studied only the tip of the iceberg by attending primarily to the formal, official action and actors.

For feminists, these unofficial, less visible structures have taken on great importance, for as Pauline Bart (1971) notes, women have had to get by informal power some of what they have been denied formally. However, informal networks also serve to support and protect the official, formal, social structures. Judith Lorber shows how an informal, fraternal system of male sponsorship and patronage insures that only male doctors will find their way into prestigious residencies and medical specialties. She argues that this informal network may be more consequential than the factors traditionally cited for why women doctors are disproportionately clumped in low-paying, low-prestige specialties.

In similar arguments, Roby, Kanter, and Daniels show how informal male friendship networks at work isolate women employees and circumvent the alleged goals of affirmative action programs. Millman demonstrates how research in deviance and social control has focused on dramatic incidents in official locations, such as courtrooms and mental hospitals, paying little attention to the equally important subject of long-term accommodation to deviance. She also argues that sociologists have not recognized the importance of studying everyday, interpersonal social control and the subtle, continuous series of maneuvers that individuals use to keep each other in line during ordinary, mundane activities. Additionally, she indicates how sociologists have focused upon the relationship between persons officially labeled deviant and the official agents of social control, while excluding victims, family members, and other individuals closely involved but having no place in formal procedures.

In its emphasis on the visible, official portion of social life, sociology has also overlooked important support structures to social enterprises because they are not in public view. Kanter discusses the need to consider these structures in studies of organizations where the vast layers of female secretaries and clerks and the "auxiliary organization" composed of wives are ignored. Tuchman argues that sociologists of culture have mistakenly placed their emphasis upon the individual "genius" artists (usually men, since women are frequently excluded from such opportunities), but says that we cannot understand the production of art without taking into account all of the social structures that support changes and developments in artistic forms. She argues that women have been central in creating important developments in art, taking as evidence the women who sponsored the salons in seventeenth- and eighteenth-century France, the middle-class women in the eighteenth century who supported the development of the novel and other literary institutions, and the philanthropic women of the social elite who fund the performing arts in contemporary United States. These analyses illustrate the point that prior sociological perspectives not only ignore the participation of women, but also result in a failure to understand many aspects of the operation of social systems (whether cultural, organizational, interpersonal, or medical).

Finally, there are various "local" settings, largely populated by women in their daily rounds of life, which have received no serious sociological attention. As Lofland argues, such important facets of urban life as the behavior of customers and clerks in stores, mothers and children in parks, women at beauty parlors, and widows at coffee shops are completely overlooked by sociologists who claim to study the "community." The importance of the mundane aspects of our social life becomes more prominent in a feminist perspective (although it is a feature of both women's and men's lives) because, as Daniels points out, women have traditionally been chained to an existence of cleaning up and caring for others.

3. *Sociology often assumes a "single society" with respect to men and women, in which generalizations can be made about all participants, yet men and women may actually inhabit different social worlds, and these must be taken into account.*

Jessie Bernard (1973) notes how it is easy to demonstrate that men and women frequently inhabit different worlds while they are living in the same physical location. Bernard's own research (1972) illustrates how the same marriage may constitute a different reality for the husband and the wife. Yet sociologists do not always take seriously this essential principle, and instead they assume that generalizations can be applied to everyone in a setting, irrespective of location and position. Several of the authors in the collection take exception to this oversight.

Hochschild argues that despite the popular notion that emotions are the great "equalizer" in society, in fact, feelings such as love and anger are distributed unevenly in the social structure (anger is aimed downward and love upward in status and power ladders). Therefore, powerless and powerful people inhabit different emotional as well as social and physical worlds. McCormack proposes that although voting studies have assumed a single political culture for both sexes (in which women frequently come out looking conservative or politically apathetic), in fact it is more accurate to assume that men and women inhabit two different political cultures. Consequently, their behavior cannot be evaluated by the same (male) criteria. Myers is critical of the social-science assumption that black women adopt the same standards as white (male) society, and the consequent assumption of researchers that therefore low self-esteem is inevitable among black women who are heads of households. Myers argues, instead, that black women evaluate themselves according to their own standards and values, and are proud of their strong positions as heads of matriarchal families. Finally, Roby discusses the special concerns and situations of blue-collar, industrial, and service working women (as opposed to their male counterparts), and outlines what research is needed to understand their living and working circumstances.

4. *In several fields of study, sex is not taken into account as a factor in behavior, yet sex may be among the most important explanatory variables.*

In her critique of literature on the sociology of education, Lightfoot points out that sociologists have failed to consider questions associated with the fact that most teachers are women. For example, research has neglected consideration of such issues as the impact of women occupying a dominant position in the classroom (and no other place) on male and female children, or how the teacher's sexuality affects her interactions with boys and girls. Similarly, Lorber points out that since studies of doctors have generally excluded women from consideration, we do not know how the sex of the physician affects patient-doctor interactions. Kanter argues that the informal organization of the managerial world may be highly masculine and the ideologies of management supportive of a "masculine ethic." Tuchman points out that studies of recruitment into artistic careers have failed to consider the relevance of sex is a variable, a glaring oversight when sex is such an important factor in career choices and patterns. In some cases these oversights come from the assumption by researchers that all of their subjects are male (in the case of doctors, managers, artists); in other cases, social scientists may not see male dominance as a problem to be explained. Thus they do not discern the significance of the distribution of the sexes in various locations. When male sociologists (or men in general) look at a meeting of a board of trustees and see only men, they think they are observing a sexually neutral or sexless world rather than a masculine world. For, as Kanter suggests, women are the bearers of sex.

5. *Sociology frequently explains the status quo (and therefore helps provide rationalizations for existing power distributions); yet social science should explore needed social transformations and encourage a more just, humane society.*

Social scientists must be mindful of what impact their research might have on social policy and on the legitimatization of present social arrangements and attend instead to indicating how needed transformations could be accomplished. As Roby argues, social scientists are needed to act on behalf of blue-collar working women by focusing public attention on the group's needs and by providing these women with information that would make them more effective in protecting themselves and attaining their goals. Similarly, Daniels argues that there is a special need at this time for research concerned not only with analyzing the conditions of women's lives and understanding the causes and consequences of women's oppression, but also concerned with improving the quality of their lives. Therefore, she argues that knowledge can best be advanced by alternating between organizing actual efforts at social reform and reflecting on the processes of such social movements.

6. *Certain methodologies (frequently quantitative) and research situations (such as having male social scientists studying worlds involving women) may systematically prevent the elicitation of certain kinds of information, yet this undiscovered information may be the most important for explaining the phenomenon being studied.*

Methodological assumptions and techniques may limit the researcher's vision and produce questionable findings. Tresemer analyzes how most statistical studies of sex differences have been misleading because of their exaggeration of differences through the inappropriate use of bipolar, unidimensional, continuous, normal distributions. Tresemer suggests alternative quantitative methods for exploring gender differences statistically in a less biased fashion. But the problems of quantitative analysis may not be restricted to the use of inappropriate distributions: as we noted earlier, several of the authors stated a preference for qualitative as opposed to the more conventional quantitative approaches, which deal with variables rather than persons, and which may be associated with an unpleasantly exaggerated masculine style of control and manipulation.

Lorber and Millman point to the difficulties of male sociologists doing research on women: the males have a serious handicap because they are frequently unable to "take the role of" their female subjects. Male actors and subjects are portrayed by male sociologists with "loving empiricism," so that we "see the world through their eyes, watch them in the process of defining, coping, interacting," but the researchers have often been unable to achieve the same empathy with female subjects. As Lofland reflects, we may look forward to the time when socially defined categories will not create such severe separations between groups of people that each group lacks access to the other's places and minds. At that time we shall fulfill the potential of all human beings to take the role of all others.

EDITOR'S NOTES

1. As Dorothy Smith points out later in this volume, women sociologists, too, must learn how to recover what the world looks like through women's eyes.

2. Judith Stacey and Barrie Thorne, "The Missing Feminist Revolution in Sociology," *Social Problems* 32, no. 4 (1985):301.

3. Pauline Bart, in conversation.

4. Kanter's best known book is *Men and Women of the Corporation* (New York: Basic Books, 1979). Millman's most recent one is *Such a Pretty Face: Being Fat in America* (Berkeley, Calif.: Berkeley Publishing Co., 1986).

REFERENCES

Bart, Pauline. 1971. "Sexism and Social Science: From the Gilded Cage to the Iron Cage, or, The Perils of Pauline," *Journal of Marriage and the Family* 33(4):734–45.

Bernard, Jessie. 1973. "My Four Revolutions: An Autobiographical History of the ASA," *American Journal of Sociology* 78(4).

Carlson, Rae. 1972. "Understanding Women: Implications for Personality Theory and Research," *Journal of Social Issues* 28(2):17–32.

Huber, Joan. 1973. *American Journal of Sociology* 78(4).

IV.

BIAS IN PSYCHOLOGY

Carolyn Wood Sherif

Carolyn Wood Sherif is well known as the author of many psychology texts and research reports. In this first part of a long essay, she points to the historical and sociological reasons why psychologists have preferred some research methods over others and held certain beliefs about how to pursue knowledge.

She argues that by the 1940s there was a hierarchy of research methods in psychology that was intended to reflect the high value given to the natural sciences by the philosophers known as logical positivists.[1] On such a scale, experimentalists, "mental testers," and statisticians ranked highest, while developmental, clinical, and social psychologists ranked lowest. She points out that in subsequent decades "each of the fields and specialities in psychology sought to improve its status by adopting . . . the perspectives, theories, and methodologies as high on the hierarchy as possible." However, she argues that this practice only mimicked the *form* of the natural sciences, not their standards for evidence gathering. Fundamental to this scientism were beliefs about the appropriate subject matters, languages, and methods of science which, in fact, wildly distorted the beliefs and practices of the natural sciences that they were intended to imitate. They also led directly to false beliefs about how to pursue knowledge—and to ones that seriously undermined psychology's ability to explain much at all about women and gender.

Of course we can give more than historical and sociological explanations for why a culture (or a subculture such as professional psychology) adopts certain beliefs and practices at a given time: some beliefs and practices *are* better than others, and social conditions permit the culture to recognize this. However, the stories which disciplines themselves tell about why their recommended beliefs and practices *should* be regarded as desirable rarely mention the kinds of real determinants Sherif mentions. One needs to keep these in mind as one listens to the criticisms of traditional research methods, methodologies, and epistemologies.

Presumably, sexists are not the only psychologists to formulate ideas about scientific problems, concepts, theories, methods, and purposes of inquiry which clearly bear the fingerprints of the social projects of their cultures. How might the offending psychological agendas Sherif identifies (and others she may not have identified) have racist consequences? What are the sociological, historical, and institutional projects that are influencing the way feminist psychologists think about their subject matters? Which of these interests and values might be increasing and which decreasing the *scientific value* of this research?

Almost a decade ago, Naomi Weisstein fired a feminist shot that ricocheted down the halls between psychology's laboratories and clinics, hitting its target dead center. The shot was a paper, of course, and thanks to the woman's movement, it later found its way into print under the title "Psychology Constructs the Female, or The Fantasy Life of the Male Psychologist." Her thesis was that "psychology has nothing to say about what women are really like, what they need and what they want, essentially because psychology does not know."[1]

Weisstein's critique focused on the male-centeredness of psychology and upon theories that attribute women's lower status in society and personal problems to psychological qualities that make both appear to be inevitable. She correctly directed attention to social-psychological research demonstrating the impact of social circumstances upon an individual's private experiences and actions.

Still earlier, a woman whose academic study had been in psychology made similar critical points in *The Feminine Mystique*.[2] The year that book appeared I spoke at a symposium at Rice University on the status of the "educated woman," declaring that ignorance about women pervaded academic disciplines in higher education where the "requirements for the degree seldom include thoughtful inquiry into the status of women, as part of the total human condition."[3] A reading of Georgene Seward's *Sex and the Social Order*[4] had long ago convinced me that the orthodox methods of studying and interpreting sex differences were capable of delivering only mischievous and misleading trivia. Apart from the hoary sex-differences tradition (euphemistically called the "study of individual differences"), psychology's treatment of the sexes contained several brands of psychoanalytic thought and a growing accumulation of research on socialization to "sex-appropriate behaviors," which was actually the old sex-difference model mixed with psychoanalytic notions and served in a new disguise.

Since the 1960s, the woman's movement has provided the needed context for critical examination of biased theoretical assumptions and working practices in psychology's diverse areas. While referring to that critical literature and the more positive efforts to proceed toward reconstruction, I will concentrate here on examining the following questions, which I believe must be answered if there is to be an equitable pursuit of knowledge about human individuals in psychology:

1. Why have demonstrations of theoretical and research bias, some dating to the earliest days of academic psychology, been no more effective than they have been in correcting theory and research practice? Is the problem simply that there have not been enough women in psychology, or is there something in psychology's assumptions and working practices that also needs attention?

2. What are the dominant beliefs in psychology about the proper ways to pursue knowledge? Where do they come from and what supports them, despite the documented fact that they can encourage biased perspectives?

3. What assumptions about the human individual lie beneath the diversity of psychological theories and their associated procedures for studying that individual?

4. What can we learn from an examination of the state of psychology today that will further an equitable pursuit of knowledge?

Ethnocentrism, Androcentrism, and Sexist Bias
in Psychology

The growth of academic psychology over the past century has been compellingly a United States' phenomenon, despite European origins and the non-American backgrounds of a number of its stimulating theorists and researchers. A few decades after William James at Harvard and Wilhelm Wundt at Leipzig started psychological laboratories (1875, according to Boring's history),[5] their students had started psychology departments or laboratories at major universities, including the newly forming women's colleges. Work by women Ph.D.'s began to appear, and two of them (Mary Calkins and Margaret Washburn) served early in this century as presidents of the American Psychological Society, which had formed toward the end of the nineteenth century. In Cattell's *American Men of Science* of 1903, three women were included among fifty psychologists starred as "eminent," two ranked in twelfth and nineteenth ranks (Mary Calkins and C. Ladd-Franklin, respectively), and the third among the last twenty (Margaret Washburn).[6] Not a high proportion, to be sure.

The problem of bias in psychological research was encountered early in the discipline's history, as E. G. Boring's *History of Experimental Psychology* makes clear. "Laboratory atmospheres," or the little Geister within the Zeitgeist (to use his favorite term), were repeatedly found to affect the results coming from different laboratories on the same problem, whether the problem concerned such issues as the presence or absence of images in thought, insightful learning vs. slow trial-and-error learning, or the accumulating research on sex difference. In his history, Boring dismissed sex bias once and for all when assessing the results of Francis Galton's psychological assessments on 9,337 persons at the 1884 International Health Exhibition: "No important generalizations as regards human individual differences appeared; however, unless we should note Galton's erroneous conclusion that women tend in all their capacities to be inferior to men."[7]

Helen Thompson Woolley had critically exposed the bias in sex-difference research, dismissing much of it as drivel, in 1903 and 1910.[8] Leta S. Hollingworth completed doctoral research at Columbia on whether performance on several tasks suffered during menstruation, finding no decrement despite the contrary conviction of her major professor, E. L. Thorndike. Like Mary Calkins earlier, she repeatedly wrote against the hypothesis that women's intellectual capacities varied less than men's. She penned an article in 1916 called "Social Devices for Impelling Women to Bear and Rear Children" that can still rock complacent heels.[9]

And surely someone must have read the dissertation by Mary Putman Jacobi that won the distinguished Boylston Prize from Harvard University in 1876 on the question, "Do women require mental and bodily rest during menstruation, and to what extent?" Dr. Jacobi began her dissertation with the following caution: "An inquiry into the limits of activity and attainments that may be imposed by sex is very frequently carried on in the same spirit as that which hastens to ascribe to permanent differences in race all the peculiarities of a class, and this because the sex that is supposed to be limiting in its nature, is nearly always different from that of the person conducting the inquiry."[10] Then she reviewed historical evidence both on medical views of menstruation and on women as workers. She collected complete case histories on 268 women, including on their health, took physiological measures during one to three months, and conducted a small performance experiment. She concluded that, yes, short rest periods during the working day would be helpful for menstruating women, as they also would be for women and men during the rest of the month, all of whom would benefit even more by an eight-hour day in place of the twelve or more hours they then labored.

Admittedly, I have chosen cases of women who were keenly aware of the actualities of sex bias, and who were vigorously protesting its manifestations. If, instead, we were to look at the work of the other forty-seven eminent psychologists on Cattell's list in 1903 or at the bulk of writings on sex differences during the early part of this century or at the writings of Sigmund Freud, we would find tons of exemplars for the conclusion reached by my colleague and former student, Stephanie Shields, in her highly original paper reviewing the early years to document social myth in psychology. Her conclusion was as follows: "That science played handmaiden to social values cannot be denied."[11] A similar conclusion could be reached by examining the literature in psychology on race. Yet some mental testers will deny that racism has anything to do with contemporary controversies over intelligence testing.[12]

One could go on and on with further examples of theoretical and research controversies involving bias in psychology on large and on small problems. But I come to a major question: If the possibility and the existence of sexist bias was recognized by the turn of this century, why and how could academic and nonacademic psychology continue to perpetuate its myths up to the present?

Hierarchy in Psychology

It has been thirty-four years since I entered psychology as a graduate student, having learned as an undergraduate at Purdue University that there was such a thing as social psychology. My desire to be a social psychologist was then unorthodox. Nevertheless, I was accepted, even welcomed into the psychology department of the University of Iowa as a graduate assistant. It was 1943, during World War II, when qualified male applicants to graduate programs were scarcer than hen's teeth. As we should know, women are valued more when men are scarce, as today's volunteer army demonstrates. My first lessons at Iowa concerned the status criteria and norms valued by psychologists.

At the peak of the status hierarchy were the experimentalists. At that time and place, being an experimentalist meant being self-consciously scientific, reading the philosophy of science as expounded by logical positivists, and studying hungry rats learning the way to food, or humans responding to a puff of air to the eyelid. One way to determine who "counts" to an elite is to learn whose arguments the elite attends to and whose viewpoints they try to demolish. At the time, the only people worthy of attention from experimentalists were other experimentalists.

The next rung in the hierarchy was occupied by the "mental testers" and statistical buffs, who represented a quite different tradition in psychology but had to be listened to by experimentalists who wanted to analyze their data in the currently fashionable way. The testing tradition, which began in Great Britain, had been fueled by the practical success of the French psychologists Binet and Simon in developing a workable test for singling out school children with potential learning problems. The Stanford version of their test, the development of group tests, and their use during World War I put testers of all kinds into an orbit that is now a $120 million industry by conservative estimate.[13] Interestingly enough, a survey of the interests of women psychologists just after World War II revealed that proportionally more were in the ranks of the testers than of the experimentalists.[14] So perhaps it is no accident that the two women (Anne Anastasi and Leona Tyler) who were elected presidents of the American Psychological Association in the past decade were recognized as experts in the mental testing tradition of differential psychology as well as active contributors to the professional organization. Somewhat more predictably, their terms followed immediately upon that of the first and only black president of the association (Kenneth B. Clark).

On the next lowest rung of the hierarchy at Iowa in 1943 were the developmental psychologists, whose work at the time focused heavily on preschool children. They were housed in the same building, but under the separate roof of the Institute for Child Welfare (a less prestigious locale, you may be sure), and included the only women faculty. Although regarded as the "child study people," they were headed by an experimentalist from the same major university as the psychology chairman; hence, a few of them were regarded as acceptable by experimentalists. But the testers and the developmentalists had more to talk about, since Iowans were in the forefront of the attack on a fixed, inherited "intelligence," battling Minnesotans and Californians who defended the alleged constancy of IQ.

One distinguished member of the Child Welfare faculty was Kurt Lewin. Lewin had published the famous studies on the effects of adult modes of interaction on the behavior of small boys in leisure-time groups, the authoritarian, democratic, and laissez-faire leadership experiments.[15] At the time, he was often in Washington, involved in the equally well-known studies on group decision. (These studies demonstrated that women volunteers in Red Cross activities were not easily persuaded by lectures to alter long-ingrained food customs, but were quite capable of changing the family diet to include unpopular foods to help the war effort when presented with the problem of food shortages and encouraged to arrive at a joint decision to make the change.)[16] Like many of their experimental colleagues in Washington, in military service, or with the Office of War Information, the experimentalists at Iowa regarded these as "applied" activities, necessary at the time but not the stuff of which a science is made. At the bottom of the Iowa ladder and also classified as "applied" were the one other social psychologist and the clinical psychologists.

The hierarchy was male, of course. Thirty years ago, it was the experimentalists at the top, the testers and statisticians next, then the developmentalists, and finally the social psychologists, including some interested in what was called personality, along with the clinicians. After World War II, there were notable changes, the most striking being the enormous increase in number of clinical psychologists, with federal funds to support their activities and student training. Today, about 40 percent of APA members are clinical psychologists. The numbers and the standing of social psychologists changed, less through their following the example of Kurt Lewin than through their self-conscious efforts to be accepted as *experimental* social psychologists and their quoting Lewin's injunction against historicalism, one of his least defensible points. A host of new specialties was born of postwar prosperity. You name it, we have it, including in 1973 a division on psychology of women and by 1976 a division "interested in religion."

So why do I bring up the hierarchy of three decades ago? It is my contention that each of the fields and specialities in psychology sought to improve its status by adopting (as well and as closely as stomachs permitted) the perspectives, theories, and methodologies as high on the hierarchy as possible. The way to "respectability" in this scheme has been the appearance of rigor and scientific inquiry, bolstered by highly restricted notions of what science is about. The promise was that theirs was the true path to general psychological principles, applicable with slight modification to any human being and, in some cases, to any organism, even rats, monkeys, and chimpanzees.

Never mind that in practice, psychology treated women, blacks, and other minorities, as well as residents of certain other countries, as more "different" than a well-behaved laboratory chimpanzee. We are talking of myth, or more accurately, the ideology of psychology's elite. In that perspective, work outside of the laboratory was suspect. Research in naturalistic settings was regarded as necessarily less "pure," even "contaminated." Efforts to change social life or individual circumstances were regarded as merely "applied" work, typically as premature attempts to apply psychological principles.

The irony is that the preservation of psychology's hierarchy and the expansion of the entire enterprise was supported by those psychologists making inroads into major institutions—educational, business, industrial, military, governmental, the growing mass media, and the "mental health" institutions and industry—in short, the "applied" psychologists. Without their inroads, psychology would have been small potatoes in academia, but it need not have worried. The growing number of psychologists in major institutions needed the academic hierarchy to support its claims at being scientific.

Dominant Beliefs Conducive to Bias in Psychology

Certain of its dominant beliefs about the proper ways to pursue knowledge have made psychological research peculiarly prone to bias in its conception, execution, and interpretation. It is on these that I shall focus here—and I shall be highly critical. If I thought that these were the only beliefs in psychology or that they characterized everything within its bounds, I would not still be a psychologist. But I have seen a number of battles and skirmishes over psychological findings, many of them possible because of fundamental flaws in the orthodox modes of seeking knowledge.

A historical perspective is useful in understanding the issues. One year after psychology's entry onto the academic scene, the Centennial Exposition of 1876 opened in Philadelphia. As the Smithsonian's 1976 recreation vividly reminds us, rhapsodic praise of science and technology was a major theme. From its birth, academic psychology cast its lot within the bright promise of a scientific future. Similarly, founders of the notion of psychotherapy—all physicians, including Sigmund Freud—were immersed in that same promise. Freud reserved special indignation for those critics, like Havelock Ellis, who suggested that he was dealing in allegory and myth rather than in science.[17] In this respect alone, Freud was brother under the skin to the best-known psychologist of our day, B. F. Skinner.

I shall not be exploring the larger historical trends toward faith in science. Instead, I am concerned with the subsidiary impulse of psychologists to seek acceptance and prestige for their new discipline through imitating the more established scientific disciplines. Over time, those who became the most prominent psychologists were those who imitated the most blindly, grasping what brought prestige in their society even though it was more a caricature of the more established sciences.

Undeniably, the prestigious and successful sciences in the late nineteenth and early twentieth century were those securely focused on the physical world and the physical processes of the organic world. Psychologists, in their strivings to gain status with other scientists, did not pause long on issues raised by the differences between studying a rock, a chemical compound, or an animal, on one hand, and a human individual, on the other. Instead, methods that had been successful in the physical and biological sciences were embraced as models for psychology. Researchers were soon deep into analogy, comparing the human individual to the chemical compound or to the animal as the subject of research, with all of the power that such an analogy gives to the scientific investigator, at least if the animal is captive and small. Unlike the natural scientist, however, the psychologist had only social power over the research subject, not the greater power to explore, observe, and analyze that had unlocked so many of nature's secrets for the physical sciences.

Beliefs about What Is "Basic"

The methodology promoted in psychology, in its strivings for social acceptability and prestige, rested on the assumption that the causes of an event can be determined by breaking down the event into component parts, or elements, and studying those parts and their relationships to one another. The more "basic" these parts or elements are, the more "basic" is the inquiry.

What psychology defined as basic was dictated by slavish devotion to the more prestigious disciplines. Thus, a physiological or biochemical part or element was defined as more basic than a belief that Eve was created from Adam's rib, not because the former can necessarily tell us more about a human individual, but because physiology and biochemistry were more prestigious than religious history or sociology. On the environmental side, a physical element that could be counted or that one of the physical sciences had already measured was regarded as more "basic" than poverty; thus, the social disciplines that wrote about poverty in any way other than by counting income had even less standing than psychology. Turning to the humanities for an understanding of what is basic in being human was considered absurd. What could scholars in English or Spanish, in history or classics, possibly tell psychologists? Psychologists did look to history and philosophy to find out about the history and philosophy of science, but then, that was all about mathematics, physics, and chemistry, and therefore respectable.

Narrowing the Space and Time Framework

The event to be studied and the elements to be considered basic or peripheral were to be those that occurred in the here-and-now of the researcher's observation or of the other techniques for data collection. In many respects, Kurt Lewin's call for ahistoricalism in psychology—that is, for concerning oneself with history only as its forces were revealed in the immediate situation at the time of study—was merely confirmation of existing research practice.[18] Nonetheless, it provided justification for developmental, social, and personality psychologists to view as "scientific" the conduct of research on human individuals about whose past, personal loyalties, and social ties, about whose place in a larger historical-cultural nexus, they knew next to nothing. Consequently, they seldom looked for or found evidence of history, culture, or organizational ties in the specific research situations they studied. Mary Putnam Jacobi's surveys of the history of cultural and medical thought about menstruation and of the historical experiences of working women were now to be considered excess baggage in a study of particular women at a particular period of time. Even her case histories would come to be seen as unnecessary, except insofar as they contained evidence of physiologic malfunction, since physiological factors were defined as basic.

"Objective" Language as a Disguise for Ignorance or Bias

By the mid-twentieth century the elementism practiced by orthodox psychology became thoroughly blended with the language of applied mathematical statistics, especially as applied to biological and agricultural research. Thus, the elements became abstract "variables." The psychologist in pursuit of knowledge was attempting to seek causation by discovering lawful relationships among variables. Paraphrasing E. L. Thorndike, the psychologist came to believe that "anything that exists, exists in some quantity, hence can be measured" and hence is a variable.[19]

In causation, not all variables are created equal, however. Some are designated "independent variables," and it is to these that one looks for causality, despite textbook cautions to the contrary. One may find the independent variable in nature, as when an agronomist selects garden plots with soil rich or poor in nitrogen in which to plant corn. The yield or height of the growing corn is then the "dependent" variable caused by the independent variable (rich or poor soil), unless the soil or the seed or the air contain other "contaminating" variables.

It goes without saying that a person's sex is considered an independent variable, not a dependent one, despite the fact that everyone and no one knows what that means. Psychologists seem to think they know, when they pronounce that the sex of the researcher or the sex of the research subject, or both, are independent variables in research; but it should not take a Renée Richards to demonstrate that the assumption of causality by the "independent variable" of sex is misleading. Why? Because the "variable" called sex is like a railroad boxcar: everyone knows what it is called and what it is used for, but no one knows what is inside. Older psychologists had no doubt that it contained "biology." Modern psychologists follow suit, or add culture, or subtract biology as well. Result? Utter confusion in almost all discussions of the variable "sex" or of sex differences.

Glorifying the Experiment: An Example

The highly abstract belief that knowledge is to be gained by studying parts, elements, or variables and by seeking lawfulness in their relationships, is translated into reality during psychological research. The most prestigious way to make this translation is the experiment. In the experiment, certain selected "independent," presumably causative, elements are deliberately varied, while other possible choices are controlled or kept in a constant state.

What this description of the experiment means is that in the human experiment much of what goes on is simply ignored. The researcher may choose the independent variable by selecting persons according to sex, race, etc., or according to their performance on a psychological test. But the experiment is considered much more valid if the researcher attempts to create the independent variable by "manipulating" the circumstances in the research situation—for example, by controlling what people see or hear or do. Thus created, the variable is somehow regarded as purer, less "contaminated" by past experiences. History is ignored, and the researcher has the illusion of creating history at the moment.

While I was looking for an example of an experiment, the mail brought the current issue of the *Journal of Personality and Social Psychology*, the most widely read and cited journal in that area of psychology. The second article, by the journal editor and his students, concerned the effects of three "independent variables" upon reactions to messages intended to persuade college students for or against some viewpoint, for example, for or against faculty tenure. Other independent variables were also introduced in a series of eight separate experiments. All of these experiments studied the ratings of messages on thirty-six different topics made by persons described as follows: "Subjects were either unpaid undergraduate volunteers who were enrolled in introductory psychology courses or were paid respondents to classified advertisements in the university newspaper. . . . Subjects were recruited without regard to sex and were assigned randomly to a persuasion . . .

group and to an identification number within that group. . . . a total of 616 subjects provided data."[20]

Eighteen of the messages concerned past presidents of the United States, and eighteen
others concerned arbitrarily selected social issues—that is, the researchers simply picked
them. The experiments are presented as a novelty, with considerable pride, because the
messages were presented to subjects by computer on video screen, and the subjects responded to them by pushing the computer's buttons. "The computerized method assures
a standardized experimental procedure for each subject . . . it minimizes interaction of the
subject with a human experimenter. These characteristics are responsible for a desirably
high degree of situational control and assurance that possible sources of experimenter bias
are minimized."[21] But it was the researchers who selected the topics, presented them in
certain orders, varied the contents of the screen, etc. Moreover, the researchers were forced
to add the caution that "although the relationship of experimenter to subject is mediated
by the computer, that relationship nonetheless exists."[22] They make less issue about the
undeniable possibility of significant effects from interacting with a computer.

The researchers present their findings on the persuasive effects of the messages in typical
fashion, as the means or averages of all the students' single ratings on each issue after
they had read the message. The individual differences among the students, including what
their opinions about the presidents or the social issues were before messages were presented, were treated in the statistical analysis as a "random-effect" factor.

In short, this experiment typifies the assumption in a great deal of experimentation that
"general laws" about the relationships among variables can be obtained by comparing
averages of the responses made by a sizable number of individuals, who are regarded as
being without a background, personal history, or gender that might have anything to do
with their response in the situation. In this case, the situation itself is described only in
terms of the equipment, which is shown in a photograph. Its duration appears to have
been well within the academic hour.

Are These the Beliefs of "Hard Science"?

Doing "basic" research on "variables" that are given numbers, and hence can be treated
statistically, and, especially, performing experiments are sometimes called the "hard science" ways of seeking knowledge in psychology. What these beliefs describe, instead, are
efforts by some members of a newer, less established discipline to imitate what they, as
outsiders, see as the ways the physical sciences achieved knowledge successfully. It is the
physical sciences that are called "hard sciences," as we all know, and the human disciplines
that are "soft."

The adoption of the "hard" and "soft" analogy within psychology and within other social disciplines obscures the real issues, which are about the ways to extend scientific
methods to the study of human beings by other human beings. Those who use these
adjectives have almost always been men trying to put down other men and their work,
attempting to enhance their own status by associating their own efforts with the more

prestigious physical or natural sciences.[23] For this reason, I think it particularly misleading to suggest that "hard" also implies "masculine," while "soft" implies "feminine." After all, in the physical sciences there have been a few women, and some of the women minority in the "soft" disciplines follow the hard line.

Within psychology, the "hard" vs. "soft" name-calling is also to be heard when issues of "scientific" vs. "humanistic" psychology are discussed. Again, the controversies do not divide the men from the women; they have been quite divisive of male psychologists. But "humanistic" psychologists need to cease accepting their opponents' definitions of what is "scientific" and start to assess science as a human endeavor. The self-consciously scientific experimental psychologists need to start thinking about the unique problems raised in the history of science when human individuals turn to studying other individuals.

Meanwhile, the equitable pursuit of knowledge will be better served if we recognize psychologists' self-annointment as "hard" researchers for what it is: a put-down of critics who do not accept their orthodoxies. Those who proclaim the hardness of their methods and their hardware the loudest are the most guilty of producing research findings with the durability of a marshmallow. And now, we shall see why.

Critique of Psychological Orthodoxy's Beliefs on Its Objectivity

I have intended my description of the standard in psychological research, which admittedly was almost a caricature, to make clear that the standard research situation is loaded with opportunity for bias. The opportunity starts when a researcher decides what to study and it continues to widen during decisions about how to study the subject. What is the individual being studied to do during the research? The researcher decides, of course, often in highly arbitrary ways dictated by custom in previous research, not by what the person does or is doing in daily life. What are to be included as the all-important independent variables? Which aspects of the individual's behavior are to be noticed and which ignored during the research experience? The researcher makes all of these decisions, often forgetting at times that he or she is a human being who is part of the research situation too.

Research as an Interpersonal and Cultural Event

Now we can see, I trust, why Robert Rosenthal and many others after him were able to demonstrate in the late 1950s and the 1960s the phenomenon of researcher bias—specifically, that the researcher's expectations of the outcome in research affect what is actually found.[24] Rosenthal's findings should have come as no surprise. Studies of interviewing had already shown that middle-class interviewers obtained answers from working-class respondents that differed from those obtained by working-class interviewers, that white interviewers got answers from black respondents differing from those obtained by black interviewers, and that women respond differently to men and to women, as men respond differently to women and to men.[25]

Why should the effect of one human being upon another be a surprise, especially the effect of a much more powerful researcher upon a person who has agreed to cooperate in an institutional setting that defines the person as "subject"? Did someone believe that the psychology of researcher and the psychology of subject, both human beings, are altogether different?

There was also the failure to recognize other sociocultural aspects of the research situation. The research setting, whether experiment or interview, packs a cultural wallop through its physical location, especially if defined as a place to do research, and through the plethora of equipment, clipboards, forms, tape recorders, and audiovisual equipment that researchers pack about. Two-way mirrors, intended to hide the researcher, in fact alert the person observed that his or her actions are being watched and evaluated. A simple button placed in the room in the event that the subject wants to leave becomes a signal to "panic" ("if it's there, it's there to be used"). The supposedly neutral and objective paper-and-pencil test or information blank turns out to be a signal to the individual that someone who knows more than she does is evaluating something about her, perhaps even her worth as a person—an unnerving thought at best and at worst a promoter of apprehension or of an active effort to appear "socially desirable." Finally, evidence has accumulated indicating that people who volunteer for research tend to be those with more interest in psychology, research, and science, who do respond to the research situation differently from a person somehow mousetrapped in the research situation. The difference is typically in a direction congenial to the researcher's interest, although it need not be, especially since the researcher has often been unaware of the impact of these research impedimenta or of the active attempts by subjects to evaluate and deal with the research situation.[26]

The impact of the research situation is nowhere more convincingly shown than in Stanley Milgram's study of obedience by research subjects to a researcher's commands to deliver increasingly more severe electric shocks to another person who is ostensibly another innocent subject. Actually, the latter played a prescribed role, exhibiting discomfort and objecting to the procedures, though never actually being shocked. Once a "subject," man or woman, agreed to participate in the experiment, typically for pay, the highly institutional setting, the white-coated experimenter, and the structured procedures took precedence, at least for 65 percent of the subjects, so long as the apparent victim was out of sight in the next room. Milgram understood the power of that institutional setting, its equipment, and the authoritative researcher. He showed that obedience dropped sharply when the procedures called for closer proximity to the apparent victim, and that another person refusing to cooperate blew the game. The standard personality tests purporting to measure proclivities toward aggression proved worthless in predicting reactions to the research situation. On the other hand, certain past experiences in the subject's life did appear to relate to his or her decision on whether to continue shocking the victim or whether to stop, as 35 percent of Milgram's subjects did even in his most compelling situation. These past experiences related much more to the individual's perspectives on authority, on science, and on self than they did to abstractly defined personality characteristics.[27]

More Culture in Study of Persons

The final cultural wallop packed by a research situation concerns the activity performed by the research subject. What is the individual to do for research? How does she or he regard the tasks—as easy or difficult, fun or boring, familiar or strange? The researcher's choice of what is to be done, and hence, of what behaviors are to be examined, is critical.

By now, we know that the standard procedures developed in an influential line of research to study achievement motivation were biased by the choice of tasks and of instructions that were male-oriented. They were inappropriate for studying achievement orientations of women who had been brought up to believe that certain activities and institutions—e.g., the military—were off-limits for women.[28] We also know that the effort to patch up that theory on achievement by adding a new motivation—avoidance or fear of success—produced over two hundred studies with conflicting results.[29]

Both efforts failed largely because the researchers, in defining the research situation, forgot that outside of it and for years, success had been defined by others who count in our eyes—our reference persons and groups—and that what success meant has been quite different for the reference persons and groups of different men and women in our society. In fact, *success* has been defined so differently that both women and men who have tried to achieve success in ways ruled more appropriate for the other gender—for example, career women or male ballet dancers—have been targets for derogatory labels and negative adjectives so widely used as to be social stereotypes. Especially in a society where some of these divisions have begun to change, indeed where some people are actively rejecting both the definitions and the possibility of "success" in traditional terms, what kind of a theory on motivations to achieve, or fears of failure, or motives to avoid success, can ignore the issues of who defines success or failure for whom, and whether individuals accept those definitions as their own? A little history, a little sociology and economics, a little attention to the historic pleas of feminists and antiracist movements, would have helped.

Another example of bias induced by the selection of activities is a whole line of research on influenceability or suggestibility. One of the old saws in many social psychology texts up through 1974 (though not in any of the four authored by the Sherifs) was that women are more susceptible to persuasive influences or suggestions than men. The research evidence to lay that old saw to rest was collected by my former student Ben Tittler over ten years ago, when he showed that both men and women were more suggestible when the topic at hand was of very little concern to them (e.g., the reputation of General von Hindenburg) than when the topic was deeply and personally involving (e.g., the appropriate personal qualities for men and women). More recently, Judy Morelock's Ph.D. research at Pennsylvania State University has demonstrated that whether men or women are easily influenced by persuasive suggestions depends upon the gender of the researcher in relation to the topic—specifically, that women are more suggestible with a male re-searcher when the topic is socially defined as one of male interest, while men respond in parallel fashion when a woman researcher tries to influence them on a topic socially defined as interesting to women. Finally, Alice Eagley has performed the arduous task of surveying all available research on short-term persuasion and suggestion, and has found no basis whatsoever for the blanket conclusion that one sex is more suggestible than the other.[30] There is, however, a great deal of evidence that anyone may be suggestible or influenced when he or she is placed in an ambiguous situation where one's responsiveness to the situation itself seems more important at the time than personal integrity or self-definition as individual man or woman. When some aspect of the person's self becomes highly involved or is at stake, neither sex is readily or easily influenced by the opinions or per-suasiveness of another person during a brief encounter, especially if that other person is a stranger.[31]

Short Course in How to Perpetuate Social Myth

The lesson for those who want to perpetuate sex bias in psychological research is clear: Restrict the framework for study to a narrow span of time. Attend only to what you decide is important, ignoring as much else as possible. Label these important aspects in the language of "variables," both to sound objective and to mask your ignorance. Arrange the research situation as you choose. If you are biased, the situation will be. Record your selectively chosen data and discuss them as though dealing with eternal verities.

If anyone tries to refer to historical, cultural, or organizational circumstances outside of your own narrow framework, either (1) derogate such talk as referring to "soft" facts and "soft" disciplines which you see as being of little relevance to your carefully controlled variables and findings; or (2) suggest that everyone has different interests, and that yours happens to be in psychology, whatever its limitations, not in history, culture, etc. In either case, you will have removed the most effective and, ultimately, the only effective means by which your critic can expose your bias and show what you have done wrong. You will have put the critic in the position either of confining the discussion to your limited frame-work, or of going out to do another study to show that your research does not hold up—that it cannot be replicated or that it crumbles when another variable is introduced.

Suppose that your critic does the latter. The attempt to replicate a study with a few well-chosen variations is the means many psychologists choose if they want to do serious battle in order to gain victory within the establishment's walls. The history of our field and the analysis of the "social psychology of the psychological experiment" that I just reviewed both suggest that the critic's chance of scoring a critical point is very high. Findings in the area will become "controversial."

Now, what should you, the researcher, do to your critic? By far the best tactic is to withdraw from the field, murmuring about the weaknesses of the research design that has become controversial. Find another way to score your point with a research design so different that the ongoing controversy is no longer relevant.

In fact, that is exactly what has happened over and over again in psychology on many topics, but almost invariably on topics where sex bias is charged. For example, most research from Putnam-Jacobi's and Hollingworth's to the present shows insignificant variations in women's performance attributable to the menstrual cycle on a variety of laboratory tasks. So proponents of the view that menstruation is debilitating by definition switched grounds. Instead of looking at what women do, they started looking at the way women said they *felt*—at their reported moods and especially at their bad ones. The switch amounted to saying, in effect, that bad moods *are* debilitating, whether women perform differently or not. Then new critics showed quite convincingly that the culture is loaded with stereotyped notions about menstruation and bad moods, some authors almost seeming to say that women report bad moods because they think they are supposed to. The debilitator school chuckles tolerantly and points to hormonal fluctuations during the cycle. Can such hormonal "storms" be ignored?

Meanwhile, women who experience discomfort during menstruation are wondering whether to blame the experience on their *really* being the "weaker sex," or on their society, or on themselves. Women who experience no discomfort wonder what all the fuss is about. Fortunately, a small minority of researchers is beginning to realize that an unbiased view of this universal, greatly neglected cyclic phenomenon can be developed only over considerable time through enlarging the framework for study. That framework has to include historical perspective and study, as well as unbiased physiological study that sees hormonal variations as normal and universal for both genders, each with characteristic patterns. It has to include a vastly expanded perspective on what women and men do, their relationships to one another and in a variety of periodic activities, as these relate to the most underdeveloped problem area in psychological research—namely, how people feel and experience themselves, and why, when, and how these self-experiences affect their actions.

If the issues of bias in psychological research were as simple as turning the methods and instruments prized by psychology into the service of defeating bias, many battles would have been won long ago. My short course in how to perpetuate myths has already been learned too well by too many to allow such a defeat. The long course in how to destroy myths has to begin with the essentials: Broaden the framework within which knowledge is sought, then persist in the difficult tasks of relating events within that broadened framework through a variety of methods and research techniques. This is the only course toward an unbiased psychology. Otherwise, those who hold biased viewpoints, either wittingly or unwittingly, will return a decade later, dredge up the old research evidence, reinterpret it by clothing it in new words, and start the argument again before public audiences who like the message. This is what happened in the so-called race and intelligence controversy, which many psychologists believed had been laid to rest a generation ago.

Buttresses in Society for Psychology's Orthodoxy

In view of the openness of psychological research to bias, who in society buttresses the continuation of its research traditions by supporting them or by drawing upon their conclusions? It is popular in academia to say "no one"; but such scholarly aloofness is far from true, historically. Since World War I, the military has been one of the strongest sources of support for psychological tests on what psychologists called "intelligence," then came to define as "what my test measures." Tests of "abilities" and of variously labeled aptitudes followed. Another source of support has been our vast educational system, from preschool through graduate school, in order to place students into educational tracks and channel them into different slots for future training or education. In fact, the goals of education became defined in terms of test performance, rather than tests serving as a means of seeing whether the educational establishment was meeting its own goals or those considered desirable in society.

The logical extension of the so-called intelligence or ability tests to the assessment of various aspects of the personality and of motivation followed, especially after World War II. These tests became so standard that incoming freshmen at the University of Minnesota accepted the practice of taking the Minnesota Multiphasic Personality Inventory along with placement tests in academic subjects. They were widely used in government and industry, which also adopted large batteries of aptitude tests for use in selecting employees and in promotion. Desirous of an "instant criterion" for selecting able and docile employees, these institutions did not, typically, develop tests demonstrably predictive of success in a job, but purchased commercial tests often developed for entirely different purposes. The use of such tests, both in educational placement and in fateful decisions about employment, have figured recently in several court decisions on affirmative action practices.[32] I am told also that a well known vocational interest test for high school students has ceased printing its separate tests for women and men, which were on pink and blue forms.

Aside from the testing industry, the military and other agencies of government have poured huge sums into research on problems that concerned them at the moment. During and after World War II, the popular topic was propaganda; then came studies of small groups and leadership; and by the early sixties all the money was for cross-cultural research and studies on how to change people's attitudes. The relationship between what was supported, what psychologists in those periods studied, and what problems were concerning government and the military is clear, though seldom discussed. Similarly, the record of what is supported in the study of child development mirrors the social problems of concern to authorities at the time and the programs they hope to justify by research. A whole new research industry whose sole aim is to evaluate social programs by the government has recently been born in academia and in commercial firms. Such evaluation research is prone to bias in the direction of confirming what policymakers want to perpetuate and what they hope fails, as one of the earliest papers on the topic makes abundantly clear.[33] More recently, we learn from daily papers that, all the while, the CIA has been supporting research through a variety of phony foundations and social agencies.

Finally, the emergence of clinical psychology as the largest specialty by psychologists after World War II reflects the fact that wars are very hard on people, creating problems that last far beyond their duration. Clinical psychology grew from the lack of enough psychiatrists to handle war-related human problems and from the growing numbers of human casualties at the community level who raised community, hence governmental issues. And once we had the problems and a growing army of professionals, the definition of what is to be done with human problems in living changed: many now required, not friends, not better working conditions, not a social worker, not a job interview, not a minister or loving parent, but a therapist. Benefitting from the aura already created by the medical profession, clinical psychologists came into demand, in preference to a minister or a social worker or a counselor, because their claims to expertise rested on a discipline that said it was scientific, that based its procedures on research findings.

It has become customary for women to deplore the practices of testing for psychological assessment, placement, and hiring, but to regard these practices as not especially biased against their gender. This misconception probably arose because the early intelligence testers in this country made the deliberate decision not to construct tests indicating overall male-female differences in intelligence. The decision was dictated perhaps less by lack of sex bias (though indeed, it was made when the suffrage movement was at its height), than by the necessity of having a test that correlated with the only available criterion of validity—performance in elementary school, in which the sexes did not differ systematically. Nevertheless, this sagacious decision by the early testers did not apply to those women, or men, who happened to have been born into a poor family or came from a minority group with problems and opportunities differing markedly from those more fortunate.

The extension of the early testers' logic to issues of aptitudes, personal motivation, and interests has been loaded with gender bias. Society has persisted in attempting to define women and men as creatures with entirely different capabilities and fates, despite the historic social trends in employment, family, and other activities of the kind documented so well by Jessie Bernard in discussing "tipping points."[34] The indiscriminate use of tests developed primarily for males is both biased and inappropriate as society changes. Necessarily their use assumes that the standards based on male performance in the past will be retained when the very institutions in which performance is to occur will have changed by admitting women. The situation is remarkably similar to that in cross-cultural research when the researcher attempts to use the methods and procedures developed in the United States to study, say, India.

The Indian psychologist Durganand Sinha has commented on this practice perceptively. "Psychology," he said, "appears to be method-bound. Sometimes it is ridiculed as a science without content but with plenty of methodology. Modeling itself after physical sciences and in its zeal for precision and universality of its principles, it has not only adopted a micro approach but has fought shy of highly complex social processes. When the study of a social phenomenon is not easily amenable to its methods, it is ignored." Sinha then goes on to relate his own experience in attempting to apply standard research methods and procedures in Indian villages, giving examples of the need for "culturally appropriate models, tools and techniques."[35] With the same logic, we may see that particular methods and procedures which may have been useful to a society content with its unequal division of labor and unequal opportunities in education are misleading when the same society finds its institutions changing to include those hitherto relegated to different or markedly inferior status.

Thus, U.S. society contains many major and central institutions with interests bolstering psychology's claims to be scientific and bolstering the particular version of scientific methodology adopted as its most prestigious resource. I do not intend at all to pose a dichotomy between so-called basic and so-called applied research. On the contrary, both have been constrained by a particular vision of what is worth doing and how to do that scientifically. That particular vision is not the only one available, nor does it lead to unbiased definition of problems, results, or conclusions. Its most powerful weapons against charges of bias have been not dazzling scientific accomplishments, but its support by elites in psychology and the larger society based on consensus of opinion.

EDITOR'S NOTE

1. See Carolyn Merchant, *The Death of Nature: Women, Ecology and the Scientific Revolution* (New York: Harper & Row, 1980), for a history of misogynous influences on the formation of modern science itself.

NOTES

1. Naomi Weisstein, "Psychology Constructs the Female, or The Fantasy Life of the Male Psychologist," in *Roles Women Play: Readings toward Women's Liberation*, ed. Michele H. Garskof (Belmont, Calif., 1971), pp. 68–83.

2. Betty Friedan, *The Feminine Mystique* (New York, 1963).

3. Carolyn W. Sherif, "Women's Role in the Human Relations of a Changing World," in *The Role of the Educated Woman*, ed. C. M. Class (Houston, 1964), pp. 29–41.

4. Georgene Seward, *Sex and the Social Order* (New York, 1946).

5. E. G. Boring, *A History of Experimental Psychology*, 2nd ed. (New York, 1950), p. 509.

6. Ibid., p. 548.

7. Ibid., p. 487.

8. Helen B. Thompson, *The Mental Traits of Sex* (Chicago, 1903); Helen T. Woolley, "Psychological Literature: A Review of the Recent Literature on the Psychology of Sex," *Psychological Bulletin* 7 (1910): 335–42.

9. For an account of Leta S. Hollingworth's career and the views of prominent male psychologists during the early period of her work, see Stephanie A. Shields, "Ms. Pilgrim's Progress: The Contributions of Leta Stetter Hollingworth to the Psychology of Women," *American Psychologist* 30 (1975): 852–57. The title quoted was published in *American Journal of Sociology* 22 (1916): 19–29.

10. Mary Putnam Jacobi, *The Question of Rest for Women during Menstruation* (New York, 1877), pp. 1–2.

11. Stephanie A. Shields, "Functionalism, Darwinism, and the Psychology of Women," *American Psychologist* 30 (1975): 739–54.

12. See Lee J. Cronbach, "Five Decades of Public Controversy over Mental Testing," *American Psychologist* 30 (1975): 1–14.

13. *AAP Advance*, August-September 1977, p. 2.

14. Boring, *A History of Experimental Psychology*, p. 583.

15. See Ronald Lippitt and Ralph K. White, "An Experimental Study of Leadership and Group Life," in *Basic Studies in Social Psychology*, ed. Harold Proshansky and Bernard Seidenberg (New York, 1965), pp. 523–37. Lewin's first publication on this research appeared in 1939.

16. Kurt Lewin, "Studies in Group Decision," reprinted in *Group Dynamics: Research and Theory*, ed. Dorwin Cartwright and Alvin Zander, 2nd ed. (New York, 1956).

17. See Carol Tavris and Carole Offir, *The Longest War* (New York, 1977), pp. 151–52.

18. A penetrating critique of ahistoricalism and its psychologizing of the social environment was written by one of Lewin's most ardent admirers, Roger G. Barker, "On the Nature of the Environment," *Journal of Social Issues* 19 (1963): 15–38.

19. Masculinity-femininity as a "variable" or polarized dimension is one example of the mischief created in psychology by "thinking in variables" and accepting the implied dictum about measurement. See Anne Constantinople, "Masculinity-Feminity: An Exception to a Famous Dictum?" *Psychological Bulletin* 80 (1973): 389–407; and Lawrence Kohlberg "A Cognitive-Developmental Analysis of Children's Sex-Role Concepts and Attitudes," in *The Development of Sex Differences*, ed. Eleanor E. Maccoby (Stanford, Calif., 1966), pp. 82–173. Very different views on the proper way to seek knowledge are achieved when the definition of what is "masculine" and "feminine" is sought by analyzing divisions of people and their activities in human social life. See Muzafer Sherif and Carolyn W. Sherif, *Social Psychology* (New York, 1969).

20. D. L. Ronis, M. H. Baumgardner, M. R. Leippe, J. J. Cacioppo, and A. G. Greenwald, "In Search of Reliable Persuasion Effects, I: A Computer-Controlled Procedure for Studying Persuasion," *Journal of Personality and Social Psychology* 35 (1977): 551.

21. Ibid., p. 567.

22. Ibid.

23. For a sociologial analysis of conditions promoting such efforts by psychologists, see J. Ben-David and R. Collins, "Social Factors in the Origin of a New Science: The Case of Psychology," *American Sociological Review* 31 (1966): 451–65.

24. Robert Rosenthal, *Experimenter Effects in Behavioral Research* (New York, 1966).

25. See Hadley Cantril, *Gauging Public Opinion* (Princeton, 1944); Howard Schuman and Shirley Hatchett, *Black Racial Attitudes: Trends and Complexities* (Ann Arbor, 1974); Charles F. Cannell and Robert L. Kahn, "Interviewing," in *Handbook of Social Psychology*, ed. Gardner Lindzey and Elliott Aronson, (Reading, Mass., 1968); vol. 2.

26. Some of the vast literature on the "social psychology of the research situation" is summarized in Robert Rosenthal and Ralph L. Rosnow, eds., *Artifact in Behavioral Research* (New York, 1969). A more recent and readable introduction is James G. Adair, *The Human Subject: The Social Psychology of the Psychological Experiment* (Boston, 1973). Both tend to ignore the earlier work on "social desirability" effects; see Allen L. Edwards; *The Social Desirability Variable in Personality Assessment and Research* (New York, 1957). Both also tend toward trying to "eliminate" or reduce the effects they have studied, rather than using their understanding toward reconstruction of psychology's methodology. For alternative perspectives with the latter aim, see Sherif and Sherif, *Social Psychology*, esp. chap. 6, and Carolyn W. Sherif, *Orientation in Social Psychology* (New York, 1976).

27. The most complete review of the obedience research is in Stanley Milgram, *Obedience to Authority* (New York, 1974). Cross-cultural comparisions leading to similar conclusions are summarized in M.E. Shanab and Khawla A. Yahya, "A Behavioral Study of Obedience in Children," *Journal of Personality and Social Psychology* 35 (1977): 530–36.

28. Aletha H. Stein and Margaret M. Bailey, "The Socialization of Achievement Orientation in Females," *Psychological Bulletin* 80 (1973): 345–66. See also Martha T. S. Mednick, Sandra J. Tangri, and Lois W. Hoffman, eds., *Women and Achievement: Social and Motivational Analysis.* (Washington, D.C., 1975); Virginia O'Leary, "Some Attitudinal Barriers to Occupational Aspirations in Women," *Psychological Bulletin* 81 (1974): 809–26.

29. John Condry and Susan Dyer, "Fear of Success: Attribution of Cause to the Victim," *Journal of Social Issues* 32 (1976): 63–83; David Tresemer, "The Cumulative Record of Research on 'Fear of Success,' " *Sex Roles* 2 (1976): 217–36.

30. See Carolyn W. Sherif, Merrilea Kelly, Lewis Rodgers, Gian Sarup, and Bennet Tittler, "Personal Involvement, Social Judgment, and Action," *Journal of Personality and Social Psychology* 27 (1973): 311–28; Judith C. Morelock, "Sex Differences in Compliance," *Sex Roles; A Journal of Research*, in press; Alice H. Eagley, "Sex Differences in Influenceability," *Psychological Bulletin* 85 (1978): 86–116.

31. This analysis of the persuasion or "suggestibility" research follows that in Muzafer Sherif and Carolyn W. Sherif, *An Outline of Social Psychology* (New York, 1956); and idem, *Social Psychology*.

32. See, for example, Phyllis A. Wallace, ed., *Equal Employment and the AT&T Case* (Cambridge, Mass., 1976.) Judith Long Laws's chapters in this book are excellent examples of the broadened perspective on women's interests and motivations that becomes possible when conditions of work and living are included in the framework of study. Other chapters particularly relevant in the present context reveal sharp divisions among psychologists on the use and interpretation of tests and interviews used in hiring or promotion.

33. Donald T. Campbell, "Reforms as Experiments," *American Psychologist* 24 (1969): 409–29.

34. Jessie Bernard, *Women, Wives, Mothers: Values and Options* (Chicago, 1975).

35. Durganand Sinha, "Social Psychologists' Stance in a Developing Country," *Indian Journal of Psychology* 50 (June 1975): 98–99.

V.

WOMAN'S PLACE IN MAN'S LIFE CYCLE

Carol Gilligan

Carol Gilligan's *In a Different Voice: Psychological Theory and Women's Development* has been widely acclaimed beyond the borders of psychology and feminist theory.[1] In this earlier essay, Gilligan previews some of the major themes of her study.

Gilligan argues that developmental theorists are wrong to see women's moral judgments as reflecting a lower level of maturity than men's. Women's ethic of caring and responsibility is simply different from the ethic of rights which men more often use. Moreover, women's ethic is as important in maintaining social relations as is the ethic of rights. In her more recent writings, Gilligan stresses the importance of recognizing that both kinds of reasoning can be found in both men and women. But the "caring" voice she identifies in this essay is more characteristic of women than of men, and it is undervalued.

The androcentric model Gilligan criticizes is fundamental not only to psychological thinking. It is assumed by philosophers and political theorists concerned with identifying the "highest" forms of morality and the policies which a "just society" should support.[2] It is also assumed by educational theorists, criminologists, and the whole array of mental health professionals. Gilligan's challenge has found broad targets in contemporary culture.

Gilligan has criticized Kohlberg for throwing away the data he had collected on women which did not fit the model he was using—one originally developed to explain masculine development. How common has this practice been? Notice that Gilligan's way of gathering evidence is not unusual at all: she interviews her subjects and asks them to respond to the same kinds of moral dilemmas that Kohlberg used. This leads us to reflect on what is unusual about Gilligan's work. For one thing, she asks us to listen to women—to people the culture silences. Moreover, she asks us not to prejudge them by forcing their responses to questions into categories which were never constructed to illuminate *their* experience at all, but to listen instead to how they think about their lives in the terms that they choose to use—in their "different voice."

We can wonder if male psychologists would have been as interested as Gilligan was to define or to explore this kind of problem. (Of course they *could* be!) People who have been evaluated as inferior moral reasoners have more interest in "correcting the record" than do those thought of as superior moral reasoners. Is there a message here about how social science can increase the objectivity of inquiry?

In the second act of *The Cherry Orchard*, Lopakhin, the young merchant, describes his life of hard work and success. Failing to convince Madame Ranevskaya to cut down the cherry orchard to save her estate, he will go on, in the next act, to buy it himself. He is the self-made man, who, in purchasing "the estate where grandfather and father were slaves," seeks to eradicate the "awkward, unhappy life" of the past, replacing the cherry orchard with summer cottages where coming generations "will see a new life" (Act III). Elaborating this developmental vision, he describes the image of man that underlies and supports this activity: "At times when I can't go to sleep, I think: Lord, thou gavest us immense forests, unbounded fields and the widest horizons, and living in the midst of them we should indeed be giants." At which point, Madame Ranevskaya interrupts him, saying, "You feel the need for giants— They are good only in fairy tales, anywhere else they only frighten us" (Act II).

Conceptions of the life cycle represent attempts to order and make coherent the unfolding experiences and perceptions, the changing wishes and realities of everyday life. But the truth of such conceptions depends in part on the position of the observer. The brief excerpt from Chekhov's play (1904/1956) suggests that when the observer is a woman, the truth may be of a different sort. This discrepancy in judgment between men and women is the center of my consideration.

This essay traces the extent to which psychological theories of human development, theories that have informed both educational philosophy and classroom practice, have enshrined a view of human life similar to Lopakhin's while dismissing the ironic commentary in which Chekhov embeds this view. The specific issue I address is that of sex differences, and my focus is on the observation and assessment of sex differences by life-cycle theorists. In talking about sex differences, however, I risk the criticism which such generalization invariably invites. As Virginia Woolf said, when embarking on a similar endeavor: "When a subject is highly controversial—and any question about sex is that—one cannot hope to tell the truth. One can only show how one came to hold whatever opinion one does hold" (1929, p. 4).

At a time when efforts are being made to eradicate discrimination between the sexes in the search for equality and justice, the differences between the sexes are being rediscovered in the social sciences. This discovery occurs when theories formerly considered to be sexually neutral in their scientific objectivity are found instead to reflect a consistent observational and evaluative bias. Then the presumed neutrality of science, like that of language itself, gives way to the recognition that the categories of knowledge are human constructions. The fascination with point of view and the corresponding recognition of the relativity of truth that has informed the fiction of the twentieth century begin to infuse our scientific understanding as well when we begin to notice how accustomed we have become to seeing life through men's eyes.

A recent discovery of this sort pertains to the apparently innocent classic by Strunk and White (1959), *The Elements of Style*. The Supreme Court ruling on the subject of discrimination in classroom texts led one teacher of English to notice that the elementary rules of English usage were being taught through examples which counterposed the birth of Napoleon, the writings of Coleridge, and statements such as, "He was an interesting talker, a man who had traveled all over the world and lived in half a dozen countries" (p.7) with "Well, Susan, this is a fine mess you are in" (p. 3) or, less drastically, "He saw a woman, accompanied by two children, walking slowly down the road" (p. 8).

Psychological theorists have fallen as innocently as Strunk and White into the same observational bias. Implicitly adopting the male life as the norm, they have tried to fashion women out of a masculine cloth. It all goes back, of course, to Adam and Eve, a story which shows, among other things, that, if you make a woman out of a man you are bound to get into trouble. In the life cycle, as in the Garden of Eden, it is the woman who has been the deviant.

The penchant of developmental theorists to project a masculine image, and one that appears frightening to women, goes back at least to Freud (1905/1961), who built his theory of psychosexual development around the experiences of the male child that culminate in the Oedipus complex. In the 1920s, Freud struggled to resolve the contradictions posed for his theory by the different configuration of female sexuality and the different dynamics of the young girl's early family relationships. After trying to fit women into his masculine conception, seeing them as envying that which they missed, he came instead to acknowledge, in the strength and persistence of women's pre-Oedipal attachments to their mothers, a developmental difference. However, he considered this difference in women's development to be responsible for what he saw as women's developmental failure.

Deprived by nature of the impetus for a clear-cut Oedipal resolution, women's superego, the heir to the Oedipus complex, consequently was compromised. It was never, Freud observed, "so inexorable, so impersonal, so independent of its emotional origins as we require it to be in men" (1925/1961, p. 257). From this observation of difference, "that for women the level of what is ethically normal is different from what it is in men" (p. 257), Freud concluded that "women have less sense of justice than men, that they are less ready to submit to the great exigencies of life, that they are more often influenced in their judgments by feelings of affection and hostility" (pp. 257–258).

Chodorow (1974, 1978) addresses this evaluative bias in the assessment of sex differences in her attempt to account for "the reproduction within each generation of certain general and nearly universal differences that characterize masculine and feminine personality and roles" (1974, p. 43). Writing from a psychoanalytic perspective, she attributes these continuing differences between the sexes not to anatomy but rather to "the fact that women, universally, are largely responsible for early child care and for (at least) later female socialization" (1974, p. 43). Because this early social environment differs for and is experienced differently by male and female children, basic sex differences recur in personality development. As a result, "in any given society, feminine personality comes to define itself in relation and connection to other people more than masculine personality does. (In psychoanalytic terms, women are less individuated than men; they have more flexible ego boundaries.)" (1974, p. 44).

In her analysis, Chodorow relies primarily on Stoller's research on the development of gender identity and gender-identity disturbances. Stoller's work indicates that male and female identity, the unchanging core of personality formation, is "with rare exception firmly and irreversibly established for both sexes by the time a child is around three" (Chodorow, 1978, p. 150). Given that for both sexes the primary caretaker in the first three years of life is typically female, the interpersonal dynamics of gender identity formation are different for boys and girls. Female identity formation takes place in a context of ongoing relationship as "mothers tend to experience their daughters as more like, and continuous with, themselves. Correspondingly, girls tend to remain part of the dyadic primary mother-child relationship itself. This means that a girl continues to experience herself as involved in issues of merging and separation, and in an attachment characterized by primary identification and the fusion of identification and object choice" (1978, p. 166).

In contrast, "mothers experience their sons as a male opposite" and, as a result, "boys are more likely to have been pushed out of the preoedipal relationship and to have had to curtail their primary love and sense of empathic tie with their mother" (1978, p. 166). Consequently, boys' development entails a "more emphatic individuation and a more defensive firming of ego boundaries." For boys, but not for girls, "issues of differentiation have become intertwined with sexual issues" (1978, p. 167).

Thus Chodorow refutes the masculine bias of psychoanalytic theory, claiming that the existence of sex differences in the early experiences of individuation and relationship "does not mean that women have 'weaker ego boundaries' than men or are more prone to psychosis" (1978, p. 167). What it means instead is that "the earliest mode of individuation, the primary construction of the ego and its inner object-world, the earliest conflicts and the earliest unconscious definitions of self, the earliest threats to individuation, and the earliest anxieties which call up defenses, all differ for boys and girls because of differences in the character of the early mother-child relationship for each" (1978, p. 167). Because of these differences, "girls emerge from this period with a basis for 'empathy' built into their primary definition of self in a way that boys do not" (1978, p. 167). Chodorow thus replaces Freud's negative and derivative description of female psychology with a more positive and direct account of her own:

> Girls emerge with a stronger basis for experiencing another's needs and feelings as one's own (or of thinking that one is so experiencing another's needs and feelings). Furthermore, girls do not define themselves in terms of the denial of preoedipal relational modes to the same extent as do boys. Therefore, regression to these modes tends not to feel as much a basic threat to their ego. From very early, then, because they are parented by a person of the same gender . . . girls come to experience themselves as less differentiated than boys, as more continuous with and related to the external object-world, and as differently oriented to their inner object-world as well. (1978, p. 167)

Consequently, "issues of dependency, in particular, are handled and experienced differently by men and women" (Chodorow, 1974, p. 44). For boys and men, separation and individuation are critically tied to gender identity since separation from the mother is essential for the development of masculinity. "For girls and women, by contrast, issues of femininity or feminine identity are not problematic in the same way" (1974, p. 44); they do not depend on the achievement of separation from the mother or on the progress of individuation. Since, in Chodorow's analysis, masculinity is defined through separation while femininity is defined through attachment, male gender identity will be threatened by intimacy while female gender identity will be threatened by individuation. Thus males will tend to have difficulty with relationships while females will tend to have problems with separation. The quality of embeddedness in social interaction and personal relationships that characterizes women's lives in contrast to men's, however, becomes not only a descriptive difference but also a developmental liability when the milestones of childhood and adolescent development are described by markers of increasing separation. Then women's failure to separate becomes by definition a failure to develop.

The sex differences in personality formation that Chodorow delineates in her analysis of early childhood relationships as well as the bias she points out in the evaluation of these differences, reappear in the middle childhood years in the studies of children's games. Children's games have been considered by Mead (1934) and Piaget (1932/1965) as the crucible of social development during the school years. In games children learn to take the role of the other and come to see themselves through another's eyes. In games they learn respect for rules and come to understand the ways rules can be made and changed.

Lever (1976), considering the peer group to be the agent of socialization during the elementary school years and play to be a major activity of socialization at that time, set out to discover whether there were sex differences in the games that children play. Studying 181 fifth-grade, white, middle-class, Connecticut children, ages 10 and 11, she observed the organization and structure of their playtime activities. She watched the children as they played during the school recess, lunch, and in physical education class, and, in addition, kept diaries of their accounts as to how they spent their out-of-school time.

From this study, Lever reports the following sex differences: boys play more out of doors than girls do; boys more often play in large and age-heterogeneous groups; they play competitive games more often than girls do, and their games last longer than girls' games (Lever, 1976). The last is in some ways the most interesting finding. Boys' games appeared to last longer not only because they required a higher level of skill and were thus less likely to become boring, but also because when disputes arose in the course of a game, the boys were able to resolve the disputes more effectively than the girls: "During the course of this study, boys were seen quarrelling all the time, but not once was a game terminated because of a quarrel and no game was interrupted for more than seven minutes. In the gravest debates, the final word was always to 'repeat the play,' generally followed by a chorus of 'cheater's proof' " (1976, p. 482). In fact, it seemed that the boys enjoyed the legal debates as much as they did the game itself, and even marginal players of lesser size or skill participated equally in these recurrent squabbles. In contrast, the eruption of disputes among girls tended to end the game.

Thus Lever extends and corroborates the observations reported by Piaget (1932/1965) in his naturalistic study of the rules of the game, where he found boys becoming increasingly fascinated with the legal elaboration of rules and the development of fair procedures for adjudicating conflicts, a fascination that, he noted, did not hold for girls. Girls, Piaget observed, had a more "pragmatic" attitude toward rules, "regarding a rule as good as long as the game repaid it" (1932/1965, p. 83). As a result, he considered girls to be more tolerant in their attitudes toward rules, more willing to make exceptions, and more easily reconciled to innovations. However, and presumably as a result, he concluded that the legal sense which he considered essential to moral development "is far less developed in little girls than in boys" (1932/1965, p. 77).

This same bias that led Piaget to equate male development with child development also colors Lever's work. The assumption that shapes her discussion of results is that the male model is the better one. It seems, in any case, more adaptive since as Lever points out it fits the requirements Riesman (1961) describes for success in modern corporate life. In contrast, the sensitivity and care for the feelings of others that girls develop through their primarily dyadic play relationships have little market value and can even impede professional success. Lever clearly implies that, given the realities of adult life, if a girl does not want to be dependent on men, she will have to learn to play like a boy.

Since Piaget argues that children learn the respect for rules necessary for moral development by playing rule-bound games, and Kohlberg (1971) adds that these lessons are most effectively learned through the opportunities for role-taking that arise in the course of resolving disputes, the moral lessons inherent in girls' play appear to be fewer than for boys. Traditional girls' games like jump rope and hopscotch are turn-taking games where competition is indirect in that one person's success does not necessarily signify another's failure. Consequently, disputes requiring adjudication are less likely to occur. In fact, most of the girls whom Lever interviewed claimed that when a quarrel broke out, they ended the game. Rather than elaborating a system of rules for resolving disputes, girls directed their efforts instead toward sustaining affective ties.

Lever concludes that from the games they play boys learn both independence and the organizational skills necessary for coordinating the activities of large and diverse groups of people. By participating in controlled and socially approved competitive situations, they learn to deal with competition in a relatively forthright manner—to play with their enemies and compete with their friends, all in accordance with the rules of the game. In contrast, girls' play tends to occur in smaller, more intimate groups, often the best-friend dyad, and in private places. This play replicates the social pattern of primary human relationships in that its organization is more cooperative and points less toward learning to take the role of the generalized other than it does toward the development of the empathy and sensitivity necessary for taking the role of the particular other.

Chodorow's analysis of sex differences in personality formation in early childhood is thus extended by Lever's observations of sex differences in the play activities of middle childhood. Together these accounts suggest that boys and girls arrive at puberty with a different interpersonal orientation and a different range of social experiences. While Sullivan (1953), tracing the sequence of male development, posits the experience of a close same-sex friendship in preadolescence as necessary for the subsequent integration of sexuality and intimacy, no corresponding account is available to describe girls' development at this critical juncture. Instead, since adolescence is considered a crucial time for separation and individuation, the period of "the second individuation process" (Blos, 1967), it has been in adolescence that female development has appeared most divergent and thus most problematic.

"Puberty," Freud said, "which brings about so great an accession of libido in boys, is marked in girls by a fresh wave of repression" (1905/1961, p. 220) necessary for the transformation of the young girls' "masculine sexuality" into the "specifically feminine" sexuality of her adulthood. Freud posits this transformation on the girl's acknowledgement and acceptance of "the fact of her castration." In his account puberty brings for girls a new awareness of "the wound to her narcissism" and leads her to develop, "like a scar, a sense of inferiority" (Freud, 1925/1961, p. 253). Since adolescence is, in Erikson's expansion of Freud's psychoanalytic account, the time when the ego takes on an identity which confirms the individual in relation to society, the girl arrives at this juncture in development either psychologically at risk or with a different agenda.

The problem that female adolescence presents for psychologists of human development is apparent in Erikson's account. Erikson (1950) charts eight stages of psychosocial development in which adolescence is the fifth. The task of this stage is to forge a coherent sense of self, to verify an identity that can span the discontinuity of puberty and make possible the adult capacity to love and to work. The preparation for the successful resolution of the adolescent identity crisis is delineated in Erikson's description of the preceding four stages. If in infancy the initial crisis of trust vs. mistrust generates enough hope to sustain the child through the arduous life cycle that lies ahead, the task at hand clearly becomes one of individuation. Erikson's second stage centers on the crisis of autonomy versus shame and doubt, the walking child's emerging sense of separateness and agency. From there, development goes on to the crisis of initiative versus guilt, successful resolution of which represents a further move in the direction of autonomy. Next, following the inevitable disappointment of the magical wishes of the oedipal period, the child realizes with respect to his parents that to beat them he must first join them and learn to do what they do so well. Thus in the middle childhood years, development comes to hinge on the crisis of industry versus inferiority, as the demonstration of competence becomes critical to the child's developing self-esteem. This is the time when children strive to learn and master the technology of their culture in order to recognize themselves and be recognized as capable of becoming adults. Next comes adolescence, the celebration of the autonomous, initiating, industrious self through the forging of an identity based on an ideology that can support and justify adult commitments. But about whom is Erikson talking?

Once again it turns out to be the male child—the coming generation of men like George Bernard Shaw, William James, Martin Luther, and Mahatma Gandhi—who provide Erikson with his most vivid illustrations. For the woman, Erikson (1968) says, the sequence is a bit different. She holds her identity in abeyance as she prepares to attract the man by whose name she will be known, by whose status she will be defined, the man who will rescue her from emptiness and loneliness by filling "the inner space" (Erikson, 1968). While for men, identity precedes intimacy and generativity in the optimal cycle of human separation and attachment, for women these tasks seem instead to be fused. Intimacy precedes, or rather goes along with, identity as the female comes to know herself as she is known, through her relationships with others.

Two things are essential to note at this point. The first is that, despite Erikson's observation of sex differences, his chart of life-cycle stages remains unchanged: identity continues to precede intimacy as the male diagonal continues to define his life-cycle conception. The second is that in the male life cycle there is little preparation for the intimacy of the first adult stage. Only the initial stage of trust versus mistrust suggests the type of mutuality that Erikson means by intimacy and generativity and Freud by genitality: The rest is separateness, with the result that development itself comes to be identified with separation and attachments appear as developmental impediments, as we have repeatedly found to be the case in the assessment of women.

Erikson's description of male identity as forged in relation to the world and of female identity as awakened in a relationship of intimacy with another person, however controversial, is hardly new. In Bettelheim's discussion of fairy tales in *The Uses of Enchantment* (1976) an identical portrayal appears. While Bettelheim argues, in refutation of those critics who see in fairy tales a sexist literature, that opposite models exist and could readily be found, nevertheless the ones upon which he focuses his discussion of adolescence conform to the pattern we have begun to observe.

The dynamics of male adolescence are illustrated archetypically by the conflict between father and son in "The Three Languages" (Bettelheim, 1976). Here a son, considered hopelessly stupid by his father, is given one last chance at education and sent for a year to study with a famous master. But when he returns, all he has learned is "what the dogs bark" (1976, p. 97). After two further attempts of this sort, the father gives up in disgust and orders his servants to take the child into the forest and kill him. The servants, however, those perpetual rescuers of disowned and abandoned children, take pity on the child and decide simply to leave him in the forest. From there, his wanderings take him to a land beset by furious dogs whose barking permits nobody to rest and who periodically devour one of the inhabitants. Now it turns out that our hero has learned just the right thing: he can talk with the dogs and is able to quiet them, thus restoring peace to the land. The other knowledge he acquires serves him equally well, and he emerges triumphant from his adolescent confrontation with his father, a giant of the life-cycle conception.

In contrast, the dynamics of female adolescence are depicted through the telling of a very different story. In the world of the fairy tale, the girl's first bleeding is followed by a period of intense passivity in which nothing seems to be happening. Yet in the deep sleep of Snow White and Sleeping Beauty, Bettelheim sees that inner concentration which he considers to be the necessary counterpart to the activity of adventure. The adolescent heroines awaken from their sleep not to conquer the world but to marry the prince. Their feminine identity is inwardly and interpersonally defined. As in Erikson's observation, for women, identity and intimacy are more intricately conjoined. The sex differences depicted in the world of the fairy tales, like the fantasy of the woman warrior in Maxine Hong Kingston's (1977) recent autobiographical novel (which in turn echoes the old stories of Troilus and Cressida and Tancred and Chlorinda) indicate repeatedly that active adventure is a male activity, and if women are to embark on such endeavors, they must at least dress like men.

These observations about sex difference support the conclusion reached by McClelland that "sex role turns out to be one of the most important determinants of human behavior.

psychologists have found sex differences in their studies from the moment they started doing empirical research" (1975, p. 81). But since it is difficult to say "different" without saying "better" or "worse," and since there is a tendency to construct a single scale of measurement, and since that scale has been derived and standardized on the basis of men's observations and interpretations of research data predominantly or exclusively drawn from studies of males, psychologists have tended, in McClelland's words, "to regard male behavior as the 'norm' and female behavior as some kind of deviation from that norm" (1975, p. 81). Thus when women do not conform to the standards of psychological expectation, the conclusion has generally been that something is wrong with the women.

What Horner (1972) found to be wrong with women was the anxiety they showed about competitive achievement. From the beginning, research on human motivation using the Thematic Apperception Test (TAT) was plagued by evidence of sex differences which appeared to confuse and complicate data analysis. The TAT presents for interpretation an ambiguous cue—a picture about which a story is to be written or a brief story stem to be completed. Such stories in reflecting projective imagination are considered to reveal the ways in which people construe what they perceive—that is, the concepts and interpretations they bring to their experience and thus presumably the kind of sense that they make of their lives. Prior to Horner's work, it was clear that women made a different kind of sense than men of situations of competitive achievement, that in some way they saw the situation differently or the situation aroused in them some different response.

On the basis of his studies of men, McClelland (1961) had divided the concept of achievement motivation into what appeared to be its two logical components, a motive to approach success ("hope success") and a motive to avoid failure ("fear failure"). When Horner (1972) began to analyze the problematic projective data on female achievement motivation, she identified as a third category the unlikely motivation to avoid success ("fear success"). Women appeared to have a problem with competitive achievement, and that problem seemed, in Horner's interpretation, to emanate from a perceived conflict between femininity and success, the dilemma of the female adolescent who struggles to integrate her feminine aspirations and the identifications of her early childhood with the more masculine competence she has acquired at school. Thus Horner reports, "When success is likely or possible, threatened by the negative consequences they expect to follow success, young women become anxious and their positive achievement strivings become thwarted" (1972, p. 171). She concludes that this fear exists because for most women, the anticipation of success in competitive achievement activity, especially against men, produced anticipation of certain negative consequences, for example, threat of social rejection and loss of femininity.

It is, however, possible to view such conflicts about success in a different light. Sassen (1980), on the basis of her reanalysis of the data presented in Horner's thesis, suggests that the conflicts expressed by the women might instead indicate "a heightened perception of the 'other side' of competitive success, that is, the great emotional costs of success achieved through competition, or an understanding which, while confused, indicates an awareness that something is rotten in the state in which success is defined as having better grades than everyone else" (Sassen, 1980). Saesen points out that Horner found success anxiety to be present in women only when achievement was directly competitive, that is, where one person's success was at the expense of another's failure.

From Horner's examples of fear of success, it is impossible to differentiate between neurotic or realistic anxiety about the consequences of achievement, the questioning of conventional definitions of success, or the discovery of personal goals other than conventional success. The construction of the problem posed by success as a problem of identity and ideology that appears in Horner's illustrations, if taken at face value rather than assumed to be derivative, suggests Erikson's distinction between a conventional and neohumanist identity, or, in cognitive terms, the distinction between conventional and postconventional thought (Loevinger, 1970; Inhelder & Piaget, 1958; Kohlberg, 1971; Perry, 1968).

In his elaboration of the identity crisis, Erikson discusses the life of George Bernard Shaw to illustrate the young person's sense of being co-opted prematurely by success in a career he cannot wholeheartedly endorse. Shaw at seventy, reflecting upon his life, describes his crisis at the age of twenty as one caused not by lack of success or the absence of recognition, but by too much of both:

> I made good in spite of myself and found, to my dismay, that Business, instead of expelling me as the worthless imposter I was, was fastening upon me with no intention of letting me go. Behold me, therefore, in my twentieth year, with a business training, in an occupation which I detested as cordially as any sane person lets himself detest anything he cannot escape from. In March, 1876, I broke loose. (Erikson, 1968, p. 143)

At which point Shaw settled down to study and to write as he pleased. Hardly interpreted as evidence of developmental difficulty, of neurotic anxiety about achievement and competition, Shaw's refusal suggested to Erikson, "the extraordinary workings of an extraordinary personality coming to the fore" (1968, p. 144).

We might on these grounds begin to ask not why women have conflicts about succeeding but why men show such readiness to adopt and celebrate a rather narrow vision of success. Remembering Piaget's observation, corroborated by Lever, that boys in their games are concerned more with rules while girls are more concerned with relationships, often at the expense of the game itself; remembering also that, in Chodorow's analysis, men's social orientation is positional and women's orientation is personal, we begin to understand why, when Anne becomes John in Horner's tale of competitive success and the stories are written by men, fear of success tends to disappear. John is considered by other men to have played by the rules and won. He has the *right* to feel good about his success. Confirmed in his sense of his own identity as separate from those who, compared to him, are less competent, his positional sense of self is affirmed. For Anne, it is possible that the position she could obtain by being at the top of her medical school class may not, in fact, be what she wants.

"It is obvious," Virginia Woolf said, "that the values of women differ very often from the values which have been made by the other sex" (1929, p. 76). Yet, she adds, it is the masculine values that prevail. As a result, women come to question the "normality" of their feelings and to alter their judgments in deference to the opinion of others. In the nineteehth-century novels written by women, Woolf sees at work "a mind slightly pulled from the straight, altering its clear vision in the anger and confusion of deference to external authority" (1929, p. 77). The same deference that Woolf identifies in nineteenth-century fiction can be seen as well in the judgments of twentieth-century women. Women's reluctance to make moral judgments, the difficulty they experience in finding or speaking publicly in their own voice, emerge repeatedly in the form of qualification and self-doubt, in intimations of a divided judgment, a public and private assessment which are fundamentally at odds (Gilligan, 1977).

Yet the deference and confusion that Woolf criticizes in women derive from the values she sees as their strength. Women's deference is rooted not only in their social circumstances but also in the substance of their moral concern. Sensitivity to the needs of others and the assumption of responsibility for taking care lead women to attend to voices other than their own and to include in their judgment other points of view. Women's moral weakness, manifest in an apparent diffusion and confusion of judgment, is thus inseparable from women's moral strength, an overriding concern with relationships and responsibilities. The reluctance to judge can itself be indicative of the same care and concern for others that infuses the psychology of women's development and is responsible for what is characteristically seen as problematic in its nature.

Thus women not only define themselves in a context of human relationship but also judge themselves in terms of their ability to care. Woman's place in man's life cycle has been that of nurturer, caretaker, and helpmate, the weaver of those networks of relationships on which she in turn relies. While women have thus taken care of men, however, men have in their theories of psychological development tended either to assume or devalue that care. The focus on individuation and individual achievement that has dominated the description of child and adolescent development has recently been extended to the depiction of adult development as well. Levinson in his study, *The Seasons of a Man's Life* (1978), elaborates a view of adult development in which relationships are portrayed as a means to an end of individual achievement and success. In the critical relationships of early adulthood, the "Mentor" and the "Special Woman" are defined by the role they play in facilitating the man's realization of his "Dream." Along similar lines Vaillant (1977), in his study of men, considers altruism a defense, characteristic of mature ego functioning and associated with successful "adaptation to life," but conceived as derivative rather than primary in contrast to Chodorow's analysis, in which empathy is considered "built-in" to the woman's primary definition of self.

The discovery now being celebrated by men in mid-life of the importance of intimacy, relationships, and care is something that women have known from the beginning. However, because that knowledge has been considered "intuitive" or "instinctive," a function of anatomy coupled with destiny, psychologists have neglected to describe its development. In my research, I have found that women's moral development centers on the elaboration of that knowledge. Women's moral development thus delineates a critical line of psychological development whose importance for both sexes becomes apparent in the intergenerational framework of a life-cycle perspective. While the subject of moral development provides the final illustration of the reiterative pattern in the observation and assessment of sex differences in the literature on human development, it also indicates more particularly why the nature and significance of women's development has for so long been obscured and considered shrouded in mystery.

The criticism that Freud (1961) makes of women's sense of justice, seeing it as compromised in its refusal of blind impartiality, reappears not only in the work of Piaget (1934) but also in that of Kohlberg (1958). While girls are an aside in Piaget's account of *The Moral Judgment of the Child* (1934), an odd curiosity to whom he devotes four brief entries in an index that omits "boys" altogether because "the child" is assumed to be male, in Kohlberg's research on moral development, females simply do not exist. Kohlberg's six stages that describe the development of moral judgment from childhood to adulthood were derived empirically from a longitudinal study of eighty-four boys from the United States. While Kohlberg (1973) claims universality for his stage sequence and considers his conception of justice as fairness to have been naturalistically derived, those groups not included in his original sample rarely reach his higher stages (Edwards, 1975; Gilligan, 1977). Prominent among those found to be deficient in moral development when measured by Kohlberg's scale are women whose judgments on his scale seemed to exemplify the third stage in his six-stage sequence. At this stage morality is conceived in terms of relationships, and goodness is equated with helping and pleasing others. This concept of goodness was considered by Kohlberg and Kramer (1969) to be functional in the lives of mature women insofar as those lives took place in the home and thus were relationally bound. Only if women were to go out of the house to enter the arena of male activity would they realize the inadequacy of their Stage Three perspective and progress like men toward higher stages where morality is societally or universally defined in accordance with a conception of justice as fairness.

In this version of human development, however, a particular conception of maturity is assumed, based on the study of men's lives and reflecting the importance of individuation in their development. When one begins instead with women and derives developmental constructs from their lives, then a different conception of development emerges, the expansion and elaboration of which can also be traced through stages that comprise a developmental sequence. In Loevinger's (1966) test for measuring ego development that was drawn from studies of females, fifteen of the thirty-six sentence stems to complete begin with the subject of human relationships (for example, "Raising a family. . . .; If my mother. . . .; Being with other people. . . .; When I am with a man. . . .; When a child won't join in group activities. . . .") (Loevinger & Wessler, 1970, p. 141). Thus ego development is described and measured by Loevinger through conception of relationships as well as by the concept of identity that measures the progress of individuation.

Research on moral judgment has shown that when the categories of women's thinking are examined in detail (Gilligan, 1977) the outline of a moral conception different from that described by Freud, Piaget, or Kohlberg begins to emerge and to inform a different description of moral development. In this conception, the moral problem is seen to arise from conflicting responsibilities rather than from competing rights and to require for its resolution a mode of thinking that is contextual and inductive rather than formal and abstract.

This conception of morality as fundamentally concerned with the capacity for understanding and care also develops through a structural progression of increasing differentiation and integration. This progression witnesses the shift from an egocentric through a societal to the universal moral perspective that Kohlberg described in his research on men, but it does so in different terms. The shift in women's judgment from an egocentric to a conventional to a principled ethical understanding is articulated through their use of a distinct moral language, in which the terms "selfishness" and "responsibility" define the moral problem as one of care. Moral development then consists of the progressive reconstruction of this understanding toward a more adequate conception of care.

The concern with caring centers moral development around the progressive differentiation and integration that characterize the evolution of the understanding of relationships just as the conception of fairness delineates the progressive differentiation and balancing of individual rights. Within the responsibility orientation, the infliction of hurt is the center of moral concern and is considered immoral whether or not it can otherwise be construed as fair or unfair. The reiterative use of the language of selfishness and responsibility to define the moral problem as a problem of care sets women apart from the men whom Kohlberg studied and from whose thinking he derived his six stages. This different construction of the moral problem by women may be seen as the critical reason for their failure to develop within the constraints of Kohlberg's system.

Regarding all constructions of responsibility as evidence of a conventional moral understanding, Kohlberg defines the highest stages of moral development as deriving from a reflective understanding of human rights. That the morality of rights differs from the morality of responsibility in its emphasis on separation rather than attachment, in its consideration of the individual rather than the relationship as primary, is illustrated by two quotations that exemplify these different orientations. The first comes from a twenty-five-year-old man who participated in Kohlberg's longitudinal study. The quotation itself is cited by Kohlberg to illustrate the principled conception of morality that he scores as "integrated [Stage] Five judgment, possibly moving to Stage Six."

> [What does the word morality mean to you?] Nobody in the world knows the answer. I think it is recognizing the right of the individual, the rights of other individuals, not interfering with those rights. Act as fairly as you would have them treat you. I think it is basically to preserve the human being's right to existence. I think that is the most important. Secondly, the human being's right to do as he pleases, again without interfering with somebody else's rights.
>
> [How have your views on morality changed since the last interview?] I think I am more aware of an individual's rights now. I used to be looking at it strictly from my point of view, just for me. Now I think I am more aware of what the individual has a right to.[1]

"Clearly," Kohlberg states,

> these responses represent attainment of the third level of moral theory. Moving to a perspective outside of that of his society, he identifies morality with justice (fairness, rights, the Golden Rule), with recognition of the rights of others as these are defined naturally or intrinsically. The human's right to do as he pleases without interfering with somebody else's rights is a formula defining rights

prior to social legislation and opinion which defines what society may expect rather than being defined by it.[2]

The second quotation comes from my interview with a woman, also twenty-five years old and at the time of the interview a third-year student at Harvard Law School. She described her conception of morality as follows:

[Is there really some correct solution to moral problems or is everybody's opinion equally right?] No, I don't think everybody's opinion is equally right. I think that in some situations . . . there may be opinions that are equally valid and one could conscientiously adopt one of several courses of action. But there are other situations which I think there are right and wrong answers, that sort of inhere in the nature of existence, of all individuals here who need to live with each other to live. We need to depend on each other and hopefully it is not only a physical need but a need of fulfillment in ourselves, that a person's life is enriched by cooperating with other people and striving to live in harmony with everybody else, and to that end, there are right and wrong, there are things which promote that end and that move away from it, and in that way, it is possible to choose in certain cases among different courses of action, that obviously promote or harm that goal.

[Is there a time in the past when you would have thought about these things differently?] Oh, yah. I think that I went through a time when I thought that things were pretty relative, that I can't tell you what to do and you can't tell me what to do, because you've got your conscience and I've got mine. . . .

[When was that?] When I was in high school, I guess that it just sort of dawned on me that my own ideas changed and because my own judgments changed, I felt I couldn't judge another person's judgment . . . but now I think even when it is only the person himself who is going to be affected, I say it is wrong to the extent it doesn't cohere with what I know about human na- ture and what I know about you, and just from what I think is true about the operation of the universe, I could say I think you are making a mistake.

[What led you to change, do you think?] Just seeing more of life, just recognizing that there are an awful lot of things that are common among people . . . there are certain things that you come to learn promote a better life and better relationships and more personal fulfillment than other things that in general tend to do the opposite and the things that promote these things, you would call morally right.

These responses also represent a reflective reconstruction of morality following a period of relativistic questioning and doubt, but the reconstruction of moral understanding is based not on the primacy and universality of individual rights, but rather on what she herself describes as a "very strong sense of being responsible to the world." Within this construction, the moral dilemma changes from how to exercise one's rights without interfering with the rights of others to how "to lead a moral life which includes obligations to myself and my family and people in general." The problem then becomes one of limiting responsibilities without abandoning moral concern. When asked to describe herself, this woman says that she values

having other people that I am tied to and also having people that I am responsible to. I have a very strong sense of being responsible to the world, that I can't just live for my enjoyment, but just the fact of being in the world gives me an obligation to do what I can to make the world a better place to live in, no matter how small a scale that may be on.

Thus while Kohlberg's subject worries about people interfering with one another's rights, this woman worries about "the possibility of omission, of your not helping others when you could help them."

The issue this law student raises is addressed by Loevinger's fifth "autonomous" stage of ego development. The terms of its resolution lie in achieving partial autonomy from an excessive sense of responsibility by recognizing that other people have responsibility for their own destiny (Loevinger, 1968). The autonomous stage in Loevinger's account witnesses a relinquishing of moral dichotomies and their replacement with "a feeling for the complexity and multifaceted character of real people and real situations" (1970, p. 6).

Whereas the rights conception of morality that informs Kohlberg's principled level [Stages Five and Six] is geared to arriving at an objectively fair or just resolution to the moral dilemmas to which "all rational men can agree" (Kohlberg, 1976), the responsibility conception focuses instead on the limitations of any particular resolution and describes the conflicts that remain. This limitation of moral judgment and choice is described by a woman in her thirties when she says that her guiding principle in making moral decisions has to do with "responsibility and caring about yourself and others, not just a principle that once you take hold of, you settle [the moral problem].The principle put into practice is still going to leave you with conflict."

Given the substance and orientation of these women's judgments, it becomes clear why a morality of rights and noninterference may appear to women as frightening in its potential justification of indifference and unconcern. At the same time, however, it also becomes clear why, from a male perspective, women's judgments appear inconclusive and diffuse, given their insistent contextual relativism. Women's moral judgments thus elucidate the pattern that we have observed in the differences between the sexes, but provide an alternative conception of maturity by which these differences can be developmentally considered. The psychology of women that has consistently been described as distinctive in its greater orientation toward relationships of interdependence implies a more contextual mode of judgment and a different moral understanding. Given the differences in women's conceptions of self and morality, it is not surprising that women bring to the life cycle a different point of view and that they order human experience in terms of different priorities.

The myth of Demeter and Persephone, which McClelland cites as exemplifying the feminine attitude toward power, was associated with the Eleusinian Mysteries celebrated in ancient Greece for over two thousand years (1975, p. 96). As told in the Homeric *Hymn to Demeter* (1971), the story of Persephone indicates the strengths of "interdependence, building up resources and giving" (McClelland, 1975, p. 96) that McClelland found in his research on power motivation to characterize the mature feminine style. Although, McClelland says, "it is fashionable to conclude that no one knows what went on in the Mysteries, it is known that they were probably the most important religious ceremonies, even partly on the historical record, which were organized by and for women, especially at the onset before men by means of the cult of Dionysus began to take them over" (1975, p. 96). Thus McClelland regards the myth as "a special presentation of feminine psychology" (1975). It is, as well, a life-cycle story par excellence.

Persephone, the daughter of Demeter, while out playing in the meadows with her girl friends, sees a beautiful narcissus which she runs to pick. As she does so, the earth opens and she is snatched away by Pluto, who takes her to his underworld kingdom. Demeter, goddess of the earth, so mourns the loss of her daughter that she refuses to allow anything to grow. The crops that sustain life on earth shrivel and dry up, killing men and animals alike, until Zeus takes pity on man's suffering and persuades his brother to return Persephone to her mother. But before she leaves, Persephone eats some pomegranate seeds, which insures that she will spend six months of every year in the underworld.

The elusive mystery of women's development lies in its recognition of the continuing importance of attachment in the human life cycle. Woman's place in man's life cycle has been to protect this recognition while the developmental litany intones the celebration of separation, autonomy, individuation, and natural rights. The myth of Persephone speaks directly to the distortion in this view by reminding us that narcissism leads to death, that the fertility of the earth is in some mysterious way tied to the continuation of the mother-daughter relationship, and that the life cycle itself arises from an alternation between the world of women and that of men. My intention in this essay has been to suggest that only when life-cycle theorists equally divide their attention and begin to live with women as they have lived with men will their vision encompass the experience of both sexes and their theories become correspondingly more fertile.

EDITOR'S NOTES

1. Carol Gilligan, *In a Different Voice: Psychological Theory and Women's Development* (Cambridge, Mass.: Harvard University Press, 1982).
2. The philosophers contributing to *Women and Moral Theory*, ed. Eva Kittay and Diana Meyers (Totowa, N.J.: Rowman and Allenheld, 1987), examine the implications of Gilligan's work for the thought of Kant, John Rawls, and other moral theorists.

NOTES

1. L. Kohlberg, *Continuities and discontinuities in childhood and adult moral development revisited.* (Unpublished manuscript, Harvard University, 1973), pp.29.
2. Ibid., pp.29–30.

REFERENCES

Bettelheim, B. *The uses of enchantment.* New York: Knopf, 1976.
Blos, P. The second individuation process of adolescence. In A. Freud (Ed.), *The psychoanalytic study of the child* (Vol. 22). New York: International Universities Press, 1967.

Chekhov, A. *The cherry orchard*. (Stark Young, trans.). New York: Modern Library, 1956. (Originally published, 1904.)

Chodorow, N. Family structure and feminine personality. In M. Rosaldo & L. Lamphere (Eds.), *Women, culture and society*. Stanford, Calif.: Stanford University Press, 1974.

——*The reproduction of mothering*. Berkeley: University of California Press, 1978.

Edwards, C. P. Societal complexity and moral development: A Kenyan study. *Ethos*, 1975, 3, 505–527.

Erikson, E. *Identity: Youth and crisis*. New York: Norton, 1968.

Freud, S. Female sexuality. In J. Strachey (Ed.), *The standard edition of the complete psychological works of Sigmund Freud* (Vol. 21). London: Hogarth Press., 1961. (Orginally published 1931.)

——Some psychical consequences of the anatomical distinction between the sexes. In J. Strachey (Ed.), *The standard edition of the complete psychological works of Sigmund Freud* (Vol. 19). London: Hogarth Press, 1961. (Originally published, 1925.)

——Three essays on sexuality. In J. Strachey (Ed.), *The standard edition of the complete psychological works of Sigmund Freud* (Vol. 7). London: Hogarth Press, 1961. (Originally published, 1905.)

Gilligan, C. In a different voice: Women's conceptions of the self and of morality. *Harvard Educational Review*, 1977, **47**, 481–517.

The Homeric Hymn (C. Boer, trans.). Chicago: Swallow Press, 1971.

Horner, M. Toward an understanding of achievement-related conflicts in women. *Journal of Social Issues*, 1972, **28** (2), 157–174.

Inhelder, B., & Piaget, J. *The growth of logical thinking from childhood to adolescence*. New York: Basic Books, 1958.

Kingston, M. H. *The woman warrior*. New York: Vintage Books, 1977.

Kohlberg, L., & Kramer, R. Continuities and discontinuities in childhood and adult moral development, *Human Development*, 1969, **12**, 93–120.

Kohlberg, L. From is to ought: How to commit the naturalistic fallacy and get away with it in the study of moral development. In T. Mischel (Ed.), *Cognitive development and epistemology*. New York: Academic Press, 1971.

Lever, J. Sex differences in the games children play. *Social Problems*, 1976, **23**, 478–487.

Levinson, D. *The seasons of a man's life*. New York: Knopf, 1978.

Loevinger, J., and Wessler, R. *The meaning and measurement of ego development*. San Francisco: Jossey-Bass, 1970.

McClelland, D. *The achieving society*. New York: Van Nostrand, 1961.

——*Power: The inner experience*. New York: Irvington Publishers, 1975.

Mead, G. H. *Mind, self and society*. Chicago: University of Chicago Press, 1934.

Perry, W. *Forms of intellectual and ethical development in the college years*. New York: Holt, Rinehart & Winston, 1968.

Piaget, J. *The moral judgment of the child*. New York: Free Press, 1965. (Originally published, 1932.)

Riesman, D. *The lonely crowd*. New Haven: Yale University Press, 1961.

Sassen, G. Success-anxiety in women: A constructivist theory of its sources and its significance. *Harvard Educational Review*, 1980, **50**, 13–24.

Strunk, W., & White, E. B. *The elements of style*. New York: Macmillan, 1959.

Sullivan, H. S. *The interpersonal theory of psychiatry*. New York: Norton, 1953.

Vaillant, G. *Adaptation to life*. Boston: Little, Brown, 1977.

Woolf, V. *A room of one's own*. New York: Harcourt, Brace & World, 1929.

VI.

INTRODUCTION TO
TOMORROW'S TOMORROW
THE BLACK WOMAN

Joyce A. Ladner

Joyce Ladner's introduction to her study of poor Black girls in the city provides a thought-provoking analysis of relationships between methodological, theoretical, epistemological, political, and ethical dimensions of social science research.[1]

She points out that her work violates the "rules of inquiry" in sociology—rules which we can see are similar to the scientistic, positivist-inspired ones Carolyn Sherif identified in psychology. Ladner is aware that she brought to her research the "attitudes, values, beliefs, and in effect, a Black perspective," that were central to her own identity. It was this perspective that enabled her to see the importance of mediating the tensions between her own identity and the rules of sociological inquiry. Sociological theory and methodology directed her to distance herself from her subjects, to take a dispassionate and "objective" attitude toward their condition (what I have referred to as "objectivism"), and to view them as deviant. But her ability to recognize in these young women reflections of her own Black perspective led her, instead, to regard their struggles as heroic: "a very healthy and successful adaptation, given their limited resources, had been made by all of these girls to a set of very unhealthy environmental conditions."

Ladner's paper raises a host of pertinent questions: here are five the reader will find it valuable to keep in mind as she/he enters Ladner's discourse. First, Ladner redefines the problem to be addressed from the deviance of urban Black girls to institutional racism. Could there be a value-neutral, nonpolitical definition of a social science problem? Second, as Ladner herself asks, why should anyone think it good to be "objective" (indifferent, disinterested, dispassionate, value-neutral) about racism or poverty? Third, does and must social research replicate a colonial political relationship? What difference to the conduct and probable results of research does it make if the researcher and her subjects are in the same dominated social group (e.g., both are Black)? If the researcher is a member of the dominated group and the researched is in the dominant group (e.g., Blacks studying whites)? Fourth, is the "double-consciousness" which comes from being defined as inferior, as an outsider, or as a stranger a more valuable perspective from which to gain a critical perspective on social life than is a consciousness which is in perfect fit with the dominant culture?[2] Finally, feminism teaches us that there is no single exemplar of "the human"; there are only men and women. What does a Black perspective teach us about such concepts as "man" and "woman"?

It is very difficult to determine whether this work had its beginnings when I was growing up in rural Mississippi and experiencing all the tensions, conflicts, joys, sorrows, warmth, compassion, and cruelty that was associated with *becoming a Black woman*; or whether it originated with my graduate school career when I became engaged in research for a doctoral dissertation. I *am* sure that the twenty years I spent being socialized by my family and the broader Black community prior to entering graduate school shaped my perception of life, defined my emotive responses to the world and enhanced my ability to survive in a society that has not made survival for Blacks easy. Therefore, when I decided to engage in research on what approaching womanhood meant to poor Black girls in the city, I brought with me these attitudes, values, beliefs and in effect, a Black perspective. Because of this cultural sensitivity I had to the life-styles of the over one hundred adolescent, preadolescent and adult females I "studied," I had to mediate tensions that existed from day to day between the *reality* and *validity* of their lives *and* the tendency to view it from the *deviant perspective* in accordance with my academic training.

Deviance is the invention of a group that uses its own standards as the *ideal* by which others are to be judged. Howard Becker states that

> Social groups create deviance by making the rules whose infraction constitutes deviance, and by applying these rules to particular people and labeling them as outsiders. From this point of view, deviance is *not* a quality of the act the person commits, but rather a consequence of the application by others of rules and sanctions to an "offender." The deviant is one to whom that label has successfully been applied; deviant behavior is behavior that people so label.[1]

Other students of social problems have adhered to the same position.[2] Placing Black people in the context of the deviant perspective has been possible because Blacks have not had the necessary power to resist the labels. This power could have come only from the ability to provide the *definitions* of one's past, present and future. Since Blacks have always, until recently, been defined by the majority group, that group's characterization was the one that was predominant.

The preoccupation with *deviancy*, as opposed to *normalcy*, encourages the researcher to limit his scope and ignore some of the most vital elements of the lives of the people he is studying. It has been noted by one sociologist that:

> It is probably a fact and one of which some contemporary students of deviance have been cognizant—that the greater portion of the lives of deviant persons or groups is spent in normal, mundane, day-to-day living. In the researcher's focus on deviance and this acquisition of the deviant perspective, not only is he likely to overlook these more conventional phenomena, and thus become insensitive to them, but he may in the process overlook that very data which helps to explain that deviance he studies.[3]

Having been equipped with the *deviant perspective* in my academic training, yet lacking strong commitment to it because it conflicted with my objective knowledge and responses to the Black women I was studying, I went into the field equipped with a set of preconceived ideas and labels that I intended to apply to these women. This, of course, meant that I had gone there only to validate and elaborate on what was *alleged to exist*. If I had continued within this context, I would have concluded the same thing that most social scientists who study Black people conclude: that they are pathology-ridden.

However, this role was difficult, if not impossible, for me to play because all of my life experiences invalidated the deviant perspective. As I became more involved with the subjects of this research, I knew that I would not be able to play the role of the dispassionate scientist, whose major objective was to extract certain data from them that would simply be used to *describe* and *theorize* about their conditions. I began to perceive my role as a Black person, with empathy and attachment, and, to a great extent, their day-to-day lives and future destinies became intricately interwoven with my own. This did not occur without a considerable amount of agonizing self-evaluation and conflict over "whose side I was on." On the one hand, I wanted to conduct a study that would allow me to fulfill certain academic requirements, i.e., a doctoral dissertation. On the other hand, I was highly influenced by my *Blackness*—by the fact that I, on many levels, was one of them and had to deal with their problems on a personal level. I was largely unable to resolve these strands, this "double consciousness," to which W. E. B. DuBois refers.[4] It is important to understand that Blacks are at a juncture in history that has been unprecedented for its necessity to grope with and clarify and *define* the status of our existence in American society. Thus, I was unable to resolve the dilemmas I faced as a Black social scientist because they only symbolized the larger questions, issues and dilemmas of our times.

Many books have been written about the Black community[5] but very few have really dealt with the intricate lives of the people who live there. By and large, they have attempted to analyze and describe the pathology which allegedly characterizes the lives of its inhabitants while at the same time making its residents responsible for its creation. The unhealthy conditions of the community such as drug addiction, poverty, crime, dilapidated housing, unemployment, and the multitude of problems which characterize it have caused social analysts to see these conditions as producing millions of "sick" people, many of whom are given few chances ever to overcome the wretchedness which clouds their existence. Few authorities on the Black community have written about the vast amount of strength and adaptability of the people. They have ignored the fact that this community is a force which not only acts upon its residents but which is also acted upon. Black people are involved in a dynamic relationship with their physical and cultural environment in that they both influence and are influenced by it. This reciprocal relationship allows them to exercise a considerable amount of power over their environs. This also means that they are able to exercise control over their futures, whereas writers have tended to view the low-income Black community as an all-pervasive force which is so devastating as to compel its powerless residents to succumb to its pressures. Their power to cope and adapt to a set of unhealthy conditions—not as stereotyped sick people but as normal ones—is a factor which few people seem to accept or even realize. The ways Blacks have adapted to poverty and racism, and yet emerged relatively unscarred, are a peculiar quality which Americans should commend.

The concept of social deviance is quite frequently applied to the values and behavior of Blacks because they represent a departure from the traditional white middle-class norm, along with criminals, homosexuals and prostitutes.

But these middle-class standards should not have been imposed because of the distinctiveness that characterizes the Black life-style, particularly that of the masses.

Most scholars have taken a dim view of any set of distinct life-styles shared by Blacks, and where they were acknowledged to exist, have of course maintained that these forces were negative adaptations to the larger society. There has never been an admission that the Black community is a product of American social policy, *not* the cause of it—the structure of the American social system, through its practices of institutional racism, is designed to create the alleged "pathology" of the community, to perpetuate "the social disorganization" model of Black life. Recently, the Black culture thesis has been granted some legitimization as an explanatory variable for much of the distinctiveness of Black life. As a result of this more positive attitude toward understanding the strengths of life in the Black community, many scholars, policy makers et al. are refocusing their attention and reinterpreting the many aspects of life that comprise the complex existence of American Blacks.

There must be a strong concern with redefining the problem. Instead of future studies being conducted on *problems* of the Black community as represented by the *deviant perspective*, there must be a redefinition of the *problem as being that of institutional racism*. If the social system is viewed as the *source* of the deviant perspective, then future research must begin to analyze the nature of oppression and the mechanisms by which institutionalized forms of subjugation are initiated and act to maintain the system intact. Thus, studies which have as their focal point the alleged deviant *attitudes* and *behavior* of Blacks are grounded within the racist assumptions and principles that only render Blacks open to further exploitation.

The challenge to social scientists for a redefinition of the basic *problem* has been raised in terms of the "colonial analogy." It has been argued that the relationship between the *researcher* and his *subjects*, by definition, resembles that of the oppressor and the oppressed, because it is the oppressor who defines the problem, the nature of the research, and, to some extent, the quality of interaction between him and his subjects. This inability to understand and research the fundamental problem—*neo-colonialism*— prevents most social researchers from being able accurately to observe and analyze Black life and culture and the impact racism and oppression have upon Blacks. Their inability to understand the nature and effects of neo-colonialism in the same manner as Black people is rooted in the inherent bias of the social sciences. The basic concepts and tools of white Western society are permeated by this partiality to the conceptual framework of the oppressor. It is simple enough to say that the difference between the two groups—the oppressor and the oppressed—prevents the former from adequately comprehending the essence of Black life and culture because of a fundamental difference in perceptions, based upon separate histories, life-styles, and purposes for being. Simply put, the slave and his master do not view and respond to the world in the same way. The historian Lerone Bennett addresses this problem below:

> George Washington and George Washington's slaves lived different realities. And if we extend that insight to all the dimensions of white American history we will realize that blacks lived at a

different time and a different reality in this country. And the terrifying implications of all this is that there is another time, another reality, another America. . . .

Bennett states further that:

> It is necessary for us to develop a new frame of reference which transcends the limits of white concepts. It is necessary for us to develop a total intellectual offensive against the false universality of white concepts whether they are expressed by William Styron or Daniel Patrick Moynihan. By and large, reality has been conceptualized in terms of the narrow point of view of the small minority of white men who live in Europe and North America. We must abandon the partial frame of reference of our oppressors and create new concepts which will release our reality, which is also the reality of the overwhelming majority of men and women on this globe. We must say to the white world that there are things in the world that are not dreamt of in your history and your sociology and your philosophy.[6]

Currently there are efforts underway to "de-colonize" social research on the *conceptual* and *methodological* levels.[7]

Although I attempted to maintain some degree of objectivity, I soon began to minimize and, very often, negate the importance of being "value-free," because the very selection of the topic itself reflected a bias, i.e., I studied Black women because of my strong interest in the subject.

I decided whose side I was on and resolved within myself that as a Black social scientist I must take a stand and that there could be no value-free sanctuary for me. The controversy over the question of values in social research is addressed by Gouldner:

> If sociologists ought not express their personal values in the academic setting, how then are students to be safeguarded against the unwitting influence of these values which shape the sociologist's selection of problems, his preferences for certain hypotheses or conceptual schemes, and his neglect of others? For these are unavoidable and, in this sense, there is and can be no value-free sociology. The only choice is between an expression of one's values as open and honest as it can be, this side of the psychoanalytic couch, and a vain ritual of moral neutrality which, because it invites men to ignore the vulnerability of reason to bias, leaves it at the mercy of irrationality.[8]

I accepted this position as a guiding premise and proceeded to conduct my research with the full knowledge that I could not divorce myself from the problems of these women, nor should I become so engrossed in them that I would lose my original purpose for being in the community.

The words of Kenneth Clark, as he describes the tensions and conflicts he experienced while conducting the research for his classic study of Harlem, *Dark Ghetto*, typify the problems I faced:

> I could never be fully detached as a scholar or participant. More than forty years of my life had been lived in Harlem. I started school in Harlem public schools. I first learned about people, about love, about cruelty, about sacrifice, about cowardice, about courage, about bombast in

Harlem. For many years before I returned as an "involved observer," Harlem had been my home. My family moved from house to house, and from neighborhood to neighborhood within the walls of the ghetto in a desperate attempt to escape its creeping blight. In a very real sense, therefore, *Dark Ghetto* is a summation of my personal and lifelong experiences and observations as a prisoner within the ghetto long before I was aware that I was really a prisoner.[9]

The inability to be *objective* about analyzing poverty, racism, disease, self-destruction, and the gamut of problems which faced these females only mirrored a broader problem in social research. That is, to what extent should any scientist—white or Black—consider it his duty to be a dispassionate observer and not intervene, when possible, to ameliorate many of the destructive conditions he studies. On many occasions I found myself acting as a counselor, big sister, etc. Certainly the question can be raised as to whether researchers can continue to gather data on impoverished Black communities without addressing these findings to the area of social policy.

This raises another important question, to which I will address myself. That is, many people will read this book because they are seeking answers to the dilemmas and problems facing Black people in general and Black women in particular. A great number of young Black women will expect to find forever-sought formulas to give them a new sense of direction as *Black women*. Some Black men will read this work because they are concerned about this new direction and want to become involved in the shaping of this process. Others, of course, will simply be curious to find out what a Black woman has to say about her peers. I expect traditional-type scholars to take great issue with my thesis and many of my formulations because I am consciously attempting to break away from the traditional way in which social science research has analyzed the attitudes and behavior patterns of Blacks. Finally, a small but growing group of scholars will find it refreshing to read a work on Black women which does not indict them for all kinds of alleged social problems, which, if they exist, they did not create.

All of these are problems and questions which I view as inescapable for one who decides to attempt to break that new ground and write about areas of human life in ways in which they are not ordinarily approached.

There are no standard answers for the dilemmas I faced, for they are simply microcosms of the larger Black community. Therefore, this work is not attempting to resolve the problems of Black womanhood but to shed light on them. More than anything else, I feel that it is attempting to depict what the Black woman's life has been like in the past, and what barriers she has had to overcome in order to survive, and how she is coping today under the most strenuous circumstances. Thus, I am simply saying, "This is what the Black woman was, this is how she has been solving her problems, and these are ways in which she is seeking to alter her roles." I am not trying to chart a course of action for her to follow. This will, in large measure, be dictated by, and interwoven with, the trends set in that vast Black American community. My primary concern here is with depicting the strength of the Black family and Black girls within the family structure. I will seek to depict the lives of Black people I knew who were utilizing their scant resources for survival purposes, but who on the whole were quite successful with making the necessary adaptive and creative responses to their oppressed circumstances. I am also dealing with the somewhat abstract white middle-class system of values as it affects Blacks. It is hoped that the problems I encountered with conducting such a study, as well as the positive approach I was eventually able to take toward this work, will enable others to be equally as effective in breaking away from an intellectual tradition which has existed far too long.

One of the primary preoccupations of every American adolescent girl, regardless of race and social class background, is that of eventually becoming a woman. Every girl looks forward to the time when she will discard the status of child and take on the role of adult, wife and possibly mother.

The official entry into womanhood is usually regarded as that time when she reaches the prescribed legal age (eighteen and sometimes twenty-one), when for the first time she is granted certain legal and other rights and privileges. These rights, such as being allowed to vote, to go to certain "for adults only" events, to join certain social clubs and to obtain certain types of employment, are accompanied by a type of informal understanding that very few privileges, either formal or informal, are to be denied her where age is the primary prerequisite for participation. Entry into womanhood is the point at which she is considered by older adults to be ready to join their ranks because she has gone through the necessary apprenticeship program—the period of adolescence. We can observe differences between racial and social class groups regarding, for instance, the time at which the female is considered to be ready to assume the duties and obligations of womanhood. Becoming a woman in the low-income Black community is somewhat different from the routes followed by the white middle-class girl. The poor Black girl reaches her status of womanhood at an earlier age because of the different prescriptions and expectations of her culture. There is no single set of criteria for becoming a woman in the Black community; each girl is conditioned by a diversity of factors depending primarily upon her opportunities, role models, psychological disposition, and the influence of the values, customs and traditions of the Black community. It will be demonstrated that the resources which adolescent girls have at their disposal, combined with the cultural heritage of their communities, are crucial factors in determining what kind of women they become. Structural *and* psychological variables are important as focal points because neither alone is sufficient to explain the many factors involved with psychosocial development. Therefore, the concepts of motivation, roles and role model, identity, and socialization, as well as family income, education, kin, and peer group relations are important to consider in the analysis. These diverse factors have rarely been considered as crucial to an analysis of Black womanhood. This situation exists because previous studies have substituted simplistic notions for rigorous multivariate analysis. Here, however, these multiple factors and influences will be analyzed as a "Black cultural" framework which has its own autonomous systems of values, behavior, attitudes, sentiments, and beliefs.

Another significant dimension to be considered will be the extent to which Black girls are influenced by the distinct culture of their community. Certain historical as well as contemporary variables are very important when describing the young Black woman. Her cultural heritage, I feel, has played a stronger role than has previously been stated by most writers in shaping her into the entity she has become.

Life in the Black community has been conditioned by poverty, discrimination, and institutional subordination. It has also been shaped by African cultural survivals. From slavery until the present, many of the African cultural survivals influenced the way Blacks lived, responded to others, and, in general, related to their environment. Even after slavery many of these survivals have remained and act to forge a distinct and viable set of cultural adaptive mechanisms because discrimination acted as an agent to perpetuate instead of to destroy the culture.

I will illustrate, through depicting the lives of Black pre-adolescent and adolescent girls in a big-city slum, how distinct sociohistorical forces have shaped a very positive and practical way of dealing and coping with the world. The values, attitudes, beliefs, and behavior emerge from a long tradition, much of which has characterized the Black community from its earliest beginnings in this country.

What is life like in the urban Black community for the "average" girl? How does she define her roles, behaviors, and from whom does she acquire her models for fulfilling what is expected of her? Is there any significant disparity between the resources she has with which to accomplish her goals in life and the stated aspirations? Is the typical world of the teenager in American society shared by the Black girl or does she stand somewhat alone in much of her day-to-day existence?

In an attempt to answer these and other questions, I went to such a community and sought out teenagers whom I felt could provide me with some insights. I was a research assistant in 1964 on a study of an all-Black low-income housing project of over ten thousand residents in a slum area of St. Louis. (This study was supported by a grant from the National Institute of Mental Health, Grant No. MH–9189, "Social and Community Problems in Public Housing Areas.") It was geographically located near the downtown section of St. Louis, Missouri, and within one of the oldest slum areas of the city. The majority of the females were drawn from the Pruitt-Igoe housing project, although many resided outside the public housing project in substandard private housing.

At that time my curiosity was centered around the various activities in which the girls engaged that frequently produced harmful consequences. Specifically, I attempted to understand how such social problems as pregnancy, premarital sex, school dropout, etc. affected their life chances for success. I also felt, at the time, that a less destructible adaptation could be made to their impoverished environments. However, I was to understand later that perhaps a very healthy and successful adaptation, given their limited resources, had been made by all of these girls to a set of very unhealthy environmental conditions. Therefore, I soon changed my focus and attempted to apply a different perspective to the data.

I spent almost four years interviewing, testing (Thematic Apperception Test), observing, and, in general, "hanging out" with these girls. I attempted to establish a strong rapport with all of them by spending a considerable amount of time in their homes with them and their families, at church, parties, dances, in the homes of their friends, shopping, at my apartment, and in a variety of other situations. The sample consisted of several peer groups which over the years changed in number and composition. I always endeavored to interview their parents, and in some cases became close friends of their mothers. The field work carried me into the community at very unregulated hours—weekends, occasional evenings, and during school hours (when I usually talked to their mothers). Although a great portion of the data collected is exploratory in nature, the majority of it is based on systematic open-ended interviews that related to (1) life histories and (2) attitudes and behavior that reflected approaching womanhood. During the last year and a half I randomly selected thirty girls between the ages of thirteen and eighteen and conducted a systematic investigation that was designed to test many of my preliminary conclusions drawn from the exploratory research. All of the interviews and observations were taped and transcribed. The great majority of the interviews were taped *live*, and will appear as direct quotations throughout this book. (All of the girls have been given pseudonyms.)

I feel that the data are broad in scope and are applicable to almost any group of low-income Black teenage girls growing up in any American city. The economic, political, social and racial factors which have produced neo-colonialism on a national scale operate in Chicago, Roxbury, Detroit, Watts, Atlanta—and everywhere else.

The total misrepresentation of the Black community and the various myths which surround it can be seen in microcosm in the Black female adolescent. Her growing-up years reflect the basic quality and character of life in this environment, as well as anticipations for the future. Because she is in perhaps the most crucial stage of psychosocial development, one can capture these crucial forces—external and internal—which are acting upon her, and which, more than any other impact, will shape her life-long adult role. Thus, by understanding the nature and processes of her development, we can also comprehend the more intricate elements that characterize the day-to-day lives of the Black masses.

EDITOR'S NOTES

1. *Tomorrow's Tomorrow: The Black Woman* (Garden City, N.Y.: Doubleday & Co., 1972.) See also her edited collection, *The Death of White Sociology* (New York: Random House, 1973).

2. Dorothy Smith also takes up this issue in her essay in this volume.

NOTES

1. Howard S. Becker, *The Outsiders*, New York: Free Press, 1963, p.9.

2. See the works of Edwin Lemert, *Social Pathology*, New York, McGraw-Hill, 1951; John Kituse, "Societal Reaction to Deviance: Problems of Theory and Method," *Social Problems*, Winter 1962, pp. 247–56; and Frank Tannenbaum, *Crime and the Community*, New York, Columbia University Press, 1938.

3. See Ethel Sawyer, "Methodological Problems in Studying Socially Deviant Communities," in Joyce A. Ladner, ed., *The Death of White Sociology*, New York, Random House 1973.

4. W.E.B. DuBois, *Souls of Black Folk*, New York, Fawcett World Library, 1961.

5. I am using the term "Black commuinity" to refer to what is traditionally called the "ghetto." I am speaking largely of the low-income and working-class masses, who comprise the majority of the Black population in this country.

6. Lerone Bennett, *The Challenge of Blackness*, Chicago: Johnson Publishing Co., 1972.

7. Refer to Robert Blauner, "Internal Colonialism and Ghetto Revolt," *Social Problems*, Vol. 16, No. 4, Spring 1969, pp. 393–408; and see Robert Blauner and David Wellman, "Toward the Decolonization of Social Research," in Ladner, *The Death of White Sociology*.

8. Alvin W. Gouldner, "Anti-Minotaur: The Myth of a Value-Free Sociology," *Social Problems*, Winter 1962, pp. 199–213.

9. Kenneth Clark, *Dark Ghetto*, New York, Harper & Row, 1965, p. xv.

VII.

WOMEN'S PERSPECTIVE AS A RADICAL CRITIQUE OF SOCIOLOGY

Dorothy E. Smith

Dorothy Smith, the Canadian sociologist of knowledge, has written a series of influential papers analyzing how sociology must be transformed in order to be able to explain social life for women instead of for male administrators.[1] This essay is the first of these, and it both borrows from and transforms Marxist and phenomenological approaches to social research. Though her concern in these papers is specifically with sociology, her arguments are applicable to every social science—and perhaps even to the natural sciences, literature, and the arts. The reader may want to test this out for her/himself by transposing Smith's analysis into one about history, political theory, legal theory, psychology, and so forth.

Smith's argument here is a densely packed one. Her main theme is that there is an unfortunate fit between men's characteristic understandings of social life, sociology's favored conceptual schemes, and the kinds of knowledge needed for "ruling" others. Sociology is part of the practices by which we are governed. It is part of the conceptual imperialism by which ruling is done in our kind of administratively managed society. Sociology works up the conceptual procedures, models, and methods by which immediate and concrete features of experience can be read into the conceptual mode in which governing is done.

Thus, Smith argues that learning to be a sociologist is learning to substitute the concerns of an administrator's world for the concerns of our experienced world. Men can enter this conceptual mode only if they don't have to focus on their own or anyone else's bodily existence. This kind of sociology depends upon someone else—women, blacks, other subservient groups—taking care of the bodies of administrators and the local places where they exist. Smith argues that women's perspective on sociology discredits sociology's claim to constitute an objective knowledge which is independent of the sociologist's situation. Women's perspective reveals that the subject matter of sociology is *organized from* a determinate position in society—a ruling-class, white, male one.

Smith is one of the thinkers who has made clear the importance of trying to recover the entire social relations of research in the results of that research.[2] The inquirer must be located in the same critical plane as the subject of research. Traditional sociological theory and practice recover only the object of research, as if that stood by itself. Such a sociology hides the way those objects are constituted, constructed, in the actual concrete social relations in which the sociologist participates day by day as she/he conducts research.

Women's daily experience must generate the "problems" requiring sociological explanation. It provides the starting point for a more adequate sociology. But though women's experiences can generate important problems, they do not offer any answers; the determinants of women's daily experience are not to be found *in* that experience, but elsewhere—in the political, economic, social order. Thus the project for sociology must be not only to make visible the daily, concrete social relations through which the worlds of men and women are brought into existence, but also to explain the relationship between these worlds; why they are separate, in what ways men's world dominates women's, how women's can/does resist that domination, and so forth. For a woman sociologist, this means that "the grasp and exploration of her own experience as a method of discovering society restores her to a center which in this enterprise at least is wholly hers."

1. The women's movement has given us a sense of our right to have women's interests represented in sociology, rather than just receiving as authoritative the interests traditionally represented in a sociology put together by men. What can we make of this access to a social reality that was previously unavailable, was indeed repressed? What happens as we begin to relate to it in the terms of our discipline? We can of course think as many do merely of the addition of courses to the existing repertoire—courses on sex roles, on the women's movement, on women at work, on the social psychology of women and perhaps somewhat different versions of the sociology of the family. But thinking more boldly or perhaps just thinking the whole thing through a little further might bring us to ask first how a sociology might look if it began from the point of view of women's traditional place in it and what happens to a sociology which attempts to deal seriously with that. Following this line of thought, I have found, has consequences larger than they seem at first.

From the point of view of "women's place" the values assigned to different aspects of the world are changed. Some come into prominence while other standard sociological enterprises diminish. We might take as a model the world as it appears from the point of view of the afternoon soap opera. This is defined by (though not restricted to) domestic events, interests, and activities. Men appear in this world as necessary and vital presences. It is not a woman's world in the sense of excluding men. But it is a women's world in the sense that it is the relevances of the women's place that govern. Men appear only in their domestic or private aspects or at points of intersection between public and private as doctors in hospitals, lawyers in their offices discussing wills and divorces. Their occupational and political world is barely present. They are posited here as complete persons, and they are but partial—as women appear in sociology predicated on the universe occupied by men.

But it is not enough to supplement an established sociology by addressing ourselves to what has been left out, overlooked, or by making sociological issues of the relevances of the world of women. That merely extends the authority of the existing sociological procedures and makes of a women's sociology an addendum. We cannot rest at that because it does not account for the separation between the two worlds and it does not account for or analyze for us the relation between them. (Attempts to work on that in terms of biology operate within the existing structure as a fundamental assumption and are therefore straightforwardly ideological in character.)

The first difficulty is that how sociology is thought—its methods, conceptual schemes, and theories—has been based on and built up within, the male social universe (even when women have participated in its doing). It has taken for granted not just that scheme of relevances as an itemized inventory of issues or subject matters (industrial sociology, political sociology, social stratification, etc.) but the fundamental social and political structures under which these become relevant and are ordered. There is a difficulty first then of a disjunction between how women find and experience the world beginning (though not necessarily ending up) from their place and the concepts and theoretical schemes available to think about it in. Thus in a graduate seminar last year, we discussed on one occasion the possibility of a women's sociology and two graduate students told us that in their view and their experience of functioning in experimental group situations, theories of the emergence of leadership in small groups, etc. just did not apply to what was happening as they experienced it. They could not find the correlates of the theory in their experiences.

A second difficulty is that the two worlds and the two bases of knowledge and experience don't stand in an equal relation. The world as it is constituted by men stands in authority over that of women. It is that part of the world from which our kind of society is governed and from which what happens to us begins. The domestic world stands in a dependent relation to that other and its whole character is subordinate to it.

The two difficulties are related to one another in a special way. The effect of the second interacting with the first is to impose the concepts and terms in which the world of men is thought as the concepts and terms in which women must think their world. Hence in these terms women are alienated from their experience.

The profession of sociology is predicated on a universe which is occupied by men and is itself still largely appropriated by men as their "territory." Sociology is part of the practice by which we are all governed and that practice establishes its relevances. Thus the institutions which lock sociology into the structures occupied by men are the same institutions which lock women into the situations in which they find themselves oppressed. To unlock the latter leads logically to an unlocking of the former. What follows then, or rather what then becomes possible—for it is of course by no means inevitable—is less a shift in the subject matter than a different conception of how it is or might become relevant as a means to understand our experience and the conditions of our experience (both women's and men's) in corporate capitalist society.

2. When I speak here of governing or ruling I mean something more general than the notion of government as political organization. I refer rather to that total complex of activities differentiated into many spheres, by which our kind of society is ruled, managed, administered. It includes that whole section which in the business world is called "management." It includes the professions. It includes of course government more conventionally defined and also the activities of those who are selecting, training, and indoctrinating those who will be its governors. The last includes those who provide and elaborate the procedures in which it is governed and develop methods for accounting for how it is done and predicting and analyzing its characteristic consequences and sequences

of events, namely the business schools, the sociologists, the economists, etc. These are the institutions through which we are ruled and through which we, and I emphasize this we, participate in ruling.

Sociology then I conceive as much more than ideology, much more than a gloss on the enterprise which justifies and rationalizes it, and, at the same time as much less than "science." The governing of our kind of society is done in concepts and symbols. The contribution of sociology to this is that of working up the conceptual procedures, models and methods by which the immediate and concrete features of experience can be read into the conceptual mode in which the governing is done. What is actually observed or what is systematically recovered by the sociologist from the actualities of what people say and do, must be transposed into the abstract mode. Sociology thus participates in and con- tributes to the formation and facilitation of this mode of action and plays a distinctive part in the work of transposing the actualities of people's lives and experience into the con- ceptual currency in which it is and can be governed.

Thus the relevances of sociology are organized in terms of a perspective on the world which is a view from the top and which takes for granted the pragmatic procedures of governing as those which frame and identify its subject matter. Issues are formulated as issues which have become administratively relevant not as they are significant first in the experience of those who live them. The kinds of facts and events which are facts for us have already been shaped up and given their character and substance as facts, as relations, etc., by the methods and practice of governing. Mental illness, crimes, riots, violence, work satisfaction, neighbors and neighborhoods, motivation, etc., these are the constructs of the practice of government. In many instances, such as mental illness, crimes, neigh- borhoods, etc., they are constituted as discrete phenomena primarily by administrative procedures and others arise as problems in relation to the actual practice of government, as for example concepts of motivation, work satisfaction, etc.

The governing processes of our society are organized as social entities constituted ex- ternally to those persons who participate in and perform them. The managers, the bu- reaucrats, the administrators, are employees, are people who are *used*. They do not own the enterprises or otherwise appropriate them. Sociologists study these entities under the heading of formal organization. They are put together as objective structures with goals, activities, obligations, etc., other than those which its employees can have as individuals. The academic professions are also set up in a mode which externalizes them as entities vis-à-vis their practitioners. The body of knowledge which its members accumulate is appropriated by the discipline as its body. The work of members aims at contributing to that body of knowledge.

As graduate students learning to become sociologists, we learn to think sociology as it is thought and to practice it as it is practiced. We learn that some topics are relevant and some are not. We learn to discard our experienced world as a source of reliable information or suggestions about the character of the world; to confine and focus our insights within the conceptual frameworks and relevances which are given in the discipline. Should we think other kinds of thoughts or experience the world in a different way or with edges and horizons that pass beyond the conceptual we must practice a discipline which discards them or find some procedure which makes it possible to sneak them in. We learn a way of thinking about the world which is recognizable to its practitioners as the sociological way of thinking.

We learn to practice the sociological subsumption of the actualities of ourselves and of other people. We find out how to treat the world as instances of a sociological body of knowledge. The procedure operates as a sort of conceptual imperialism. When we write a thesis or a paper, we learn that the first thing to do is to latch it on to the discipline at some point. This may be by showing how it is a problem within an existing theoretical and conceptual framework. The boundaries of inquiry are thus set within the framework of what is already established. Even when this becomes, as it happily often does, a cere-monial authorization of a project which has little to do with the theory used to authorize it, we still work within the vocabularies and within the conceptual boundaries of what we have come to know as "the sociological perspective."

An important set of procedures which serve to constitute the body of knowledge of the discipline as something which is separated from its practitioners are those known as "ob-jectivity." The ethic of objectivity and the methods used in its practice are concerned primarily with the separation of the knower from what he knows and in particular with the separation of what is known from any interests, "biases," etc., which he may have which are not the interests and concerns authorized by the discipline. I must emphasize that being interested in knowing something doesn't invalidate what is known. In the social sciences the pursuit of objectivity makes it possible for people to be paid to pursue a knowledge to which they are otherwise indifferent. What they feel and think about society can be taken apart from and kept out of what they are professionally or academically interested in.

3. The sociologist enters the conceptually ordered society when he goes to work. He enters it as a member and he enters it also as the mode in which he investigates it. He observes, analyzes, explains, and examines as if there were no problem in how that world becomes observable to him. He moves among the doings of organizations, governmental processes, bureaucracies, etc., as a person who is at home in that medium. The nature of that world itself, how it is known to him and the conditions of its existence or his relation to it are not called into question. His methods of observation and inquiry extend into it as procedures which are essentially of the same order as those which bring about the phenomena with which he is concerned, or which he is concerned to bring under the jurisdiction of that order. His perspectives and interests may differ, but the substance is the same. He works with facts and information which have been worked up from actualities and appear in the form of documents which are themselves the product of organizational processes, whether his own or administered by him, or of some other agency. He fits that information back into a framework of entities and organizational processes which he takes for granted as known, without asking how it is that he knows them or what are the social processes by which the phenomena which correspond to or provide the empirical events, acts, decisions, etc., of that

world, may be recognized. He passes beyond the particular and immediate setting in which he is always located in the body (the office he writes in, the libraries he consults, the streets he travels, the home he returns to) without any sense of having made a transition. He works in the same medium as he studies.

But like everyone else he also exists in the body in the place in which it is. This is also then the place of his sensory organization of immediate experience, the place where his coordinates of here and now before and after are organized around himself as center; the place where he confronts people face to face in the physical mode in which he expresses himself to them and they to him as more and other than either can speak. It is in this place that things smell. The irrelevant birds fly away in front of the window. Here he has indigestion. It is a place he dies in. Into this space must come as actual material events, whether as the sounds of speech, the scratchings on the surface of paper which he constitutes as document, or directly, anything he knows of the world. It has to happen here somehow if he is to experience it at all.

Entering the governing mode of our kind of society lifts the actor out of the immediate local and particular place in which he is in the body. He uses what becomes present to him in this place as a means to pass beyond it to the conceptual order. This mode of action creates then a bifurcation of consciousness, a bifurcation of course which is there for all those who participate in this mode of action. It establishes two modes of knowing and experiencing and doing, one located in the body and in the space which it occupies and moves into, the other which passes beyond it. Sociology is written in and aims at this second mode. Vide Bierstedt:

> Sociology can liberate the mind from time and space themselves and remove it to a new and tran-scendental realm where it no longer depends upon these Aristotelian categories. (1966)

Even observational work aims at its description in the categories and hence conceptual forms of the "transcendental realm."

4. Women are outside and subservient to this structure. They have a very specific re-lation to it which anchors them into the local and particular phase of the bifurcated world. For both traditionally and as a matter of occupational practices in our society, the governing conceptual mode is appropriated by men and the world organized in the natural attitude, the home, is appropriated by (or assigned to) women (Smith, 1973).

It is a condition of a man's being able to enter and become absorbed in the conceptual mode that he does not have to focus his activities and interests upon his bodily existence. If he is to participate fully in the abstract mode of action, then he must be liberated also from having to attend to his needs, etc. in the concrete and particular. The organization of work and expectations in managerial and professional circles both constitutes and depends upon the alienation of man from his bodily and local existence. The structure of work and the structure of career take for granted that these matters are provided for in such a way that they will not interfere with his action and participation in that world. Providing for the liberation from the Aristotelian categories of which Bierstedt speaks, is a woman who keeps house for him, bears and cares for his children, washes his clothes, looks after him when he is sick, and generally provides for the logistics of his bodily existence.

The place of women then in relation to this mode of action is that where the work is done to create conditions which facilitate his occupation of the conceptual mode of consciousness. The meeting of a man's physical needs, the organization of his daily life, even the consistency of expressive background, are made maximally congruent with his commitment. A similar relation exists for women who work in and around the professional and managerial scene. They do those things which give concrete form to the conceptual activities. They do the clerical work, the computer programming, the interviewing for the survey, the nursing, the secretarial work. At almost every point women mediate for men the relation between the conceptual mode of action and the actual concrete forms in which it is and must be realized, and the actual material conditions upon which it depends.

Marx's concept of alienation is applicable here in a modified form. The simplest formulation of alienation posits a relation between the work an individual does and an external order which oppresses her, such that the harder she works the more she strengthens the order which oppresses her. This is the situation of women in this relation. The more successful women are in mediating the world of concrete particulars so that men do not have to become engaged with (and therefore conscious of) that world as a condition to their abstract activities, the more complete man's absorption in it, the more effective the authority of that world and the more total women's subservience to it. And also the more complete the dichotomy between the two worlds, and the estrangement between them.

5. Women sociologists stand at the center of a contradiction in the relation of our discipline to our experience of the world. Transcending that contradiction means setting up a different kind of relation than that which we discover in the routine practice of our worlds.

The theories, concepts and methods of our discipline claim to account for, or to be capable of accounting for and analyzing the same world as that which we experience directly. But these theories, concepts, and methods have been organized around and built up out of a way of knowing the world which takes for granted the boundaries of an experience in the same medium in which it is constituted. It therefore takes for granted and subsumes without examining the conditions of its existence. It is not capable of analyzing its own relation to its conditions because the sociologist as actual person in an actual concrete setting has been cancelled in the procedures which objectify and separate him from his knowledge. Thus the linkage which points back to its conditions is lacking.

For women those conditions are central as a direct practical matter, to be somehow solved in the decision to take up a sociological career. The relation between ourselves as practicing sociologists and ourselves as working women is continually visible to us, a central feature of experience of the world, so that the bifurcation of consciousness becomes for us a daily chasm which is to be crossed, on the one side of which is this special conceptual activity of thought, research, teaching, administration, and on the other the world of concrete practical activities in keeping things clean, managing somehow the house and household and the children, a world in which the particularities of persons in their full organic immediacy (cleaning up the vomit, changing the diapers, as well as feeding) are inescapable. Even if we don't have that as a direct contingency in our lives, we are aware of that as something that our becoming may be inserted into as a possible predicate.

It is also present for us to discover that the discipline is not one which we enter and occupy on the same terms as men enter and occupy it. We do not fully appropriate its authority, i.e., the right to author and authorize the acts and knowing and thinking which are the acts and knowing and thinking of the discipline as it is thought. We cannot therefore command the inner principles of our action. That remains lodged outside us. The frames of reference which order the terms upon which inquiry and discussion are conducted originate with men. The subjects of sociological sentences (if they have a subject) are male. The sociologist is "he." And even before we become conscious of our sex as the basis of an exclusion (*they* are not talking about *us*), we nonetheless do not fully enter ourselves as the subjects of its statements, since we must suspend our sex, and suspend our knowledge of who we are as well as who it is that in fact is speaking and of whom. Therefore we do not fully participate in the declarations and formulations of its mode of consciousness. The externalization of sociology as a profession which I have described above becomes for women a double estrangement.

There is then for women a basic organization of their experience which displays for them the structure of the bifurcated consciousness. At the same time it attenuates their commitment to a sociology which aims at an externalized body of knowledge based on an organization of experience which excludes theirs and excludes them except in a subordinate relation.

6. An alternative approach must somehow transcend this contradiction without re-entering Bierstedt's "transcendental realm" (1966). Women's perspective, as I have analyzed it here, discredits sociology's claim to constitute an objective knowledge independent of the sociologist's situation. Its conceptual procedures, methods, and relevances are seen to organize its subject matter from a determinate position in society. This critical disclosure becomes, then, the basis for an alternative way of thinking sociology. If sociology cannot avoid being situated, then sociology should take that as its beginning and build it into its methodological and theoretical strategies. As it is now, these separate a sociologically constructed world from that which is known in direct experience and it is precisely that separation which must be undone.

I am not proposing an immediate and radical transformation of the subject matter and methods of the discipline nor the junking of everything that has gone before. What I am suggesting is more in the nature of a re-organization which changes the relation of the sociologist to the object of her knowledge and changes also her problematic. This reorganization involves first placing the sociologist where she is actually situated, namely at the beginning of those acts by which she knows or will come to know; and second, making her direct experience of the everyday world the primary ground of her knowledge.

We would reject, it seems to me, a sociology aimed primarily at itself. We would not be interested in contributing to a body of knowledge the uses of which are not ours and the knowers of whom are who knows whom, but generally male—particularly when it is not at all clear what it is that is constituted as knowledge in that relation. The professional sociologist's practice of thinking it as it is thought would have to be discarded. She would be constrained by the actualities of how it happens in her direct experience. Sociology would aim at offering to anyone a knowledge of the social organization and determinations of the properties and events of their directly experienced world. Its analyses would become part of our ordinary interpretations of the experienced world, just as our experience of the sun's sinking below the horizon is transformed by our knowledge that the world turns. (Yet from where we are it seems to sink and that must be accounted for.)

The only way of knowing a socially constructed world is knowing it from within. We can never stand outside it. A relation in which sociological phenomena are objectified and presented as external to and independent of the observer is itself a special social practice also known from within. The relation of observer and object of observation, of sociologist to "subject," is a specialized social relationship. Even to be a stranger is to enter a world constituted from within as strange. The strangeness itself is the mode in which it is experienced.

When Jean Briggs (1970) made her ethnographic study of the ways in which an Eskimo people structure and express emotion, what she learned and observed emerged for her in the context of the actual developing relations between her and the family with whom she lived and other members of the group. Her account situates her knowledge in the context of those relationships. Affections, tensions, and quarrels were the living texture in which she learnt what she describes. She makes it clear how this context structured her learning and how what she learnt and can speak of became observable to her. Briggs tells us what is normally discarded in the anthropological or sociological telling. Although sociological inquiry is necessarily a social relation, we have learned to disattend our own part in it. We recover only the object of its knowledgte as if that stood all by itself and of itself. Sociology does not provide for seeing that there are always two terms to this relation. An alternative sociology must be reflexive (Gouldner, 1971), i.e., one that preserves in it the presence, concerns, and experience of the sociologist as knower and discoverer.

To begin from direct experience and to return to it as a constraint or "test" of the adequacy of a systematic knowledge is to begin from where we are located bodily. The actualities of our everyday world are already socially organized. Settings, equipment, "environment," schedules, occasions, etc., as well as the enterprises and routines of actors are socially produced and concretely and symbolically organized prior to our practice. By beginning from her original and immediate knowledge of her world, sociology offers a way of making its socially organized properties first observable and then problematic.

Let me make it clear that when I speak of "experience" I do not use the term as a synonym for "perspective." Nor in proposing a sociology grounded in the sociologist's actual experience, am I recommending the self-indulgence of inner exploration or any other enterprise with self as sole focus and object. Such subjectivist interpretations of "experience" are themselves an aspect of that organization of consciousness which bifurcates it and transports us into mind country while stashing away the concrete conditions and practices upon which it depends. We can never escape the circles of our own heads if we accept that as our territory. Rather the sociologist's investigation of our directly experienced world as a problem is a mode of discovering or rediscovering the society from within. She begins from her own original but tacit knowledge and from within the acts by which she brings it into her grasp in making it observable and in understanding how it works. She aims not at a reiteration of what she already (tacitly) knows, but at an exploration through that of what passes beyond it and is deeply implicated in how it is.

7. Our knowledge of the world is given to us in the modes we enter into relations with the object of knowledge. But in this case the object of our knowledge is or originates in a "subject." The constitution of an objective sociology as an authoritative version of how things are is done from a position and as part of the practices of ruling in our kind of society. It has depended upon class and sex bases which make it possible for sociology to evade the problem that our kind of society is known and experienced rather differently from different positions within it. Our training teaches us to ignore the uneasiness at the junctures where transitional work is done—for example, the ordinary problems respondents have of fitting their experience of the world to the questions in the interview schedule. It is this exclusion which the sociologist who is a woman cannot so easily preserve, for she discovers, if she will, precisely that uneasiness in her relation to her discipline as a whole. The persistence of the privileged sociological version (or versions) relies upon a substructure which has already discredited and deprived of authority to speak, the voices of those who know the society differently. The objectivity of a sociological version depends upon a special relation with others which makes it easy for the sociologist to remain outside the other's experience and does not require her to recognize that experience as a valid contention.

Riding a train not long ago in Ontario I saw a family of Indians, woman, man, and three children standing together on a spur above a river watching the train go by. There was (for me) that moment—the train, those five people seen on the other side of the glass. I saw first that I could tell this incident as it was, but that telling as a description built in my position and my interpretations. I have called them a family; I have said they were watching the train. My understanding has already subsumed theirs. Everything may have been quite other for them. My description is privileged to stand as what actually happened, because theirs is not heard in the contexts in which I may speak. If we begin from the world as we actually experience it, it is at least possible to see that we are located and that what we know of the other is conditional upon that location as part of a relation comprehending the other's location also. There are and must be different experiences of the world and different bases of experience. We must not do away with them by taking advantage of our privileged speaking to construct a sociological version which we then impose upon them as their reality. We may not rewrite the other's world or impose upon it a conceptual framework which extracts from it what fits with ours. Our conceptual procedures should be capable of explicating and analyzing the properties of their experienced world rather than administering it. Their reality, their varieties of experience must be an unconditional datum.

8. My experience in the train epitomizes a sociological relation. The observer is already separated from the world as it is experienced by those she observes. That separation is fundamental to the character of that experience. Once she becomes aware of how her world

is put together as a practical everyday matter and of how her relations are shaped by its concrete conditions (even in so simple a matter as that she is sitting in the train and it travels, but those people standing on the spur do not) the sociologist is led into the discovery that she cannot understand the nature of her experienced world by staying within its ordinary boundaries of assumption and knowledge. To account for that moment on the train and for the relation between the two experiences (or more) and the two positions from which those experiences begin involves positing a total socio-economic order "in back" of that moment. The coming together which makes the observation possible as well as how we were separated and drawn apart as well as how I now make use of that here—these properties are determined elsewhere than in that relation itself.

Further, how our knowledge of the world is mediated to us becomes a problem. It is a problem in knowing how that world is organized for us prior to our participation as knowers in that process. As intellectuals we ordinarily receive it as a media world, of documents, images, journals, books, talk as well as in other symbolic modes. We discard as an essential focus of our practice other ways of knowing. Accounting for that mode of knowing and the social organization which sets it up for us again leads us back into an analysis of the total socio-economic order of which it is part. It is not possible to account for one's directly experienced world or how it is related to the worlds which others directly experience who are differently placed by remaining within the boundaries of the former.

If we address the problem of the conditions as well as the perceived forms and organization of immediate experience, we should include in it the events as they actually happen or the ordinary material world which we encounter as a matter of fact—the urban renewal project which uproots 400 families; how it is to live on welfare as an ordinary daily practice; cities as the actual physical structures in which we move; the organization of academic occasions such as that in which this paper originated. When we examine them, we find that there are many aspects of how these things come about of which we have little as sociologists to say. We have a sense that the events which enter our experience originate somewhere in a human intention, but we are unable to track back to find it and to find out how it got from there to here. Or take this room in which I work or that room in which you are reading and treat that as a problem. If we think about the conditions of our activity here, we could track back to how it is that there are chairs, table, walls, our clothing, our presence; how these places (yours and mine) are cleaned and maintained, etc. There are human activities, intentions, and relations which are not apparent as such in the actual material conditions of our work. The social organization of the setting is not wholly available to us in its appearance. We bypass in the immediacy of the specific practical activity, a complex division of labor which is an essential precondition to it. Such preconditions are fundamentally mysterious to us and present us with problems in grasping social relations in our kind of society with which sociology is ill equipped to deal. Our experience of the world is of one which is largely incomprehensible beyond the limits of what is known in a common sense. No amount of observation of face-to-face relations, no amount of analysis of commonsense knowledge of everyday life, will take us beyond our essential ignorance of how it is put together. Our direct experience of it consititutes it (if we will) as a problem, but it does not offer any answers. The matrix of direct experience as that from which sociology might begin discloses that beginning as an "appearance" the determinations of which lie beyond it.

We might think of the "appearances" of our direct experience as a multiplicity of surfaces, the properties and relations among which are generated by a social organization which is not observable in its effects. The structures which underlie and generate the characteristics of our own directly experienced world are social structures and bring us into unseen relations with others. Their experience is necessarily different from ours. Beginning from our experienced world and attempting to analyze and account for how it is, necessitates positing others whose experience is different.

Women's situation in sociology discloses to her a typical bifurcate structure with the abstracted conceptual practices on the one hand and the concrete realizations, the maintenance routines, etc., on the other. Taking each for granted depends upon being fully situated in one or the other so that the other does not appear in contradiction to it. Women's direct experience places her a step back where we can recognize the uneasiness that comes in sociology from its claim to be about the world we live in and its failure to account for or even describe its actual features as we find them in living them. The aim of an alternative sociology would be to develop precisely that capacity from that beginning so that it might be a means to anyone of understanding how the world comes about for her and how it is organized so that it happens to her as it does in her experience.

9. Though such a sociology would not be exclusively for or done by women it does begin from the analysis and critique originating in their situation. Its elaboration therefore depends upon a grasp of that which is prior to and fuller than its formulation. It is a little like the problem of making a formal description of the grammar of a language. The linguist depends and always refers back to the competent speakers' sense, etc. In her own langauge she depends to a large extent upon her own competence. Women are native speakers of this situation and in explicating it or its implications and realizing them conceptually, they have that relation to it of knowing it before it has been said.

The incomprehensibility of the determinations of our immediate local world is for women a particularly striking metaphor. It recovers an inner organization in common with their typical relation to the world. For women's activities and existence are determined outside them and beyond the world which is their "place." They are oriented by their training and by the daily practices which confirm it, towards the demands and initiations and authority of others. But more than that, the very organization of the world which has been assigned to them as the primary locus of their being is determined by and subordinate to the corporate organization of society (Smith, 1973). Thus as I have expressed her relation to sociology, its logic lies elsewhere. She lacks the inner principle of her own activity. She does not grasp how it is put together because it is determined elsewhere than where she is. As a sociologist then the grasp and exploration of her own experience as a method of discovering society restores to her a center which in this enterprise at least is wholly hers.

EDITOR'S NOTES

1. See also "Some Implications of a Sociology for Women," in *Woman in a Man-Made World: A Socio-economic Handbook*, ed. N. Glazer and H. Waehrer (Chicago: Rand-McNally, 1977); "A Sociology for Women," in *The Prism of Sex: Essays in the Sociology of Knowledge*, ed. J. Sherman and E. T. Beck (Madison: University of Wisconsin Press, 1979); and "The Experienced World as Problematic: A Feminist Method," Sorokin Lecture no. 12 (Saskatoon: University of Saskatchewan, 1981).

2. How was Joyce Ladner calling for such a recovery?

NOTES

This paper was originally prepared for the meetings of the American Academy for the Advancement of Science (Pacific Division) Eugene, Oregon, June, 1972. The original draft of this paper was typed by Jane Lemke and the final version by Mildred Brown. I am indebted to both of them.

REFERENCES

Briggs, Jean L. 1970. Never in Anger. Cambridge, Mass.: Harvard University Press.
Bierstedt, Robert. 1966. "Sociology and general education." In Charles H. Page (ed.), Sociology and Contemporary Education, New York: Random House.
Gouldner, Alvin. 1971. The Coming Crisis in Western Sociology. London: Heinemann Educational Books.
Smith, Dorothy E. 1973. "Women, the family and corporate capitalism." In M. L. Stephenson (ed.), Women in Canada, Toronto: Newpress.

VIII.

THE DIALECTICS
OF BLACK WOMANHOOD

Bonnie Thornton Dill

Bonnie Thornton Dill points out that black women's role in the workplace has played an important part in generating a historical ideal of womanhood that is alternative to the stereotype of femininity for white women. Paradoxically, it is much like the goals for which many white feminists strive. Dill draws attention to the poor methods and inadequate concepts and theories in the literature on black families. These flawed components of research ensure the social scientists' failure to recognize this alternative model of black womanhood.

Dill, like Joyce Ladner, challenges the tendency of white women to generalize from the situation of white, Western women to that of all women. Black feminists criticize the value of imagining a racially and culturally homogenous "woman"—one who is really a bourgeois, white, Western woman—as the agent of a more progressive history and culture. They insist that "knowers" (agents of knowledge) are racially and culturally specific, not just of specific genders as many white women have implied.

This paper leads us to reflect that the possibility of conceptualizing femininity in the way the white stereotype in this culture insists has depended on the existence of some other women—black women—to whom characteristics eliminated from the list of feminine ones could be assigned. If white women (bourgeois ones) are to be weak, virgins, passionless, and kept on a pedestal as the flower of civilization, then there must be other women—strong, rapable or forced into prostitution, super-sexual, and held up as evil, immoral, lazy, and not quite human—who would do the rest of the work the dominating class/race of men refuses to do.

Dill's analysis makes us think further about the importance of, and the political prerequisites for, an empirically more adequate social science. Our analyses of social reality must include critical accounts of women's situation in every race, class, and culture. We should know by now that this means working to provide the resources so that women in every race, class, and culture can define problematics, generate concepts and theories, design research projects, and so forth. After all, is there any more reason to think white women inherently or unproblematically capable of seeing social life from the perspective of black women than there is to think men inherently or unproblematically capable of seeing social life from the perspective of women? If our picture of social reality doesn't meet this criterion, our feminist agendas and the social policy informed by our analyses will not improve the situation of women in every race, class, and culture. It may even worsen some women's conditions. It should be a top-priority item for feminisms that we create antiracist (and anticlassist) as well as antisexist social sciences. In fact, we can see that we can't possibly achieve the latter unless we simultaneously achieve the former: how could a social science which isn't *for* all women be a feminist social science?

A new scholarship about black women, strengthened by the growing acceptance of black and women's studies as distinct areas of academic inquiry and by the need to refute myths and stereotypes about black women and black family life which helped shape social policies of the mid–1960s, is examining aspects of black family life that have been overlooked or distorted. Several studies have argued that a historical tradition of work forms an essential component in the lives of Afro-American women.[1] Beginning from that premise, this paper seeks to demonstrate that the emphasis on women's work role in Afro-American culture has generated alternative notions of womanhood contradictory to those that have been traditional in modern American society.[2]

These new models project images of female sexual and intellectual equality, economic autonomy, and legal as well as personal parity with men. While they represent a new direction in the social ideology, they reflect an aspect of life that has been dominant for generations among many Afro-American women. Dialectical analysis enables us to clarify and illuminate this contradiction, and could provide theoretical direction to the new scholarship. But understanding the dialectics of black womanhood first requires rethinking several areas of scholarship about black women and their families.

Black Women in Black Family Literature

Four major problems pervade the literature on Afro-American families. The first of these derives from the use of inadequate historical data and/or the misinterpretation of that data. The second entails erroneous or partially conceived assumptions about the relationship of blacks to white society. The third problem is a direct result of the second and arises because of the differences between the values of the researcher and those of the subject. Fourth is the general confusion of class and culture.

Problem One: Issues in Black Family History

The dominant influence on the study of the black family and the role of black women was Frazier's *The Negro Family in the United States*.[3] While his major contribution was to provide a historical and sociological analysis of black family life in a period when psychological and biological theories of racial inferiority abounded, his historical methodology had serious shortcomings.

According to Gutman, Frazier did not explain the conditions he studied but "read that condition back into the past and linked it directly to the nineteenth-century slave experience."[4] He concluded that female-headed families, which he termed the "matriarchate," had developed during the slave period and gained prominence after emancipation among those blacks who were economically unstable or otherwise removed from the direct influence of Euro-American culture. In his views, poverty and limited assimilation into the dominant culture inhibited their adopting the normative family patterns of the society. Since these conditions were characteristic of most black families, he concluded that female-headed households were prototypical of black family life. Using a linear model of historical change, Frazier argued that the subsequent crises of reconstruction and urbanization served only to intensify this type of family disorganization.

The overriding image of black women that emerged from his work is that of a strong and independent person who placed little value on marriage, engaged without conscience in free sexual activity, and had no notion of male supremacy. As a grandmother, she is depicted as the "oldest head" in a maternal family organization, ideotypically defined as a three-generation household. Thus, while Frazier identified some of the historical conditions which encouraged the development of self-reliance and autonomy in black women, the limitations of his historical interpretation resulted in his evaluating these qualities negatively, suggesting that they were contributory factors in the disorganization of Afro-American family life.

Probably the most debated of recent studies which drew heavily on Frazier's history is "The Moynihan report."[5] Moynihan accepted, without examination, Frazier's linear model of the historical development of the black family and used it as an explanation for contemporary data. The effect of his work, focusing on marital dissolution, illegitimacy rates, female-headed families, and welfare dependency, was to "prove" that Frazier's interpretation was still relevant. However, Frazier's analysis of black family history is being refuted, not only because of its methodological weakness but also because of its findings.

Gutman's recent study of black families suggests the breadth and detail required for a more accurate understanding of the history of black families, particularly with regard to its structure and normative patterns.[6] He contends that the female-headed household, while a recurrent pattern, was atypical in the period before 1925 and generally exaggerated in studies of black family life. His findings indicate that: (1) there is little evidence of a matriarchal form of household; (2) the typical household everywhere was a simple nuclear household headed by a male; (3) there is a significant difference in the household structure of field hands as opposed to artisans and house servants (this finding addresses itself directly to the issue of assimilation); (4) some of the physical movement associated with emancipation involved the reconstruction of broken slave households; and (5) sustained marriage among slaves, common everywhere, meant that the role models of marriage and family existed *within* the slave world and were constantly available to younger slaves.[7]

Gutman's work is important in developing a dialectical analysis of black women and their families because he has begun the process of examining the detailed components of family structure at specific historical moments. This permits us to begin an analysis of why and how the family and women's roles therein have changed over time. Of particular interest is the fact that he explains this trend in terms of distinct Afro-American cultural norms which emphasized marriage while refraining from stigmatizing women who gave birth out of wedlock. Since the establishment of paternity has had so profound an influence on the social position of Euro-American women, Gutman's documentation of the existence of norms which differed radically from those of the dominant culture supports the potential of Afro-American culture to generate alternative notions of womanhood and poses this contradiction as an important problem for further study.

Problem Two: Black Families in a White World

Fundamental to the proposal of a dialectical framework to analyze the condition of black women in the family is a conviction that the relationship of blacks to white society is dialectical in nature. This contention, while not new, has yet to be systematically applied to the study of black families. Frazier, influenced by the theories of Robert Park, determined that incomplete assimilation and isolation of blacks from white society explained their divergent family forms. The matriarchate was the result of the failure to assimilate, while patriarchal forms developed among those who had not been isolated from Euro-American norms and values.

A different theoretical position about the relationship of blacks to white society has been promised by Billingsley.[8] He adopted Parson's social systems model and argued that the black family must be viewed as a separate but interrelated social system within the nexus of the larger society. The functionality of black families depends on the smooth interrelationship of these systems. Applying Billingsley's model, one could analyze black women in their complex of social roles: first in terms of their roles within the family— mother, daughter, or sister; second, within the community—church member, PTA president, etc.; and third, within the wider society—secretary, housekeeper, teacher, or welfare recipient.

While this model recognizes the existence of a distinct Afro-American culture, its focus on the lives of black women as a set of interacting roles provides only a limited understanding of the dynamic and contradictory nature of their experience. Emphasis on functionality and dysfunctionality of their roles predisposes us to view black women more in relationship to the dominant culture than within Afro-American culture itself.

Valentine has suggested the concept of "biculturation" to describe the relationship of blacks to white society.[9] This concept assumes that blacks have been simultaneously socialized into two different cultural systems: white Euro-American and black Afro-American. However, much of the learning about Euro-American culture remains latent because discrimination prohibits blacks from achieving many mainstream values. While this concept may be particularly useful in explaining role conflict where role expectations derived from Afro-American culture contradict those derived from Euro-American culture, its major weakness is failure to account for the interrelatedness of these two cultural streams or to explain the basis of their unequal interaction.

Ladner's study of adolescent black girls, rather than emphasizing the shared and interacting norms which link Afro- and Euro-American traditions, illuminated the conflicts and dualities which the young women in her sample coped with as maturing adolescents.[10] She argued that the attitudes, behaviors, and interpersonal relationships of these women were adaptations to a variety of factors, including the harsh realities of their environment, Afro-American cultural images of black womanhood, and the sometimes conflicting values and norms of the wider society. This is exemplified in her discussion of attitudes toward premarital sex:

> Often in the absence of material resources, . . . sex becomes the resource that is exchanged. . . . It is here that sexual involvement transcends any conventional analysis because the standards that the individuals apply to their actions are created out of their own situations. Although many girls found it to be a means of expression in a variety of ways, they were still influenced by the conventional codes of morality. Some of them were more influenced by the conventional codes of morality than others and experienced conflict and sometimes trauma over whether or not they should defy these codes. The sharp conflict . . . had a profound effect upon their lives.[11]

At the same time, she describes the reciprocal effects of distinctive aspects of black life upon the wider society.

Ladner's work comes closest to the perspective which we are proposing in this paper. By self-consciously applying the dialectical mode of analysis to the experiences of black women, we may make explicit the complex interaction of political, social, and economic forces in shaping the broad historical trends that characterize black women as a group as well as the particular lives of individual women. In this way, we move beyond the deficit models of Frazier and Moynihan and even beyond the models of Billingsley and Valentine. These models illuminate the complexities of black and white social roles but have limitations in accounting for the impact of racial oppression on the economic, political, or social life of black Americans and in explaining the historical or geographic variations in the black experience. The dialectic permits us to focus on the dynamic and contradictory aspects of black American life and to account for this simultaneity of conflict and interdependence which characterize black-white relations in American society.

Problem Three: Value Discrepancies between Researcher and Subject

The third problem is a direct result of the second and arises because of the differences between the values of the researcher and those of the subject. The values about family life underlying the work of Frazier and Moynihan are those that form the foundation of the bourgeois family: monogamy, nuclearity, and patriarchy. Female independence of male authority and economic control is viewed as destructive of this family form. This analysis denied the existence of a distinct Afro-American culture and ignored the meaning that these behaviors might have for the people being studied. To a large extent, the matriarch thesis was based on the combination of erroneous historical interpretation with the actualities of black female labor-force participation.

As Aldridge, Jackson, Lewis, and others have pointed out, black females have historically had high participation rates in the labor force—higher than their white counterparts, even with children (see tables 1 and 2 and fig. 1). Moynihan combined these high levels of labor-force participation with notions of female dominance in husband-wife families and with the large (relative to white families) percentage of female-headed families in the black community to conclude that matriarchy was characteristic of black family life.

As a result, in much of the social science literature on black families, black women became scapegoats, responsible for the psychological emasculation of black men and for the failure of the black community to gain parity with the white community.

Table 1

Labor-Force Participation Rates of Women by Race and Year

Selected Years	All Women	Black	White
1900	20.4	41.2	...
1910	25.2	58.2	...
1920	23.3	43.7	...
1930	24.3	...	...
1940	25.4	37.3	...
1950	29.0	46.9	32.6
1960	34.5	48.2	36.5
1970	...	49.5	42.6
1974	...	49.1	45.2

SOURCES.—Joe Feagin, "Black Women in the American Work Force," in *The Family Life of Black People*, ed. Charles Willie (Columbus, Ohio: Charles E. Merrill Publishing Co., 1970), pp. 23–24; Valerie K. Oppenheimer, *The Female Labor Force in the United States*, Population Series Monographs no. 5 (Berkeley: University of California, 1970); U.S. Commerce Department, *Negro Population 1790–1915* (Washington, D.C.: Government Printing Office, 1918).

Table 2

Percentage of Mothers in Labor Force by Age of Children, Color, and Marital Status (March 1967)

Age of Children (years)	Race of Mother		Differential
	Nonwhite	White	
Under 6*	44	27	+17
6–17	58	48	+10
Under 18	50	37	+13

SOURCE.—Adapted from Joe Feagin, "Black Women in the American Work Force" in *The Family Life of Black People*, ed. Charles Willie (Columbus, Ohio: Charles E. Merrill Publishing Co. 1970).
*Percentage participation of black and white mothers for 1973 are 54 and 31, respectively, a differential of +23.

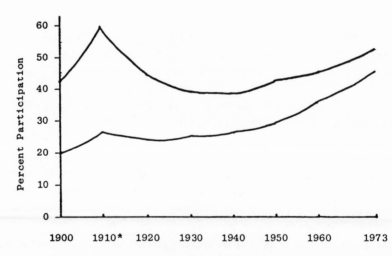

Figure 1.—Trends in labor-force participation for all women and black women, 1900–1973. *The sharp increase in 1910 has been accounted for by differing instructions to the census takers for that year.

Ryan has labeled this type of reasoning "blaming the victim." It is an ideology which, he says, " . . . attributes defect and inadequacy to the malignant nature of poverty, injustice, slum life, and racial difficulties. The stigma that marks the victim . . . is an acquired stigma, a stigma of social, rather than genetic, origin. But the stigma . . . is still located *within* the victim, inside the skin. . . . It is a brilliant ideology for justifying a perverse form of social action designed to change, not society, as one might expect, but rather society's victims."[12] In general, the justification of the matriarchy thesis has been based on the combination of erroneous historical interpretation with the actualities of black female participation in the labor force. Ten Houten states: "In modern urban society the sub-dominance of the black husband to the wife is attributed to employment behaviors."[13]

It is a cruel irony that the black woman's role as a worker has been used to represent dominance over and emasculation of black men. This predisposition ignores both historical and socioeconomic realities. Black women were brought to this country for two economic reasons: to work and to produce workers. Although they were valued for their reproductive function, as were white women settlers, it was only of equal importance with their labor.

There was no concern about the legitimacy of their children because there was nothing for them to inherit. The protective barriers which gradually forced white women out of production and changed their relationship to labor and society did not exist for most black women. Davis, in an analysis of the historical significance of black women's relationship to labor, emphasizes this point.

> It is true that she was a victim of the myth that only the woman, with the diminished capacity for mental and physical labor, should do degrading household work. Yet, the alleged benefits of the ideology of femininity did not accrue to her. She was not sheltered or protected; she would not remain oblivious to the desperate struggle for existence unfolding outside the "home." She was also there in the fields, alongside the man, toiling under the lash. . . . This was one of the supreme ironies of slavery: In order to approach its strategic goal—to extract the greatest possible surplus from the labor of slaves—the black woman had to be released from the chains of the myth of femininity. . . . The black woman shared the deformed equality of equal oppression with the black man.[14]

Problem Four: Class and Culture

Too often, social science researchers have sought to describe black women and their families as if they were a monolithic whole, without regard for differences in social class. At the other extreme is the contention that social class differences obliterate distinctions of race. In other words, social science has generally supported the idea that Afro-American culture is synonymous with lower class culture and that it disappears as black Americans gain middle class status.

To illuminate the complexities of the interaction of class and culture, Billingsley adopts Milton Gordon's concept of "ethnic subsociety." According to Gordon, "the ethnic group is the locus of a sense of *historical identification*, while the eth-class (the intersection of ethnicity and social class) is the locus of a sense of *participational identification*. With a person of the same social class but of a different ethnic group, one shares behavioral similarities but not a sense of peoplehood. With those of the same ethnic group but of a different social class, one shares the sense of peoplehood but not behavioral similarities. The only group which meets both these criteria are people of the same group *and* social class."[15]

The concept of "eth-class" is useful in that it communicates a sense of the ways in which ethnic differences interact with social class. However, it has serious limitations because it ignores the elements of domination and oppression which are at the root of black-white relations in the United States and which account for the high concentration of blacks in the lower class.

Blauner argues that black culture is not merely a phenomenon of lower-class life but a product of the experience of discrimination which cuts across all social classes.[16] More important, he links racial oppression to economic exploitation and the structure of classes within a capitalist economy. Thus his analysis goes beyond a merely descriptive portrayal of the interaction of the two variables, class and race, and focuses on the dynamic and contradictory influence that each has on the other. Thus, while he sees race as a form of stratification which has economic, political, and ideological dimensions, he argues that it is a basic rather than epiphenomenal aspect of American industrial capitalism. He concludes: "In American society, races and classes interpenetrate one another. Race affects class formation and class influences racial dynamics in ways that have not yet been adequately investigated."[17]

Implications for the Study of Black Women and Their Jobs

It is the contention of this paper, therefore, that the study of the black women and their families requires serious revision. First, it must be placed within a historical framework which is carefully researched, documented, and reinterpreted. Gutman, Pleck, Lammermeier, and others have only recently begun to provide this data.[18] Serious historical research promises to provide new information regarding the structure and organization of black families at different historical periods and in different regions of the United States. Information about values, attitudes, and the vicissitudes of daily life will remain, however, to be pieced together from oral history and other descriptive reports.

Second, black women must be studied within a dynamic and contradictory framework to understand the complexities of their relations to all aspects of society. Thus, an examination of the impact of work on the family life of women whose occupational categories result in class differences would be expected to yield important distinctions. At the same time, however, the experience of slavery, whether house servant or field hand, and the continued economic precariousness of most black families which has resulted in high rates of female labor-force participation, would be expected to have a particular impact on the growth and development of women in Afro-American culture.

Third, we must continue to research and provide good descriptive studies of the lives of black women and their families across the social class spectrum. Studies such as Stack's offer considerable insight into the ways in which economic oppression impacts on daily life, family patterns, and women's self-concepts.[19] Her work and Ladner's are examples of studies which provide the data necessary for concept development and theory building in this area.[20] They reveal the ways in which black women conceptualize work, its meaning in their lives, and its importance in the development of their models of womanhood.

Conclusion: Toward a New Model

We began developing a historical framework for the study of black women by focusing on the contradiction cited at the outset: the historical role as a laborer in a society where ideals of femininity emphasized domesticity. A dominant image of black women as "beasts of burden"[21] stands in direct contrast to American ideals of womanhood: fragile, white, and not too bright. The impact of this contradiction is profound. It has already been alluded to in discussions of the values pervading much of the pejorative literature on black women. It can also be expected to have affected self-images as well as their interpretations and expectations of various role relationships.

In concluding, however, it is important to explore the implications of this historical tradition for contemporary models of black womanhood. Ladner suggests several in her study of adolescent black girls. These revolve around the girls' images of womanhood, goals for themselves, and their relationships to their families and to boys. In developing their ideals of womanhood, Ladner reports that "the strongest conception of womanhood that exists among all pre-adult females is that of how the woman has to take a strong family role."[22] The pervasiveness of this image of an economically independent, resourceful, and hardworking woman was resented by some, adopted by others, and accepted with resignation by still others. Nevertheless, its overriding importance remained even though Ladner observed other models which existed alongside it. One of these other models, which appears to me as a variation, is that of an upwardly mobile middle-class woman. Ladner points out that education was most frequently seen as the means to this end. The choice of this model had a serious impact on the entire life of girls who chose it, particularly as it affected their relationship with boys. These girls most often avoided serious involvement with boys, particularly premarital sex and the risk of pregnancy which represented a definite end to their aspirations. Success in attaining their middle class goals was not only measured in terms of the training or job acquired but also "by the extent to which one can not only care for himself, but help others in the family."[23]

Girls who rejected the dominant model often adopted a model which Ladner calls a "carefree, laissez-faire, egalitarian model of womanhood." Different though this model was, it too encompasses a sense of self-reliance, strength, and autonomy. This image, as described by Ladner, was primarily directed toward relationships with boys. Inherent in it was an attitude of equality between men and women, a rejection of the sexual double standard, and a general belief that a woman can do whatever a man does. This practical attitude toward male-female relations was not without conflict, particularly as it was confronted by the ideals of the wider society. Neither, however, were the other models. They, too, support an image of womanhood which, until recently, has been out of step with the values of white society.

The image of independent, self-reliant, strong, and autonomous women which pervades the models of the young black women in Ladner's study has been reinforced by the work experience and social conditions of black women throughout history. The image, therefore, represents both the oppressive experiences of work and the liberating attitudes of personal autonomy and sexual equality. It may explain the findings of the *1970 Virginia Slims American Women's Opinion Poll* that "an essentially urban coalition of black women and the young and the educated of both races are ready to follow the examples of blacks and the young and challenge the stateus quo in American society."[24] This finding is particularly interesting in light of the goals of the women's liberation movement and the relationship of black women to this movement. It has been acknowledged that black women have not identified strongly with what many have seen as a movement of middle-class white women.[25] I would suggest that the image of women—as more than housewives and as sexual equals—toward which white women strive is, in large part, synonymous with the dominant image and much of the experience of black women. Ladner says it well in the closing statement on one of the chapters of *Tomorrow's Tomorrow*: "*Black womanhood* has always been the very essence of what American womanhood is attempting to become on some levels."[26] And again in her final chapter:

> . . . much of the current focus on being liberated from the constraints and protectiveness of the society which is proposed by Women's Liberation groups has never been applied to Black women, and in this sense, we have always been "free," and able to develop as individuals even under the most harsh circumstances. This freedom, as well as the tremendous hardships from which Black women suffered, allowed for the development of a female personality that is rarely described in scholarly journals for its obstinate strength and ability to survive. Neither is its peculiar humanistic character and quiet courage viewed as the epitome of what the American model of femininity should be.[27]

Thus the contradiction between the subjection of women from West Africa to the harsh deprivations of slavery, farm, factory, and domestic work and the sense of autonomy and self-reliance which developed, points in the direction of a new avenue for studying black American women. And it is the potential synthesis of these contradictions which embraces the future problems and possibilities of a new definition of femininity for *all* American women.

NOTES

This is a revision of a paper presented at the Seventieth Annual Meetings of the American Sociological Association, August 25–29, 1975, San Francisco, California. I would like to thank Elizabeth Higginbotham and Carroll Seron for their helpful comments and criticism.

1. See Delores Aldridge, "Black Women in the Economic Marketplace: A Battle Unfinished," *Journal of Social and Behavioral Scientists* 21 (Winter 1975): 48–61; Jacqueline Jackson, "Family Organization and Ideology," in *Comparative Studies of Blacks and Whites in the United States*, ed. Kent Miller and Ralph Dreger (New York: Seminar Press, 1973); and Diane K. Lewis, "A Response to Inequality: Black Women, Racism, and Sexism,"*Signs* 3 (Winter 1977): 339–61.

2. Natalie J. Sokoloff, "The Economic Position of Women in the Family," in *The Family*, ed. Peter J. Stein, Judith Richman, and Natalie Hannon (Reading, Mass.: Addison-Wesley, 1977).

3. E. Franklin Frazier, *The Negro Family in the United States* (Chicago: University of Chicago Press, 1966).

4. Herbert Gutman, "Persistent Myths about the Afro-American Family," *Journal of Interdisciplinary History*, vol. 6, no. 2 (Autumn 1975).

5. U.S. Department of Labor, Office of Policy Planning and Research, *The Negro Family: The Case for National Action* (Washington, D.C.: Government Printing Office, March 1965).

6. Herbert Gutman, *The Black Family in Slavery and Freedom* (New York: Pantheon Books, 1976).

7. These findings were quoted in Clarence Turner, "Some Theoretical and Conceptual Considerations for Black Family Studies," *Blacklines* 2 (Winter 1972): 16. The assumption that slavery was a closed system (item no. 5) without any influences from outside the plantation or from traditional African life has been hotly debated. Two people who have presented findings to the contrary are Melville Herskovitz (*The Myth of the Negro Past* [Boston: Beacon Press, 1941]) and John Blassingame (*The Slave Community* [New York: Oxford University Press, 1972]). In general, revisionist history seeks to examine the existence and influence of African survivals in Afro-American culture.

8. Andrew Billingsley, *Black Families in White America* (Englewood Cliffs, N.J.: Prentice-Hall, 1968).

9. Charles Valentine, "Deficit, Difference and Bicultural Models of Afro-American Behavior," *Harvard Educational Review*, vol. 41, no. 2 (May 1971).

10. Joyce A. Ladner, *Tomorrow's Tomorrow* (Garden City, N.Y.: Doubleday & Co., 1971).

11. Ladner, *Tomorrow's Tomorrow*, pp. 212–13.

12. William Ryan, *Blaming the Victim* (New York: Vintage, 1971), pp. 7–8.

13. Warren Ten Houten, "The Black Family: Myth and Reality," in *The Family in Transition*, ed. Arlene Skolnick and Jerome Skolnick (Boston: Little, Brown & Co., 1971) p. 420.

14. Angela Davis, "Reflections on the Black Woman's Role in the Community of Slaves," *Black Scholar* 3 (December 1971): 7.

15. Quoted in Billingsley, *Black Families*, p. 10.

16. Robert Blauner, *Racial Oppression in America* (New York: Harper & Row, 1972), chap. 4.

17. Blauner, *Racial Oppression*, pp. 28–29.

18. Particular attention is called to the work of Elizabeth Pleck, "The Two Parent Household: Black Family Structure in Late Nineteenth Century Boston," *Journal of Social History*, vol. 6 (Fall 1972); Paul Lammermeier, "The Urban Black Family of the Nineteenth Century: A Study of Black Family Structure in the Ohio Valley, 1850–1880," *Journal of Marriage and the Family*, vol. 35 (August 1973); and the developing activity in oral history of the Kinte Foundation.

19. Carol Stack, *All Our Kin* (New York: Harper & Row, 1974).

20. See forthcoming Ph.D. dissertations by Bonnie Dill (New York University), which explores the meanings of work and its perceived impact on the family lives of black female household workers; and Elizabeth Higginbotham (Brandeis University), which examines the interrelationship of education, career, and family among college-educated black women. Both studies focus on the women's self-presentations, their goals and strategies for survival, upward mobility, and its relationship to their family lives. An article by Robert D. Abrahams ("Negotiating Respect: Patterns of Presentation among Black Women," *Journal of American Folklore* 88 [January—March 1975]: 58–80) utilizes the data in novels and several sociological studies in an attempt to develop a systematic analysis of the manner in which black women attain respect. It is a preliminary step in the direction of concept development using descriptive data.

21. This conceptualization is drawn from the writings of Jeanne L. Noble. It was presented in a draft of an article being prepared for the *World Encyclopedia of Black Peoples* which the author generously shared with me.

22. Ladner, *Tomorrow's Tomorrow*, p.127.

23. Ladner, *Tomorrow's Tomorrow*, p.121.

24. Louis Harris and Associates, *The Virginia Slims American Women's Opinion Poll* (1970), p.78.

25. For discussions of black women's responses to the women's liberation movement see Robert Staples, *The Black Woman in America* (Chicago: Nelson-Hall Co., 1973); Inez Reid, *"Together" Black Women* (New York: Emerson Hall, 1972); selections in Toni Cade, ed., *The Black Woman: An Anthology* (New York: New American Library, 1970); Linda LaRue, "The Black Woman and Women's Liberation, " *Black Scholar*, vol. 1 (May 1970); and Lewis (n. 1 above) for a discussion of the structural factors affecting the variety of responses that have been noted among black women.

26. Ladner, *Tomorrow's Tomorrow*, p. 239.

27. Ladner, *Tomorrow's Tomorrow*, p. 280.

IX.

THE FAMILY AS THE LOCUS OF GENDER, CLASS, AND POLITICAL STRUGGLE

THE EXAMPLE OF HOUSEWORK

Heidi I. Hartmann

Heidi I. Hartmann is one of a small number of feminist economists. As she states early in this essay, she is concerned to develop a Marxist-feminist analysis of the family. We see her adapt political economy's dialectical, historical, and materialist theory of social relations to achieve this end.[1] Such an analysis reveals the error of many family historians (and sociologists?) who assume that there is always a unity of interests among family members and therefore tend to "downplay conflicts or differences of interest among family members." Hartmann argues that we must look at the work people do in the family and the amount of control they have over the products of that labor. When we do, we begin to see that much of the time the family is a locus of struggle over inequities in the division of labor in the family, though that same division of labor creates the interdependency which is the basis for family unity at other times.

Hartmann's example is housework—a central target of criticism and analysis from the beginnings of this latest and earlier women's movements. Hartmann asks feminist questions of some existing quantitative studies. She concludes that because men and women have different relationships to the capitalism and patriarchy that structure the division of labor in housework, by and large "men are not likely to share the burden of housework with women." Morever, this appears to be true regardless of whether their wives work full time for wages and/or have children at home. In fact, Hartmann points to the shocking fact that "men whose wives had the longest work weeks had the shortest work weeks themselves."

Both the use of quantitative studies and a Marxist methodological/theoretical framework have been favored targets of many feminist social science critics. Hartmann's fruitful uses of these lead us to reflect that there are probably few methods of gathering evidence or theoretical frameworks that cannot be made to yield gold to feminist miners (though we always have to watch out for the patriarchal assumptions which all too frequently accompany such methods and theories).[2] In part this is because feminist social science has at least as many concerns and focuses as does nonfeminist inquiry: there are many different kinds of things we want to know about social life. Some of the theories and methods which provide fruitful resources for answering one kind of question may not provide such resources for others.

Marxist-feminist (or socialist-feminist) theory is particularly useful if we want to understand how patriarchy and capitalism support each other and how they occasionally conflict.[3] It can provide valuable understandings of how institutions (such as the family) change over time (or resist change) as forms of the economy and of male domination change. It leads us to identify revealing and, possibly, emancipatory tensions and contradictions in a culture—as Hartmann does in this paper. What is usually referred to as its "method"—dialectical, historical, materialism—is well-suited to revealing aspects of social life that are otherwise easy to overlook, and that those who (consciously or unconsciously) benefit from the misery of the poor are all too happy to "overlook." It has other virtues—and, like any other theoretical approach, severe limitations. Hartmann herself raises significant challenges in her own work to antifeminist tendencies in Marxist theory.[4] Quantitative studies too, whether or not they are used within a Marxist-feminist theoretical framework, can reveal patterns of social thought and behavior that are invisible to us from the perspective of our daily experience.

Perhaps what social scientists should avoid is the assumption that Marxist-feminism, or radical feminism, or any other single theoretical framework or way of gathering evidence, can tell us everything we want to know about women, gender, and social life. Of course, to assert this is not to entertain the idea that all theoretical frameworks or ways of gathering evidence are equally valuable: sexist theories and modes of evidence gathering are less valuable than non-sexist ones—to understate the case.

Although the last decade of research on families has contributed enormously to our understanding of diversity in family structures and the relationship of family units to various other aspects of social life, it has, it seems to me, generally failed to identify and address sources of conflict within family life. Thus, the usefulness of this research for understanding women's situation has been particularly limited. The persistence and resilience of family forms in the midst of general social change, often forcefully documented in this research, have certainly helped to goad us, as feminists, to consider what women's interests may be in the maintenance of a type of family life that we have often viewed as a primary source of women's oppression. Historical, anthropological, and sociological studies of families have pointed to the many ways in which women and men have acted in defense of the family unit, despite the uneven responsibility and rewards of the two sexes in family life. In failing to focus sufficiently clearly on the differences between women's and men's experiences and interests within families, however, these studies overlook important aspects of social reality and potentially decisive sources of change in families and society as people struggle both within and outside families to advance their own interests. This oversight stems, I think, from a basic commitment shared by many conducting these studies to a view of the family as a unified interest group and as an agent of change in its own right.

Family historians, for example, have explored the role of the family in amassing wealth; in contributing to population growth or decline; in providing, recruiting, or failing to provide labor for a new industrial system; in transmitting social values to new generations; and in providing or failing to provide enclaves from new and rude social orders. They have consistently aimed to place the family in a larger social arena. The diversity of findings and the range of their interpretation is great: the size of the household has been constant before, during, and after industrialization (Peter Laslett); it has decreased as capitalism curtailed household production (Eli Zaretsky); it has been flexible, depending on the processes of rural-to-urban migration and wage levels in the new industrial employments, and has often actually increased (Michael Anderson); industrialization liberated sexuality and women (Edward Shorter); capitalism destroyed the extended family and created the nuclear (Eli Zaretsky); capitalist industrialization destroyed the nuclear (Friedrich Engels); the nuclear family facilitated industrialization (William Goode); the family and industrialization were partners in modernization (Tamara Hareven).[1] Yet despite this diversity, the consistent focus of the new family history on the interconnection between family and society implies a definition of family. The family is generally seen as a social entity that is a source of dynamic change, an actor, an agent, on a par with such other "social forces" as economic change, modernization, or individualism.[2] Such a view assumes the unity of interests among family members; it stresses the role of the family as a unit and tends to downplay conflicts or differences of interests among family members.[3]

In this essay I suggest that the underlying concept of the family as an active agent with unified interests is erroneous, and I offer an alternative concept of the family as a locus of *struggle*. In my view, the family cannot be understood solely, or even primarily, as a unit shaped by affect or kinship, but must be seen as a *location* where production and redistribution take place. As such, it is a location where people with different activities and interests in these process often come into conflict with one another. I do not wish to deny that families also encompass strong emotional ties, are extremely important in our psychic life, and establish ideological norms, but in developing a Marxist-feminist analysis of the family, I wish to identify and explore the material aspects of gender relations within family units.[4] Therefore, I concentrate on the nature of the work people do in the family and their control over the products of their labor.

In a Marxist-feminist view, the organization of production both within and outside the family is shaped by patriarchy and capitalism. Our present social structure rests upon an unequal division of labor by class and by gender which generates tension, conflict, and change. These underlying patriarchal and capitalist relations among people, rather than familial relations themselves, are the sources of dynamism in our society. The particular forms familial relations take largely reflect these underlying social forces. For example, the redistribution that occurs within the family between wage earners and non-wage earners is necessitated by the division of labor inherent in the patriarchal and capitalistic organization of production. In order to provide a schema for understanding the underlying economic structure of the family form prevalent in modern Western society—the heterosexual nuclear family living together in one household—I do not address in this essay the many real differences in the ways people of different periods, regions, races, or ethnic groups structure and experience family life. I limit my focus in order to emphasize the potential for differing rather than harmonious interests among family members, especially between women and men.

The first part of this essay explains the family's role as a location for production and redistribution and speculates about the interaction between the family and the state and about changes in family-state relations. The second part uses the example of housework to illustrate the differences in material interests among family members that are caused by their differing relations to patriarchy and capitalism. Since, as I argue, members of families frequently have different interests, it may be misleading to hold, as family historians often do, that "the family" as a unit resists or embraces capitalism, industrialization, or the state. Rather, people—men and/or women, adults and/or children—use familial forms in various ways. While they use their "familial" connection or kin groups and their locations in families in any number of projects—to find jobs, to build labor unions, to wage community struggles, to buy houses, to borrow cars, or to share child care—they are not acting only as family members but also as members of gender categories with particular relations to the division of labor organized by capitalism and patriarchy.

Yet tensions between households and the world outside them have been documented by family historians and others, and these suggest that households do act as entities with unified interests, set in opposition to other entities. This seeming paradox comes about because, although family members have distinct interests arising out of their relations to production and redistribution, those same relations also ensure their mutual dependence. Both the wife who does not work for wages and the husband who does, for example, have a joint interest in the size of his paycheck, the efficiency of her cooking facilities, or the quality of their children's education. However, the same historical processes that created households in opposition to (but also in partnership with) the state also augmented the power of men in households, as they became their household heads, and exacerbated tensions within households.

Examples of tensions and conflicts that involve the family in struggle are presented in table 1. The family can be a locus of internal struggle over matters related to production or redistribution (housework and paychecks, respectively). It can also provide a basis for struggle by its members against larger institutions such as corporations or the state. Will cooking continue to be done at home or be taken over largely by fast-food chains? Will child care continue to be the responsibility of parents or will it be provided by the state outside the home? Such

TABLE 1

Conflicts Involving the Family

Sources of Conflict	Conflicts within the Household	Conflicts between Households and Larger Institutions
Production issues	*Housework*: Who does it? How? According to which standards? Should women work for wages outside the home or for men inside the home?	*Household production versus production organized by capital and the state*: Fast-food or home-cooked meals? Parent cooperative child care or state regulated child-care centers?
Redistribution issues	*Paycheck(s)*: How should the money be spent? Who decides? Should the husband's paycheck be spent on luxuries for him or on household needs?	*Taxes*: Who will make the decisions about how to use the family's resources? Family members or representatives of the state apparatus?

questions signal tensions over the location of production. Tax protest, revolving as it does around the issue of who will make decisions for the family about the redistribution of its resources, can be viewed as an example of struggle between families and the state over redistribution. In this essay I intend to discuss only one source of conflict in any depth—housework—and merely touch upon some of the issues raised by tensions in other arenas. As with most typologies, the categories offered here are in reality not rigidly bounded or easily separable. Rather they represent different aspects of the same phenomena; production and redistribution are interrelated just as are struggles within and beyond households.[5]

Production, Redistribution, and the Household

Let me begin with a quote from Engels that has become deservedly familiar:

> According to the materialist conception, the determining factor in history is, in the final instance, the production and reproduction of immediate life. This, again, is of a twofold character: on the one side, the production of the means of existence, of food, clothing and shelter and the tools necessary for that production; on the other side, the production of human beings themselves, the propagation of the species. The social organization under which the people of a particular historical epoch live is determined by both kinds of production.[6]

Engels and later Marxists failed to follow through on this dual project. The concept of production ought to encompass both the production of "things," or material needs, and the "production" of people or, more accurately, the production of people who have particular attributes, such as gender. The Marxist development of the concept of production however, has focused primarily on the production of things. Gayle Rubin has vastly increased our understanding of how people are produced by identifying the "sex/gender system" as a "set of arrangements by which a society transforms biological sexuality into products of human activity, and in which these transformed sexual needs are satisfied."[7] This set of arrangements, which reproduces the species—and gender as well—is fundamentally social. The biological fact of sex differences is interpreted in many different ways by different groups; biology is always mediated by society.[8]

From an economic perspective, the creation of gender can be thought of as the creation of a division of labor between the sexes, the creation of two categories of workers who need each other.[9] In our society, the division of labor between the sexes involves men primarily in wage labor beyond the household and women primarily in production within the household; men and women, living together in households, pool their resources. The form of the family as we know it, with men in a more advantageous position than women in its hierarchy of gender relations, is simply one possible structuring of this human activity that creates gender; many other arrangements have been known.[10]

Although recent feminist psychoanalytic theory has emphasized the relations between children, mothers, and fathers in typical nuclear families, and the way these relations fundamentally shape personality along gender lines and perpetuate hierarchical gender relations, the pervasiveness of gender relations in all aspects of social life must be recognized.[11] In particular, the creation and perpetuation of hierarchical gender relations depends not only on family life but crucially on the organization of economic production, the production of the material needs of which Engels spoke. While a child's personality is partly shaped by who his or her mother is and her relations to others, her relations to others are products of all our social arrangements, not simply those evident within the household. Such arrangements are collectively generated and collectively maintained. "Dependence" is simultaneously a psychological and political-economic relationship. Male-dominated trade unions and professional associations, for example, have excluded women from skilled employment and reduced their opportunities to support themselves. The denial of abortions to women similarly reinforces women's dependence on men. In these and other ways, many of them similiarly institutionalized, men as a group are able to maintain control of women's labor power and thus perpetuate their dominance. Their control of women's labor power is the lever that allows men to benefit from women's provision of personal and household services, including relief from child rearing and many unpleasant tasks both within and beyond households, and the arrangement of the nuclear family, based on monogamous and heterosexual marriage, is one institutional form that seems to enhance this control.[12] Patriarchy's material base is men's control of women's labor; both in the household and in the labor market, the division of labor by gender tends to benefit men.

In a capitalist system the production of material needs takes place largely outside households, in large-scale enterprises where the productive resources are owned by capitalists. Most people, having no productive resources of their own, have no alternative but to offer their labor power in exchange for wages. Capitalists appropriate the surplus value the workers create above and beyond the value of their wages. One of the fundamental dynamics in our society is that which flows from this production process: wage earners seek to retain as much control as possible over both the conditions and products of their labor, and capitalists, driven by competition and the needs of the accumulation process, seek to wrest control away from the workers in order to increase the amount of surplus value.[13] With the wages they receive, people buy the commodities that they need for their survival. Once in the home these commodities are then transformed to become usable in producing and reproducing people. In our society, which is organized by patriarchy as well as by capitalism, the sexual division of labor by gender makes men primarily responsible for wage labor and women primarily responsible for household production. That portion of household production called housework consists largely in purchasing commodities and transforming them into usable forms. Sheets, for example, must be bought, put on beds, rearranged after every sleep, and washed, just as food must be bought, cleaned, cooked, and served to become a meal. Household production also encompasses the biological reproduction of people and the shaping of their gender, as well as their maintenance through housework. In the labor process of producing and reproducing people, household production gives rise to another of the fundamental dynamics of our society. The system of production in which we live cannot be understood without reference to the production and reproduction both of commodities—whether in factories, service centers, or offices—and of people, in households. Although neither type of production can be self-reproducing, together they create and recreate our existence.[14]

This patriarchal and capitalist arrangement of production necessitates a means of redistribution. Because of the class and gender division of labor not everyone has direct access to the economic means of survival. A schematic view of the development of capitalism in Western societies suggests that capitalism generally took root in societies where production and redistribution had taken place largely in households and villages; even though capitalism shifted much production beyond the household, it did not destroy all the traditional ways in which production and redistribution were organized. In preindustrial households, people not only carried on production but also shared their output among themselves (after external obligations such as feudal dues were met), according to established patriarchal relations of authority. In the period of capitalist primitive accumulation, capitalists had to alienate the productive resources that people previously attached to the land had controlled in order to establish the capitalist mode of production based on "free" wage labor. Laborers became "free" to work for capitalists because they had no other means of subsistence and therefore required wages to buy from the capitalists what they had formerly produced in households and villages and exchanged with each other.

With the development of the capitalist mode of production, the old, the young, and women of childbearing age participated less in economic production and became dependent on the wage earners, increasingly adult men. People continued to live in households, however, to reproduce the species and to redistribute resources. Households became primarily income-pooling units rather than income-producing units.[15] The previously established patriarchal division of labor, in which men benefited from women's labor, was perpetuated in a capitalist setting where men became primarily wage laborers but retained the personal services of their wives, as women became primarily "housewives."[16] The interdependence of men and women that arises out of the division of labor by gender was also maintained. The need for the household in capitalism to be an income-pooling unit, a place where redistribution occurs between men and women, arises fundamentally from the patriarchal division of labor. Yet it is income pooling that enables the household to be perceived as a unit with unitary interests, despite the very different relationships to production of its separate members. Because of the division of labor among family members, disunity is thus inherent in the "unity" of the family.

Recent, often speculative, anthropological and historical research, by focusing on the development of households and their role in political arenas, has contributed to my understanding of the family as an embodiment of both unity and disunity. Briefly, this research suggests that women's status has declined as political institutions have been elaborated into state apparata, although the mechanisms that connect these two phenomena are not well understood.[17] One possible connection is that the process of state formation enhanced the power of men as they became heads of "their" households. The state's interest in promoting households as political units stemmed from its need to undermine prior political apparata based on kinship. In prestate societies, kinship groups made fundamental political and eco-

nomic decisions—how to share resources to provide for everyone's welfare, how to redistribute land periodically, how to settle disputes, how to build new settlements. States
gradually absorbed these functions.

For instance, in the process of state formation that took place in England and Wales roughly
between the eighth and fifteenth centuries, Viana Muller suggests, emerging rulers attempted
to consolidate their power against kin groups by winning the allegiance of men away from
their kin. One means of doing this may have been allowing men to usurp some of the kin
group's authority, particularly over land and women and children.[18] In this view, the household, with its male head, can be seen to be a "creation" of the state. Georges Duby reports
that by 1250 the household was everywhere the basis of taxation in Western society.[19]
Lawrence Stone argues that the state's interests were served by an authoritarian household
structure, for it was generally believed that deference shown to the head of household
would be transferred to the king: "The power of kings and of heads of households grew
in parallel with one another in the sixteenth century. The state was as supportive of the
patriarchal nuclear family as it was hostile to the kin-oriented family; the one was a buttress
and the other a threat to its own increasing power."[20]

As Elizabeth Fox-Genovese points out, the authoritarianism of the new nation-state was
incompatible with developing capitalism, and Locke's concept of authority as derivative from
the individual helped to establish a new legitimating ideology for the state: it serves with the
consent of the propertied individuals. To put forward his theory with logical coherence, Locke
had to assert the authority of all individuals, including women and children. But by removing
the family from the political sphere, ideologically at least, later theorists solved the contradiction between the elevation of women to the status of individuals and the maintenance of
patriarchal authority. The family became private, of no moment in conducting the politics of
social interchange, and the head of the family came to represent its interests in the world.[21]
The ideology of individualism, by increasing the political importance of men beyond their
households, strengthened patriarchy at home; it completed the legitimation of male public
power begun during the process of state elaboration.

Yet even as the household, and particularly the man within it, became in this view an agent
of the state against collectivities organized by kinship, the household also remained the last
repository of kin ties. Even the nuclear household continues to tie its members to others
through the processes of marriage, childbirth, and the establishment of kinship. These ties
to others beyond the household (though much more limited than in the past) coupled with
the interdependence of household members stemming from their different relations to production continue to give members of households a basis for common interests vis-à-vis the
state or other outside forces. Household members continue to make decisions about pooling
incomes, caring for dependent members, engaging in wage work, and having children, but
it is important to remember that within the household as well as outside it men have more
power. Therefore, viewing the household as a unit which jointly chooses, for example, to
deploy its available labor power to maximize the interests of *all* its members (the implicit
approach of those historians who discuss family strategies and adaptations and the explicit
approach of others) obscures the reality of both the capitalist and patriarchal relations of

production in which households are enmeshed.[22] Mutual dependence by no means precludes the possibility of coercion. Women and men are no less mutually dependent in the household than are workers and capitalists or slaves and slaveowners. In environments that are fundamentally coercive (such as patriarchy and capitalism) concepts of choice and adaptation are inevitably flawed—as is the belief that workers and capitalists or men and women have unified interests. This is not to say that such unity can *never* exist.

Housework

Some observers have argued that the family is no longer a place where men exercise their power. If patriarchy exists at all for them, it does so only on impersonal, institutional levels. For some analysts working in the Marxist traditions, the inexorable progress of capitalism has eliminated patriarchy within the family and has even given rise to the women's movement, because it weakened patriarchal power just enough to enable women to confront it directly.[23] I wish to argue, however, that, although capitalism has somewhat shifted the locus of control, the family nevertheless remains a primary arena where men exercise their patriarchal power over women's labor. In this section, I review some of the empirical findings on time spent on housework by husbands and wives to support this proposition. I believe that time spent on housework, as well as other indicators of household labor, can be fruitfully used as a measure of power relations in the home.

Who Does How Much Housework?

In recent years a number of time-budget studies have measured time spent on housework, as well as other activities such as paid work and leisure. Such studies generally involve having respondents record their activities for specified time intervals (for example, fifteen minutes) for one or two days. The most comprehensively analyzed data on time spent doing housework in the United States are those collected in 1967 and 1968 by Kathryn Walker and Margaret Woods for 1,296 husband- and-wife families in Syracuse, New York.[24] Time diaries were also collected for a representative sample of families in five U.S. cities in 1965 and 1966 as part of the Multinational Comparative Time-Budget Research Project.[25] The University of Michigan Survey Research Center has collected data for representative national samples of families and individuals for 1965–1966 and for 1975.[26] Subsequently, a number of smaller studies have been conducted.[27] While the studies all differ in such data collection procedures as sampling (national vs. local, husband-and-wife families vs. individuals) and reporting (interview vs. self-report, contemporaneous vs. retrospective reporting), their findings are remarkably consistent and support rather firm conclusions about who does how much housework.[28] Because Walker and Woods have analyzed their data so extensively, their findings are relied upon here.

Women who have no paid employment outside the home work over fifty hours per week on household chores: preparing and cleaning up after meals, doing laundry, cleaning the house, taking care of children and other family members, and shopping and keeping records. Walker and Woods found that 859 full-time houseworkers (usually labeled "homemakers" or "housewives") worked an average of fifty-seven hours per week. Their husbands, as reported by their wives, spent about eleven hours a week on housework, and children were reported to do about the same amount on average.[29] A study of a national sample of 700 women in 1965 and 1966 found that 357 full-time houseworkers worked an average of 55.4 hours per week.[30] Household production is clearly more than a full-time job according to these time-budget studies.

The way that time spent on housework changes as demands on members' time increase is a good indicator of how patriarchy operates in the home, at least with respect to housework. Much has been made of the potentially equalizing effects of women's increased labor-force participation: as women earn wages they may come to exercise more power both within and outside the family. Time-budget studies show, however, that husbands of wives who work for wages do not spend more time on housework than those husbands whose wives do not work for wages. The Walker and Woods data for Syracuse families show that the more wage work women do, the fewer hours they spend on housework but the longer are their total work weeks. Women who worked for wages thirty or more hours per week had total work weeks of seventy-six hours on average, including an average of thirty-three hours per week spent on housework. Yet men whose wives had the longest work weeks had the shortest work weeks themselves (see fig. 1). The lack of responsiveness of men's housework time to women's increased wage work is also shown in time-budget data from cities in twelve industrialized countries collected by the Multinational Comparative Time-Budget Research Project in 1965 and 1966. In all countries wage-working wives worked substantially more hours every day than husbands or full-time houseworkers. Employed wives also spent substantially more time on housework on their days off (about double their weekday time), whereas husbands and even full-time houseworkers had the weekends for increased leisure.[31] These findings are corroborated by two later studies, one of 300 couples in Greater Vancouver in 1971, and one of 3,500 couples in the United States in 1976.[32]

A look at the tasks performed by husbands and wives, as well as the time spent, adds to our understanding of the relative burden of housework. Meissner and his associates, examining participation rates of husbands and wives in various tasks for 340 couples, finds that only 26 percent of the husbands reported spending some time cleaning the house (on either of two days reported, one weekday and one weekend day) while 86 percent of their wives did, and that 27 percent of the husbands contributed 2.5 hours per week to cooking, while 93 percent of the wives contributed 8.5 hours. Only seven of the 340 husbands reported doing any laundry, but nearly half their wives did.[33] Meissner and his associates conclude: "These data indicate that most married women do the regular, necessary, and most time consuming work in the household every day. In view of the small and selective contribution of their husbands, they can anticipate doing it for the rest of their lives."[34]

Walker and Woods, examining the percentage of record days that wives and husbands, as well as other household members, participated in various household tasks, conclude that while husbands of employed wives participated more often than husbands of non-

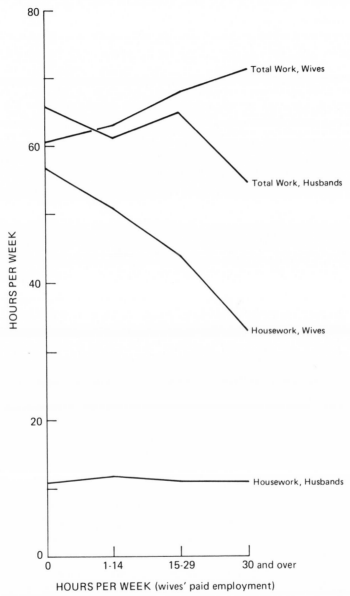

80

Total Work, Wives

60

Total Work, Husbands

HOURS PER WEEK

40

Housework, Wives

20

Housework, Husbands

0

0   1-14   15-29   30 and over

HOURS PER WEEK (wives' paid employment)

Figure 1.—Time spent on housework and total work by wives and husbands in 1,296 Syracuse, New York, families (1967–1968), by wives' hours of employment. Based on data from Kathryn E. Walker and Margaret E. Woods, *Time Use: A Measure of Household Production of Family Goods and Services* (Washington, D.C.: American Home Economics Association, 1976), p 45; and Kathyrn E. Walker, "Time-Use Patterns for Household Work Related to Homemakers' Employment" (paper presented at the 1970 National Agricultural Outlook Conference, Washington, D.C., February 18, 1970), p.5.

employed wives in almost all household tasks, their contributions to the time spent on the tasks were small.[35] One is forced to conclude that the husbands of wage-working wives appear to do more housework by participating more often, but the substance of their contributions remains insignificant.[36] Women are apparently not, for the most part, able to translate their wages into reduced work weeks, either by buying sufficient substitute products or labor or by getting their husbands to do appreciably more housework. In the absence of patriarchy, we would expect to find an equal sharing of wage work and housework; we find no such thing.

The burden of housework increases substantially when there are very young children or many children in the household. The household time-budget data from Walker and Woods's study indicate that in both cases the wife's work week expands to meet the needs of the family while the husband's does not. In families with a child under one year old, the typical full-time houseworker spent nearly seventy hours per week in housework, nearly thirty of it in family (primarily child) care. The typical husband spent five hours per week on family care but reduced his time spent on other housework, so that his total housework did not increase. When the wife was employed for fifteen or more hours per week, the average husband did spend two hours more per week on child care, and his time spent on housework increased to twenty hours (compared to twelve for the husband whose wife did less wage work). Meanwhile, however, his employed wife spent over fifty hours on housework, nearly twenty of them on child care. As figure 2 indicates, the employed wife's total housework time expands substantially with the presence of young children, while the husband's increases only moderately. Data from a national sample of about 3,500 U.S. husband-and-wife families in the 1976 Panel Study of Income Dynamics also show a pattern of longer housework time for wives with greater family responsibility (indicated by numbers of children) and nearly total lack of variability in the husbands' housework time (see fig. 3).[37]

Meissner and his associates developed a ranked set of four combinations of demands on household time and analyzed the data on changes in the housework time of husbands and wives in response to these increased levels of demands. The first level of demand is represented by households with one job and no children under ten, the second is one job and children under ten, the third is two jobs and no children under ten, and the fourth is two jobs and children under ten. The invariance of time husbands spend on housework is corroborated by their procedure. For the five activities of meals, sleep, gardening, visiting, and watching television, women lose fourteen hours a week from the least to most demanding situation, while men gain 1.4 hours a week.[38] The United States cities survey of 1965–1966 found that "among working couples with children, fathers averaged 1.3 hours more free time each weekday and 1.4 hours more on Sunday than mothers."[39]

The rather small, selective, and unresponsive contribution of the husband to housework raises the suspicion that the husband may be a net drain on the family's resources of housework time—that is, husbands may require more housework than they contribute. Indeed, this hypothesis is suggested by my materialist definition of patriarchy, in which men benefit directly from women's labor power. No direct estimates of housework required by the presence of husbands have, to my knowledge, been made. The Michigan survey data, however,

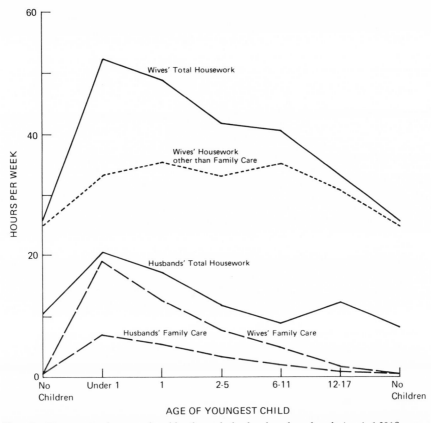

Figure 2.—Time spent on housework and family care by husbands and employed wives in 1,296 Syracuse, New York, families (1967–1968), by age of youngest child. Based on data from Walker and Woods (see legend to fig.1), pp. 50, 126.

in providing information on the housework time of single parents shed some light on this question. Single women spend considerably less time on housework than wives, for the same size families (see fig. 3). They spend less time even when they are compared only to wives who work for wages. It seems plausible that the difference in time spent on housework (approximately eight hours per week) could be interpreted as the amount of increased housework caused by the husband's presence. Unfortunately, because very few time-budget studies solicit information from single women, this estimate of "husband care" cannot be confirmed. Additional estimates can be made, however, from Walker and Woods's data of the minimum time necessary for taking care of a house. For wives who worked in the labor market less than fourteen hours per week, time spent on "regular" housework (all housework minus family care) ranged between forty and forty-five hours for all life-cycle phases (varying ages and numbers of children), while for wives who worked for wages fifteen hours per week or more, time spent on regular housework ranged between twenty-five and thirty-five hours per week (see fig. 2).

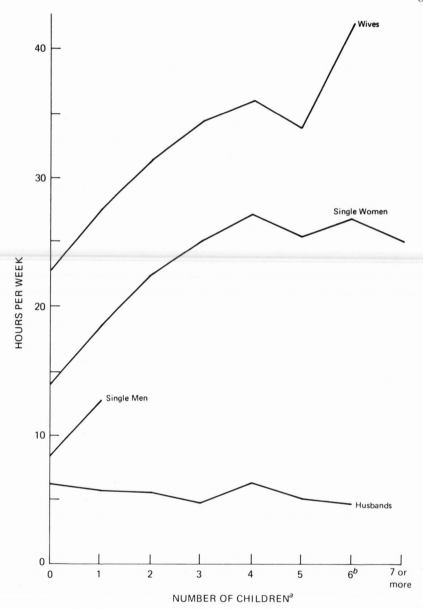

Number of other people in household besides husband and wife or single head of household.
bSix or more for husbands and wives.

Figure 3.—Time spent on house work, not including child care, by a national sample of 5,863 families (1976), by number of children. Based on data in James N. Morgan, "A Potpourri of New Data Gathered from Interviews with Husbands and Wives," in *Five Thousand American Families: Patterns of Economic Progress*, vol. 6, *Accounting for Race and Sex Differences in Earnings and Other Analyses of the First Nine Years of the Panel Study of Income Dynamics*, ed. Greg J. Duncan and James N. Morgan (Ann Arbor: University of Michigan, Institute for Social Research, 1978), p. 370.

These studies demonstrate the patriarchal benefits reaped in housework. First, the vast majority of time spent on housework is spent by the wife, about 70 percent on the average, with both the husband and the children providing about 15 percent on average.[40] Second, the wife is largely responsible for child care. The wife takes on the excess burden of housework in those families where there are very young or very many children; the husband's contribution to housework remains about the same whatever the family size or the age of the youngest child. It is the wife who, with respect to housework at least, does all of the adjusting to the family life cycle. Third, the woman who also works for wages (and she does so usually, we know, out of economic necessity) finds that her husband spends very little more time on housework on average than the husband whose wife is not a wage worker. Fourth, the wife spends perhaps eight hours per week in additional housework on account of the husband. And fifth, the wife spends, on average, a minimum of forty hours a week maintaining the house and husband if she does not work for wages and a minimum of thirty hours per week if she does.

Moreover, while we might expect the receipt of patriarchal benefits to vary according to class, race, and ethnicity, the limited time data we have relating to socioeconomic status or race indicate that time spent on housework by wives is not very sensitive to such differences.[41] The national panel study data, for example, showed no variation in housework time between racial groups.[42] With respect to class differences, I have argued elsewhere that the widespread use of household conveniences (especially the less expensive ones) and the decline in the use of servants in the early twentieth century probably increased the similarity of housework across class. In addition, no evidence was found that showed that the larger appliances effectively reduced housework time.[43] Income probably has its most important effect on housework through its effect on women's labor-force participation rates. Wives of husbands with lower incomes are more likely to be in the labor force and therefore experiencing the "double day" of wage work and housework.[44] Wage work, while it shortens the number of hours spent on housework (compared to those of the full-time houseworker), almost certainly increases the burden of the hours that remain. Even for full-time houseworkers, the number and ages of children appear to be more important than income in effect upon housework time.[45]

The relation of the household's wage workers to the capitalist organization of production places households in class relations with each other and determines the household's access to commodities; yet in viewing and understanding women's work in the home—the rearing of children, the maintenance of the home, the serving of men—patriarchy appears to be a more salient feature than class.[46]

Does It Matter?

I have suggested that women of all classes are subject to patriarchal power in that they perform household labor for men. Some would argue, however, that women's overwhelming share of housework relative to men's and their longer total work weeks should not be perceived as exploitation of one group's labor by another, that the patriarchal division of labor is not like the capitalist division of labor. Some would argue that among the working class, especially, the sexual division of labor is a division of labor without significance. Working-class husbands and wives, it is argued, recognize the fundamental coercion involved in both the homemaker and wage-earner roles.[47] The sexual division of labor, it is also argued, has no significance among the middle class, since women's lives are not especially hard.

The argument about the significance of patriarchy in women's lives revolves around whether or not women *perceive* patriarchy as oppressive. The interest behind much of the literature growing out of the women's movement has been to document women's oppression so that they may recognize exploitation when they experience it in their daily lives.[48] The sexual division of labor, so ancient that its unfairness is often accepted as normal, is an example of such oppression. Pat Mainardi, in "The Politics of Housework," captures the essence of the battle between the genders over housework. Her analysis exposes the patriarchal power underlying each response of a radical male to his wife's attempts to get him to share the housework. "The measure of your oppression is his resistance," she warns us, and goes on to point out the husband's typical response: " 'I don't mind sharing the work, but you'll have to show me how to do it.' *Meaning*: I ask a lot of questions and you'll have to show me everything every time I do it because I don't remember so good. Also don't try to sit down and read while I'm doing my jobs because I'm going to annoy hell out of you until it's easier to do them yourself."[49] The women's liberation movement has no doubt changed the perceptions of many middle-class women about the significance of patriarchy. Can the same be said for working-class women? The evidence is more limited, but working-class women are also expressing their recognition of the unfairness of male power within the working class. For example, a Southern white working-class woman recently wrote in response to a column by William Raspberry in the *Washington Post*:

> Men . . . live, speak and behave exactly by the slogans and notions of our traditional male "law and the prophets." Their creed and their litany . . . is as follows:
> All money and property, including welfare funds and old-age pensions, are "his."
> All wages, no matter who earns them, are "his." . . .
> Food, housing, medical and clothing expenses are "her" personal spending money. . . .
> *Many* wives must "steal" food from their own wages! . . .
> The sum of it all is a lifetime of ridicule, humiliation, degradation, utter denial of dignity and self-respect for women and their minor children at the hands of husband-father.
> We older women took, and take, the male abuse because (1) we thought we had to, (2) we thought rearing our children and keeping our families together was more important than life itself. . . .
> Young women can now earn their own and their children's bread, or receive it from welfare, without the abuse, ridicule and humiliation.[50]

The first step in the struggle is awareness, and the second is recognition that the situation can change.

What Are the Prospects for Change?

What is the likelihood that patriarchal power in the home, as measured by who does housework, will decline? What is the likelihood that housework will become equally shared by men and women? Might the amount of time required for housework be reduced? The prospects for change in housework time, while dependent on economic and political changes at the societal level, probably hinge most directly on the strength of the women's movement, for the amount and quality of housework services rendered, like the amount of and pay for wage work, result from historical processes of struggle. Such struggle establishes norms that become embodied in an expected standard of living. Time spent on housework by both full-time houseworkers and employed houseworkers has remained remarkably stable in the twentieth century. Kathryn Walker and Joann Vanek for the United States and Michael Paul Sacks for the Soviet Union report that total time spent on housework has not declined significantly from the 1920s to the 1960s.[51] Although time spent on some tasks, such as preparing and cleaning up after meals, has declined, that spent on others—such as shopping, record keeping, and child care—has increased. Even time spent on laundry has increased, despite new easy care fabrics and the common use of automatic home washing machines. A completely satisfactory explanation for the failure of housework time to decline, despite rapid technological change, has not yet been developed, but part of the answer lies in rising standards of cleanliness, child care, and emotional support, as well as in the inherent limitation of technology applied to small decentralized units, that is, typical homes.[52]

Gender struggle around housework may be bearing fruit. Standards may in fact be changing, allowing for a reduction in overall time spent on housework. A recent time-budget study indicates that between 1965 and 1975 housework time may have fallen by as much as six hours per week for full-time houseworkers and four hours for those also employed outside the house.[53] Such a decrease may also be the result of changing boundaries between home and market production; production formerly done by women at home may be increasingly shifted to capitalist production sites. In such cases, the products change as well; home-cooked meals are replaced by fast food.[54] Over time, the boundary between home and market production has been flexible rather than fixed, determined by the requirements of patriarchy and capitalism in reproducing themselves and by the gender and class struggles that arise from these processes.

While women's struggles, and perhaps as well capital's interests, may be successfully altering standards for housework and shifting some production beyond the home, prospects within the home for shifting some of the household tasks onto men do not appear to be as good. We have already seen, in our review of the current time-budget studies, that men whose wives work for wages do not spend more time than other married men on housework. This suggests that, even as more women increase their participation in wage labor and share with men the financial burden of supporting families, men are not likely to share the burden of housework with women. The increase in women's labor-force participation has occurred over the entire course of the twentieth century. Walker's comparison of the 1967–1968 Syracuse study with studies from the 1920s shows that husbands' work time may have increased at most about a half hour per week, while the work time of women, whether employed outside the home or full-time houseworkers, may have increased by as much as five hours per week.[55] Interestingly, a similar conclusion was reached by Sacks in his comparison of time-budget studies conducted in several cities in the Soviet Union in 1923 and 1966. He found that women's housework time has decreased somewhat, that men's time has not increased, that women still spend more than twice as much time on housework than do men, and that women have a total work week that is still seventeen hours longer than men's. In 1970, fully 90 percent of all Soviet women between the ages of twenty and forty-nine were in the labor force.[56] We are forced to conclude that the increase in women's wage labor will not *alone* bring about any sharing of housework with men. Continued struggle will be necessary.

People have different interests in the future of household production, based upon their current relation to productive activity outside the home. Their interests are not always unequivocal or constant over time. Some women might perceive their interests to lie in getting greater access to wages by mounting campaigns against employment and wage discrimination, others in maintaining as much control as possible over the home production process by resisting both capitalist inroads on household production and male specifications of standards for it. Some women might reduce housework by limiting childbirth. Some capitalists might seek to expand both the market and mass production of meal preparation if this area appears potentially profitable. Other capitalists may simply need women's labor power in order to expand production in any area or to cheapen labor power.[57] Or their interests might lie in having women in the home to produce and rear the next generation of workers. The outcome of these counteracting requirements and goals is theoretically indeterminate.

My reading of the currently dominant forces and tensions goes as follows: Women are resisting doing housework and rearing children, at least many children; the majority of women increasingly perceive their economic security to lie primarily in being self-supporting. Therefore, they are struggling with men to get out of the house and into decent jobs in the labor market. Given women's restricted access to decent jobs and wages, however, women also maintain their interests in men's continued contribution to family support. Men are relinquishing responsibility for families in some ways but are loathe to give up some of the benefits that go with it. Desertion, informal liaisons, contract cohabitation may be manifestations of this attitude; the attitude itself may be a response to capitalist inroads on patriarchal benefits, as more wives enter the labor force, providing fewer personalized services at home. Men may perceive that part-time wage labor by their wives is useful in contributing to the family's financial support without interfering very much with the provision of household services to them: To make such an arrangement compatible with their continued patriarchal power, men are on the whole struggling fairly hard to keep their better places in the labor market. Capitalists are primarily interested in using women's participation in the labor market to cheapen labor power and to allow expansion on better terms; women workers, for example, are much less unionized than men. Capitalists attempt to pass on most of the social costs—child care, for example—to the state, but the state's ability to provide is limited by a generalized fiscal crisis and by the present difficulties in capital accumulation.[58] The current period of alternating slow growth and actual production setback forces an intensification of class struggle, which in turn may exacerbate gender conflict.

Over the next twenty years, while there will be some change in the sexual division of labor resulting from conflict and struggles, patriarchy will not be eradicated. Despite at least a century of predictions and assertions that capitalism will triumph over patriarchy—a situation in which all production would take place under capitalist relations and all people would be wage earners on equal terms—patriarchy has survived. It has survived otherwise cataclysmic revolutions in the Soviet Union and China.[59] This means that a substantial amount of production will remain in the home. The irreducible minimum from the patriarchal point of view is that women will continue to raise young children and to provide men with the labor power necessary to maintain established standards of living, particularly the decentralized home system.

My assessment is that we are reaching a new equilibrium, or a new form of an old partnership, a judgment supported by data on women's employment in eight countries; these figures suggest that there may be a kind of structural limit on the participation of women in the labor force. As shown in table 2, those countries in which the proportion of women who are in the labor force is largest have the highest proportion of women working part-time. It is necessary, such findings suggest, that a substantial proportion of women's collective work hours be retained in the home if the patriarchal requirement that women continue to do housework and provide child care is to be fulfilled. In Sweden, it is most often married mothers of young children who work part-time. In the United States, the married mothers of preschool children have unemployment rates more than double those of married women with no children.[60]

We must hope that the new equilibrium will prove unstable, since without question it creates a situation in which a woman's work day is longer than it was when she served as a full-time houseworker, the male as breadwinner. As described earlier, when women's wage labor is greatest their total work weeks (wage work plus housework) are longest and men's are shortest (see fig. 1). Women have entered the labor market in greater numbers, and more husbands consequently have wives who are working for wages and contributing to the family income; the collective work effort of men as a group has decreased since men reduce their total work weeks when their wives work for wages. At the same time the collective contribution of women as a group has increased. This situation will undoubtedly continue to generate gender struggle. As more and more women become subject to the "double burden," more are moved to protest. Yet it is worth noting that husbands may not be the main beneficiaries of the recent increases in women's labor time. Although their wives' wages contribute to the family income, their wives' labor power is being used to create surplus value for capitalists and not to maintain the previous level of services at home. Eventually the decentralized home system itself may be a casualty of gender and class struggle.

TABLE 2

Women's Labor Force Participation and Part-time Employment in Eight Countries

Country and Year	Women's Labor Force Participation Rate		Women in Labor Force Part Time	
	%	Rank	% of Total Women in Labor Force	Rank
Sweden (1977)...............................	55.2*	1	45.2†	1
United States (1975)...........................	47.3*	2	33.0†	3
Canada (1977)...............................	45.9	3	23.0‡	4
United Kingdom (1975).........................	45.8*	4	40.9‡	2
France (1975)...............................	43.8*	5	14.1‡	6
Austria (1975)	42.4	6	14.0†	7
Federal Republic of Germany (1975)	37.7*	7	22.8‡	5
Belgium (1975)	30.7	8	11.6‡	8

SOURCE—Ronnie Steinberg Ratner, "Labor Market Inequality and Equal Opportunity Policy for Women, a Crossnational Comparison," paper prepared for Working Party no. 6 on the Role of Women in the Economy (Paris: Organization for Economic Cooperation and Development, June 1979), tables 1, 18.

NOTE—Women's labor force participation rate is the proportion of all women of working age (usually over fifteen) who are in the labor force (employed or looking for work).

*Figures from 1976.

†Part-time employment defined as less than thirty-five hours per week.

‡Part-time employment defined as ca. thirty hours per week or less.

Conclusion

The decentralized home system, which I see as a fundamental result of patriarchy, also meets crucial requirements for the reproduction of the capitalist system.[61] Families can provide crucial services less expensively than does the cash nexus of either the state or capital, especially when economic growth has come to a halt. From capital's point of view, however, the relationship is an uneasy one; capital and the state use the household but do not entirely control it. Despite the spread of capitalism and centralized, bureaucratic states, and their penetration into more and more areas of social life, people in households still manage to retain control over crucial resources and particular areas of decision. Family historians have helped us understand the strength and endurance of family units and their retention of power in many areas. The family historians may not have been sensitive to power relations within the family, but they have focused on another aspect of the same phenomenon—the interdependence of people within households and their common stance as a household against the incursion of forces that would alienate their resources or their control over decision making. Although I have focused on the potential for conflict among family members, particularly between men and women over housework, I want to point out that the same division of labor that creates the basis for that conflict also creates interdependence as a basis for family unity. It is this dual nature of the family that makes the behavior of families so unpredictable and problematic for both capital and the state. In the United States, for example, no one predicted the enormity of the post–World War II baby boom, the size of the subsequent increase in women's labor force participation, the rapid decrease in the birthrate in the late 1960s and early 1970s, or, most recently, the increase in divorce and single parenthood.

With the perspective developed here, these changes in people's household behavior can be understood as responses to conflicts both within and outside households. As Wendy Lutrell, who has also been working on reconceptualizing the family as a locus of tension and conflict, writes: "People can be seen as historical agents acting both independently as individuals *and* dependently as family members. This dual process fuels tensions and conflicts within the family arena and creates one potential for social change. . . . When the state, workplace, community, religion, or family are seen as arenas of struggle, we are forced to abandon a static, functional framework which can only see capitalist institutions as maintaining the status quo."[62]

In some cases, family members face capital or state actions together. In the Brookside strike, miners' wives united with their husbands, supporting their demands and even extending them to community concerns. Struggles around community issues are often initiated by women because of their ties to their neighbors and extended kin, and they are sometimes joined by men disaffected with their lot in patriarchy and capitalism. In New York City, both men and women protested government cuts for preschools and hospitals. In other cases, men and women who are in conflict within the family may seek solutions in the capitalist or state sectors. The recent rapid growth of fast-food eateries can be seen in this light, as can English women's fight for milk allowances from the state to redress income inequality within the family.

In our society both class and gender shape people's consciousness of their situation and their struggles to change those situations. At times it may be appropriate to speak of the family or the household as a unit with common interests, but the conditions which make this possible should be clearly spelled out. The conflicts inherent in class and patriarchal society tear people apart, but the dependencies inherent in them can hold people together.

EDITOR'S NOTES

1. Briefly, this theory directs us to look for what tensions and contradictions in social relations can tell us about those relations; it asks us to identify how (and why) social relationships change over time; it tells us to account for historical change in terms of changes in actual, concrete human activities—not merely in terms of ideas or mental states.

2. As I pointed out in the introductory essay, even sociobiology has been put to feminist ends. See Donna Haraway's analysis in "Animal Sociology and a Natural Economy of the Body Politic," pt. 2., in *Signs: Journal of Women in Culture and Society*, vol. 4, no. 1 (1978).

3. Many thinkers would distinguish between Marxist-feminist and socialist-feminist theories, and would

categorize Hartmann's approach as the latter. I shall retain Hartmann's terminology here. For a useful introduction to the differences between these and other varieties of feminism, see Alison Jaggar and Paula Rothenberg, eds., *Feminist Frameworks: Alternative Theoretical Accounts of the Relations between Women and Men*, 2nd ed., (New York: McGraw-Hill, 1984]. For a more extended analysis see Alison Jaggar, *Feminist Politics and Human Nature* (Totowa, N.J.: Rowman & Allenheld, 1983).

4. See, for instance, Hartmann's paper on "The Unhappy Marriage of Marxism and Feminism," in *Women and Revolution*, ed. Lydia Sargent (Boston: South End Press, 1981).

NOTES

The first draft of this paper was presented at the Rockefeller Foundation conference on Women, Work, and the Family (New York, September 21–22, 1978) organized by Catharine Stimpson and Tamara Hareven. Many people besides myself have labored over this paper. Among them are Rayna Rapp and Joan Burstyn. Jack Wells, Judy Stacey, Shelly Rosaldo, Evelyn Glenn, and my study group provided particularly careful readings; and Sam Bowles, Mead Cain, Steven Dubnoff, Andrew Kohstad, Ann Markusen, Katie Stewart, and the staff of the National Academy of Sciences provided helpful comments and aid of various sorts. I thank all of them. The views presented here are my own and do not reflect the opinion of the National Academy of Sciences or the National Research Council.

1. Peter Laslett and R. Wall, eds., *Household and Family in Past Time* (Cambridge: Cambridge University Press, 1972); Michael Anderson, *Family Structure in Nineteenth-Century Lancashire* (Cambridge: Cambridge University Press, 1971); Eli Zaretsky, "Capitalism, the Family, and Personal Life," *Socialist Revolution*, no. 13–14 (January–April 1973): 66–125; Friedrich Engels, *The Condition of the Working Class in England* (Stanford, Calif.: Stanford University Press, 1958)—of course, Engels was only the first and most prominent person who made this particular argument; Christopher Lasch, *Haven in a Heartless World: The Family Besieged* (New York: Basic Books, 1977) is a later adherent; William Goode, *World Revolution and Family Patterns* (Glencoe, Ill.: Free Press, 1963); Tamara Hareven, "Family Time and Industrial Time: The Interaction between Family and Work in a Planned Corporation Town, 1900–1924," *Journal of Urban History* 1 (May 1975): 365–89; Edward Shorter, *The Making of the Modern Family* (New York: Basic Books, 1975). Michael Gordon, ed., *The American Family in Social-Historical Perspective*, 2d ed. (New York: St. Martin's Press, 1978), provides a good introduction to family history.

2. Examples of the implicit definition can be found in the special issue of *Daedalus* (Spring 1977), later published as *The Family*, ed. Alice S. Rossi, Jerome Kagan, and Tamara K. Hareven (New York: W. W. Norton & Co. 1978).

3. See Joan Scott and Louise Tilly, "Women's Work and the Family in Nineteenth-Century Europe," *Comparative Studies in Society and History* 17, no. 1 (January 1975): 36–64; and Hareven, "Family Time."

4. In distinguishing between the household—the unit in which people actually live—and the family—the concept of the unit in which they think they should live—Rayna Rapp points to the contradictions that develop because of the juxtaposition of economic and ideological norms in the family/household ("Family and Class in Contemporary America: Notes toward an Understanding of Ideology," *Science and Society* 42 [Fall 1978]: 257–77). In addition, see Lila Leibowitz, *Females, Males, Families, a Biosocial Approach* (North Scituate, Mass.: Duxbury Press, 1978), esp. pp. 6–11, for a discussion of how the family defines ties among its members and to kin beyond it.

5. For another typology of struggle, see Gosta Esping-Anderson, Roger Friedland, and Erik Olin Wright, "Modes of Class Struggle and the Capitalist State," *Kapitalistate*, no. 4/5 (Summer 1976): 186–220; and for a critique, see Capitol Kapitalistate Collective, "Typology and Class Struggle: Critical Notes on 'Modes of Class Struggle and the Capitalist State,' " *Kapitalistate*, no. 6 (Fall 1977): 209–15.

6. Frederick Engels, *The Origin of the Family, Private Property and the State*, ed. with an introduction by Eleanor Leacock (New York: International Publishers, 1972), "Preface to the First Edition," pp. 71–72.

7. Gayle Rubin, "The Traffic in Women: Notes on the 'Political Economy' of Sex," in *Toward an Anthropology of Women*, ed. Rayna Rapp Reiter (New York: Monthly Review Press, 1975), p. 159.

8. The diverse ways in which sex differences are socially interpreted are well illustrated in both Rubin, (n. 7 above) and Leibowitz, *Females, Males, Families*.

9. See Claude Lévi-Strauss, "The Family," in *Man, Culture and Society*, ed. Harry L. Shapiro (New York: Oxford University Press, 1971).

10. Leibowitz, *Females, Males, Families,* provides examples of diverse household and family structures, especially in chaps. 4 and 5.

11. In addition to Rubin, see Nancy Chodorow, *The Reproduction of Mothering: Psychoanalysis and the Sociology of Gender* (Berkeley and Los Angeles: University of California Press, 1978); Dorothy Dinnerstein, *The Mermaid and the Minotaur: Sexual Arrangements and Human Malaise* (New York: Harper Colophon Books, 1977); and Jane Flax, "The Conflict between Nurturance and Autonomy in Mother-Daughter Relationships and within Feminism," *Feminist Studies* 4, no. 2 (June 1978): 171–89.

12. Heidi I. Hartmann, "The Unhappy Marriage of Marxism and Feminism: Towards a More Progressive Union," *Capital and Class* 8 (Summer 1979): 1–33. See also extentions and critiques in Lydia Sargent, ed., *Women and Revolution* (Boston: South End Press, 1981).

13. See Harry Braverman, *Labor and Monopoly Capital: The Degradation of Work in the Twentieth Century* (New York: Monthly Review Press, 1974), as well as Karl Marx, *Capital* (New York: International Publishers, 1967), vol. 1.

14. See Susan Himmelweit and Simon Mohun, "Domestic Labour and Capital," *Cambridge Journal of Economics* 1, no. 1 (March 1977): 15–31.

15. See Heidi Hartmann and Ellen Ross, "The Origins of Modern Marriage" (paper delivered at the Scholar and the Feminist Conference, III, Barnard College, April 10, 1976). Batya Weinbaum, "Women in Transition to Socialism: Perspectives on the Chinese Case," *Review of Radical Political Economics* 8, no. 1 (Spring 1976): 34–58, shows that the family is also an income-pooling unit in China under socialism.

16. See Heidi Hartmann, "Capitalism, Patriarchy, and Job Segregation by Sex," *Signs: Journal of Women in Culture and Society* 1, no. 3, pt. 2 (Spring 1976): 137–69, for how this came about.

17. See Rayna Rapp, "Gender and Class: An Archaeology of Knowledge concerning the Origin of the State," *Dialectical Anthropology* 2 (December 1977): 309–16; Christine Gailey, "Gender Hierarchy and Class Formation: The Origins of the State in Tonga," unpublished paper (New York: New School for Social Research, 1979); Ruby Rohrlich, "Women in Transition: Crete and Sumer," in *Becoming Visible: Women in European History,* ed. Renate Bridenthal and Claudia Koonz (Boston: Houghton Mifflin Co., 1977); Ruby Rohrlich, "State Formation in Sumer and the Subjugation of Women," *Feminist Studies* 6 (Spring 1980): 76–102; and a symposium in *Feminist Studies,* vol. 4 (October 1978), including Anne Barstow, "The Uses of Archaeology for Women's History: James Mellart's Work on the Neolithic Goddess at Çatal Hüyük," pp. 7–18; Sherry B. Orther, "The Virgin and the State," pp. 19–36; and Irene Silverblatt, "Andean Women in the Inca Empire," pp. 37–61.

18. Viana Muller, "The Formation of the State and the Oppression of Women: Some Theoretical Considerations and a Case Study in England and Wales," *Review of Radical Political Economics* 9 (Fall 1977): 7–21. Muller bases her account on the work of Tacitus, Bede, Seebohm, Phillpotts, F. M. Stenton, Whitelock, Homans, and McNamara and Wemple.

19. Georges Duby, "Peasants and the Agricultural Revolution," in *The Other Side of Western Civilization,* ed. Stanley Chodorow (New York: Harcourt Brace Jovanovich, 1979), p. 90, reprinted from *Rural Economy and Country Life in the Medieval West,* trans. Cynthia Poston (Columbia: University of South Carolina Press, 1968).

20. Lawrence Stone, "The Rise of the Nuclear Family in Early Modern England: The Patriarchal Stage," in *The Family in History,* ed. Charles E. Rosenberg (Philadelphia: University of Pennsylvania Press, 1975), p. 55. Also see Ellen Ross, "Women and Family," in "Examining Family History," by Rayna Rapp, Ellen Ross, and Renate Bridenthal, *Feminist Studies* 5, no.1 (Spring 1979): 174–200, who discusses the transition from kin to nuclear family in more detail than I do here and offers a number of useful criticisms of family history.

21. Elizabeth Fox-Genovese, "Property and Patriarchy in Classical Bourgeois Political Theory," *Radical History Review* 4 (Spring/Summer 1977): 36–59. See also Robert A. Nisbet, *The Sociological Tradition* (New York: Basic Books, 1966).

22. Scott and Tilly (n. 3 above) and Hareven (n. 1 above) use the the concepts of choice and adaptation. Louise Tilly, "Individual Lives and Family Strategies in the French Proletariat," *Journal of Family History* 4, no. 2 (Summer 1979): 137–52, employs the concept of family strategies but incorporates an understanding of potential intrafamily conflict. Jane Humphries, "The Working Class Family, Women's Liberation, and Class Struggle: The Case of Nineteenth Century British History," *Review of Radical Political Economics* 9, no. 3 (Fall 1977): 25–41, makes explicit use of the concept of family unity.

23. Stewart Ewen, *Captains of Consciousness* (New York: McGraw Hill, 1976), and Barbara Ehrenreich and Deirdre English, *For Her Own Good: 150 Years of the Experts' Advice to Women* (New York: Anchor Press, 1978), argue that patriarchal control is now exercised by the corporation or the experts, rather than the small guy out there, one to a household. The trenchant review of the weakness of family history by Wini Breines, Margaret Cerullo, and Judith Stacey, "Social Biology, Family Studies and Anti-feminist Backlash," *Feminist Studies* 4, no. 1 (February 1978): 43–67, also suggests that within the family male power over women is declining. Barbara Easton, "Feminism and the Contemporary Family," *Socialist Revolution*, no. 39 (May–June 1978): 11–36, makes a similar argument, as do Linda Gordon and Allen Hunter, "Sex, Family and the New Right: Anti Feminism as a Political Force," *Radical America* 11, no. 6 and 12, no. 1 (November 1977–February 1978): 9–25.

24. Kathryn E. Walker and Margaret E. Woods, *Time Use: A Measure of Household Production of Family Goods and Services* (Washington, D.C.: American Home Economics Association, 1976).

25. Alexander Szalai, ed., *The Use of Time* (The Hague: Mouton, 1972).

26. James N. Morgan, "A Potpourri of New Data Gathered from Interviews with Husbands and Wives," in *Five Thousand American Families: Patterns of Economic Progress*, vol. 6, *Accounting for Race and Sex Differences in Earnings and Other Analyses of the First Nine Years of the Panel Study of Income Dynamics*, ed. Greg J. Duncan and James N. Morgan (Ann Arbor: University of Michigan, Institute for Social Research [hereafter ISR], 1978), pp. 367–401; Frank Stafford and Greg Duncan, "The Use of Time and Technology by Households in the United States," working paper (Ann Arbor: University of Michigan, ISR, 1977); John P. Robinson, "Changes in Americans' Use of Time: 1965–1975: A Progress Report," working paper (Cleveland: Cleveland State University, August 1977).

27. Among the smaller studies are Martin Meissner et al., "No Exit for Wives: Sexual Division of Labour and the Cumulation of Household Demands," *Canadian Review of Sociology and Anthropology* 12 (November 1975): 424–39; Richard A. Berk and Sarah Fenstermaker Berk, *Labor and Leisure at Home: Content and Organization of the Household Day* (Beverly Hills, Calif.: Sage Publications, 1979); and Joseph H. Pleck, "Men's Family Work: Three Perspectives and Some New Data," working paper (Wellesley, Mass.: Wellesley College Center for Research on Women, 1979). New data collection efforts on a larger scale are already under way in several states, coordinated by Kathyrn Walker at Cornell University, and planned by the Survey Research Center at the University of Michigan under the coordination of Frank Stafford, Greg Duncan, and John Robinson.

28. For a discussion of the reliability of time diaries and their compatibility, see John Robinson, "Methodological Studies into the Reliability and Validity of the Time Diary," in *Studies in the Measurement of Time Allocation*, ed. Thomas Juster (Ann Arbor: University of Michigan, ISR, in press); and Joann Vanek, "Keeping Busy: Time Spent in Housework, United States, 1920–1970" (Ph.D. diss., University of Michigan, 1973). Research on the distribution of families at the extremes (e.g., where men and women may be sharing housework equally) would also be very useful.

29. Kathryn E. Walker, "Time-Use Patterns for Household Work Related to Homemakers' Employment" (paper presented at the 1970 National Agricultural Outlook Conference, Washington, D.C., February 18, 1970), p. 5.

30. John Robinson and Philip Converse, "United States Time Use Survey" (Ann Arbor, Mich.: Survey Research Center, 1965–1966), as reported by Joann Vanek, "Household Technology and Social Status: Rising Living Standards and Status and Residence Differences in Housework," *Technology and Culture* 19 (July 1978): 374.

31. John P. Robinson, Philip E. Converse, and Alexander Szalai, "Everyday Life in Twelve Countries," in Szalai, *The Use of Time*, pp. 119, 121.

32. Meissner et al. (n. 27 above); Morgan, (n. 26 above). One recent survey, the national 1977 Quality of Employment Survey, does, however, indicate that husbands of employed wives do more housework than husbands of full-time houseworkers: about 1.8 hours more per week in household tasks and 2.7 more in child care (quoted in Pleck, (n. 27 above), pp. 15, 16). These findings are based on data gathered by the retrospective self-reports of 757 married men in interviews rather than by time diaries kept throughout the day. Respondents were asked to "estimate" how much time they spent on "home chores—things like working, cleaning, repairs, shopping, yardwork, and keeping track of money and bills," and on "taking care of or doing things with your child(ren)." The child-care estimates are probably high relative to those from time-budget studies because the latter count only active care; "doing things with your children" would often be classified as leisure.

33. Meissner et al. (n. 27 above), p. 430.

34. Ibid., p. 431.

35. Husbands of employed wives reported participating in meal preparation on 42 percent of the record-keeping days, while the employed wives participated on 96 percent of the days. Yet the husbands contributed only 10 percent of the time spent on that task, while the wives contributed 75 percent. Similarly, 17 percent of the husbands of employed wives participated in after-meal cleanup, contributing 7 percent of the time. In only two of the seven tasks constituting regular housework, marketing and nonphysical care of the family, did husbands contribute as much as 25 percent of the total time spent on the tasks (tasks defined as nonphysical care of the family are activities that relate to the social and educational development of other family members, such as reading to children or helping them with lessons; pet care is also included in this task). For these two tasks, neither the participation rates nor the proportions of time contributed differed substantially between those husbands whose wives worked for wages and those whose wives did not. It should be noted that the percentage of record days husbands were reported as participating in a particular task is not the same as a straightforward participation rate. For example, a report that husbands participated on half the days could indicate either that all husbands participated every other day or that half the husbands participated both days (Walker and Woods [n. 24 above], pp. 58–59).

36. The unusual finding reported by Pleck, that husbands of employed wives estimate they spend more time on housework, could be explained by this phenomenon: men *participate* more often, and *think* they are doing more housework. The new time-budget studies will be useful in confirming or denying this change.

37. Morgan (n. 26 above). These data indicate far fewer hours spent on housework than the Walker and Woods data because they exclude child-care hours and, perhaps as well, because they are based on recall rather than actual time diaries.

38. Meissner et al. (n. 27 above), p. 433.

39. John Robinson and Philip Converse, "United States Time Use Survey" (Ann Arbor, Mich.: Survey Research Center, 1965–66), as reported in Janice N. Hedges and Jeanne K. Barnett, "Working Women and the Division of Household Tasks," *Monthly Labor Review* (April 1971), p. 11.

40. Walker and Woods (n. 24 above), p. 64.

41. Hartmann, "Unhappy Marriage."

42. Morgan (n. 26 above), p. 369.

43. Heidi I. Hartmann, "Capitalism and Women's Work in the Home, 1900–1930" (Ph.D. diss., Yale University, 1974 [Temple University Press, in press]). The Robinson-Converse study found that wives' housework time hovered around forty-two hours per week at all household incomes above $4,000 per year (1965–66 dollars) but was somewhat less, thirty-three hours, when household income was below $4,000 (reported in Vanek [n.30 above], p. 371).

44. In the Meissner study, fully 36 percent of the wives whose husbands earned under $10,000 (1971 dollars) were in the labor force, whereas no more than 10 percent of those whose husbands earned over $14,000 were in the labor force (Meissner et al. [n. 27 above] p. 429).

45. Much additional research, both of the already available data and the forthcoming data, is needed to increase our knowledge of potential variations in housework time.

46. The salience of patriarchy over class for women's work could probably be shown for many societies; Bangladesh provides one example. In 1977 Mead Cain and his associates collected data on time use from all members of 114 households in a rural Bangladesh village, where control of arable land is the key to economic survival and position. Dichotomizing people's class position by the amount of arable land owned by their households, Cain found that the work days of men with more than one-half acre of land were substantially shorter than those of men with less than one-half acre of land, whereas women in households with more land worked longer hours. The better-off men probably worked about eleven hours *less* per week than the poorer. The better-off women worked about three hours *more* per week than the poorer. In this rural village, Bangladesh women, unlike the men, did not benefit—at least in terms of lighter work loads—from the higher class position of their households (Mead Cain, Syeda Rokeya Khanam, and Shamsun Naher, "Class, Patriarchy, and Women's Work in Bangladesh," *Population and Development Review* 5, no. 3 [September 1979]: 405–38).

47. Humphries adopts this perspective (see n. 22 above). In reality, the question is not so much whether or not patriarchy is oppressive in the lives of working-class women, but rather what the trade-offs are between patriarchal and class oppression.

48. Beverly Jones, "The Dynamics of Marriage and Motherhood," in *Sisterhood Is Powerful*, ed. Robin Morgan (New York: Vintage Books, 1970), pp. 46–61; Meredith Tax, "Woman and Her Mind: The Story of Daily Life" (Boston: New England Free Press, 1970), 20 pages; Laurel Limpus, "Liberation of Women: Sexual Repression and the Family" (Boston: New England Free Press, ca. 1970), 15 pages; Betty Friedan, *The Feminine Mystique* (New York: Dell Publishing Co., 1963).

49. Pat Mainardi, "The Politics of Housework," in *Sisterhood Is Powerful*, ed. Morgan, pp. 451, 449. Mainardi begins her article with this quote from John Stuart Mill, *On the Subjection of Women*: "Though women do not complain of the power of husbands, each complains of her own husband, or of the husbands of friends. It is the same in all other cases of servitude; at least in the commencement of the emancipatory movement. The serfs did not at first complain of the power of the lords, but only of their tyranny" (p. 447).

50. William Raspberry, "Family Breakdowns: A Voice from 'Little Dixie,' " *Washington Post* (June 23, 1978). Lillian Rubin, *Worlds of Pain* (New York: Basic Books, 1976), describes current tensions between the women and men in the working-class families she interviewed.

51. Kathryn E. Walker, "Homemaking Still Takes Time," *Journal of Home Economics* 61, no. 8 (October 1969): 621–24; Joann Vanek, "Time Spent in Housework," *Scientific American* 231 (November 1974): 116–20; Michael Paul Sacks, "Unchanging Times: A Comparison of the Everyday Life of Soviet Working Men and Women between 1923 and 1966", *Journal of Marriage and the Family* 39 (November 1977): 793–805.

52. Technological innovations within the household—the washing machine, the vacuum cleaner, the dishwasher—have not been effective in reducing household time. Sophisticated robots, microwave ovens, or computer-controlled equipment may yet be able to reduce the time required for maintaining household services at established levels. Yet what technology is developed and made available is also the result of historical processes and the relative strength of particular classes and genders. See Hartmann, *Capitalism and Women's Work*.

53. Robinson, table 4 (see n. 28 above); Clair Vickry, "Women's Economic Contribution to the Family," in *The Subtle Revolution*, ed. Ralph E. Smith (Washington, D.C.: Urban Institute, 1979), p. 194.

54. One in four meals is now eaten outside the home (Charles Vaugh, "Growth and Future of the Fast Food Industry," *Cornell Motel and Restaurant Administration Quarterly* [November 1976]), cited in Christine Bose, "Technology and Changes in the Division of Labor in the American Home" (paper delivered at the annual meeting of the American Sociological Association, San Francisco, September, 1978). I suspect that the most effective means of reducing housework time involves changing the location of production from the household to the larger economy, but men, acting in their patriarchal interests, may well resist this removal of production from the home, with its attendant loss of personalized services.

55. Walker, (n.51 above).

56. Sacks, (n. 51 above), p. 801.

57. In the Marxist perspective, the wage paid to the worker is largely dependent on her or his costs of reproduction, mediated by custom, tradition, and class struggle. When there are two wage workers per family, the family's cost of reproduction can be spread over the wages of both workers; the capitalist can pay two workers the same wage one received previously and get twice as many hours of labor, cheapening the price of labor per hour. See Lise Vogel, "The Earthy Family," *Radical America* 7, no. 4–5 (July–October 1973): 9–50. Jean Gardiner, "Women's Domestic Labor," *New Left Review*, no. 89 (January–February 1975), pp. 47–58, also discusses conflicting tendencies within capitalism.

58. James O'Connor, *The Fiscal Crisis of the State* (New York: St. Martin's Press, 1973).

59. Weinbaum (see n. 15 above).

60. Hedges and Barnett (n. 39 above), p. 11.

61. Ann R. Markusen has extended the notion of decentralized households as characteristic of patriarchy to explain the development of segregated residential areas in cities. See her "City Spatial Structure, Women's Household Work, and National Urban Policy," *Signs: Journal of Women in Culture and Society* 5, no. 3, suppl. (Spring 1980): S23–S44.

62. Wendy Lutrell, "The Family as an Arena of Struggle: New Directions and Strategies for Studying Contemporary Family Life" (paper delivered at a Sociology Colloquium, University of California, Santa Cruz, May 30, 1979), pp. 19, 18.

X.

FEMINISM, MARXISM, METHOD, AND THE STATE
TOWARD FEMINIST JURISPRUDENCE

Catharine A. MacKinnon

Catharine A. MacKinnon weaves together epistemological, sociological, psychological, and po-litical perspectives to provide what is widely regarded as the most innnovative of the new femin-ist approaches to jurisprudence (the theory or philosophy of law). She produced one of the first comprehensive analyses of sexual harassment,[1] and more recently coauthored with Andrea Dworkin antipornography ordinances for several U.S. cities.

Her essay below is the second part of a two-part analysis that lays the groundwork for a (radical) feminist theory of the state. In part one, she examined problems that arise in trying to use liberal or Marxist political theory to understand women's situation and how the law treats women. Here she turns to make the startling claim that we can see that "the state is male" when we look at how the Supreme Court thinks about rape: the Court thinks about it just the way men do, and that is very different indeed from how women think about it. Moreover, the law of a liberal state conceptualizes its own virtue as men do their own reason and as scientists con-ceptualize rationality: they espouse an "objectivist epistemology" that measures rationality by "point-of-viewlessness."

MacKinnon has argued that one important distinction between radical feminism, on the one hand, and liberal or Marxist feminism, on the other hand, is the method radical feminism uses: "consciousness raising *is* feminist method" she claims in the first of these essays. Readers will be struck by her constant interrogation of unnoticed assumptions, her surprising shifts from familiar to unfamiliar questions, her striking turns of phrase, and the various other ways in which she does indeed succeed in raising the reader's consciousness. What research practices would MacKinnon have all feminist inquirers follow? Should we call this a feminist method of research? If not, what is it?

MacKinnon's radical feminism—the particular theoretical perspective she shares with other thinkers—has been criticized in a variety of ways. For one thing, its important assumptions lead MacKinnon to be more interested in what all women share than in the ways male domination is experienced differently (and *is* different) for women in different races, classes, and cultures. Moreover, it has been argued that she paints a picture of such unrelenting oppression and exploitation of women that it is hard to imagine how feminism ever got started. This extremely important social theory, like all fruitful theories, has its limitations.

Does MacKinnon provide here a radical feminist version of the feminist epistemological stand-point developed in different ways by Dorothy Smith and Nancy Hartsock?

I

Feminism has no theory of the state. It has a theory of power: sexuality is gendered as gender is sexualized. Male and female are created through the erotization of dominance and submission. The man/woman difference and the dominance/submission dynamic define each other. This is the social meaning of sex and the distinctively feminist account of gender inequality.[1] Sexual objectification, the central process within this dynamic, is at once epistemological and political.[2] The feminist theory of knowledge is inextricable from the feminist critique of power because the male point of view forces itself upon the world as its way of apprehending it.

The perspective from the male standpoint[3] enforces woman's definition, encircles her body, circumlocutes her speech, and describes her life. The male perspective is systemic and hegemonic. The content of the signification "woman" is the content of women's lives. Each sex has its role, but their stakes and power are not equal. If the sexes are unequal, and perspective participates in situation, there is no ungendered reality or ungendered perspective. And they are connected. In this context, objectivity—the nonsituated, universal standpoint, whether claimed or aspired to—is a denial of the existence or potency of sex inequality that tacitly participates in constructing reality from the dominant point of view. Objectivity, as the epistemological stance of which objectification is the social process, creates the reality it apprehends by defining as knowledge the reality it creates through its way of apprehending it. Sexual metaphors for knowing are no coincidence.[4] The solipsism of this approach does not undercut its sincerity, but it is interest that precedes method.

Feminism criticizes this male totality without an account of our capacity to do so or to imagine or realize a more whole truth. Feminism affirms women's point of view by revealing, criticizing, and explaining its impossibility. This is not a dialectical paradox. It is a methodological expression of women's situation, in which the struggle for consciousness is a struggle for world: for a sexuality, a history, a culture, a community, a form of power, an experience of the sacred. If women had consciousness or world, sex inequality would be harmless, or all women would be feminist. Yet we have something of both, or there would be no such thing as feminism. Why can women know that this—life as we have known it—is not all, not enough, not ours, not just? Now, why don't all women?[5]

The practice of a politics of all women in the face of its theoretical impossibility is creating a new process of theorizing and a new form of theory. Although feminism emerges from women's particular experience, it is not subjective or partial, for no interior ground and few if any aspects of life are free of male power. Nor is feminism objective, abstract, or universal.[6] It claims no external ground or unsexed sphere of generalization or abstraction beyond male power, nor transcendence of the specificity of each of its manifestations. How is it possible to have an engaged truth that does not simply reiterate its determinations? *Dis*-engaged truth only reiterates *its* determinations. Choice of method is choice of determinants—a choice which, for women as such, has been unavailable because of the subordination of women. Feminism does not begin with the premise that it is unpremised. It does not aspire to persuade an unpremised audience because there is no such audience. Its project is to uncover and claim as valid the experience of women, the major content of which is the devaluation of women's experience.

This defines our task not only because male dominance is perhaps the most pervasive and tenacious system of power in history, but because it is metaphysically nearly perfect.[7] Its point of view is the standard for point-of-viewlessness, its particularity the meaning of universality. Its force is exercised as consent, its authority as participation, its supremacy as the paradigm of order, its control as the definition of legitimacy. Feminism claims the voice of women's silence, the sexuality of our eroticized desexualization, the fullness of "lack," the centrality of our marginality and exclusion, the public nature of privacy, the presence of our absence. This approach is more complex than transgression, more trans-formative than transvaluation, deeper than mirror-imaged resistance, more affirmative than the negation of our negativity. It is neither materialist nor idealist; it is feminist. Neither the transcendence of liberalism nor the determination of materialism works for us. Idealism is too unreal; women's inequality is enforced, so it cannot simply be thought out of existence, certainly not by us. Materialism is too real; women's inequality has never not existed, so women's equality never has. That is, the equality of women to men will not be scientifically provable until it is no longer necessary to do so. Women's situation offers no outside to stand on or gaze at, no inside to escape to, too much urgency to wait, no place else to go, and nothing to use but the twisted tools that have been shoved down our throats. If feminism is revolutionary, this is why.

Feminism has been widely thought to contain tendencies of liberal feminism, radical feminism, and socialist feminism. But just as socialist feminism has often amounted to marxism applied to women, liberal feminism has often amounted to liberalism applied to women. Radical feminism is feminism. Radical feminism—after this, feminism unmodi-fied—is methodologically post-marxist.[8] It moves to resolve the marxist-feminist proble-matic on the level of method. Because its method emerges from the concrete conditions of all women as a sex, it dissolves the individualist, naturalist, idealist, moralist structure of liberalism, the politics of which science is the epistemology. Where liberal feminism sees sexism primarily as an illusion or myth to be dispelled, an inaccuracy to be corrected, true feminism sees the male point of view as fundamental to the male power to create the world in its own image, the image of its desires, not just as its delusory end product. Feminism distinctively as such comprehends that what counts as truth is produced in the interest of those with power to shape reality, and that this process is as pervasive as it is necessary as it is changeable. Unlike the scientific strain in marxism or the Kantian im-perative in liberalism, which in this context share most salient features, feminism neither claims universality nor, failing that, reduces to relativity. It does not seek a generality that subsumes its particulars or an abstract theory or a science of sexism. It rejects the approach of control over nature (including us) analogized to control over society (also including us) which has grounded the "science of society" project as the paradigm for political knowl-edge since (at least) Descartes. Both liberalism and marxism have been subversive on women's behalf. Neither is enough. To grasp the inadequacies for women of liberalism on one side and marxism on the other is to begin to comprehend the role of the liberal state and liberal legalism[9] within a post-marxist feminism of social transformation.

As feminism has a theory of power but lacks a theory of the state, so marxism has a theory of value which (through the organization of work in production) becomes class analysis, but a problematic theory of the state. Marx did not address the state much more explicitly than he did women. Women were substratum, the state epiphenomenon.[10] Engels, who frontally analyzed both, and together, presumed the subordination of women in every attempt to reveal its roots, just as he presupposed something like the state, or state-like social conditions, in every attempt to expose its origins.[11] Marx tended to use the term "political" narrowly to refer to the state or its laws, criticizing as exclusively political interpretations of the state's organization or behavior which took them as sui generis. Accordingly, until recently, most marxism has tended to consider political that which occurs between classes, that is, to interpret as "the political" instances of the marxist concept of inequality. In this broad sense, the marxist theory of social inequality has been its theory of politics. This has not so much collapsed the state into society (although it goes far in that direction) as conceived the state as determined by the totality of social relations of which the state is one determined and determining part—without specifying which, or how much, is which.

In this context, recent marxist work has tried to grasp the specificity of the institutional state: how it wields class power, or transforms class society, or responds to approach by a left aspiring to rulership or other changes. While liberal theory has seen the state as emanating power, and traditional marxism has seen the state as expressing power constituted elsewhere, recent marxism, much of it structuralist, has tried to analyze state power as specific to the state as a form, yet integral to a determinate social whole understood in class terms. This state is found "relatively autonomous." This means that the state, expressed through its functionaries, has a definite class character, is definitely capitalist or socialist, but also has its own interests which are to some degree independent of those of the ruling class and even of the class structure.[12] The state as such, in this view, has a specific power and interest, termed "the political," such that class power, class interest expressed by and in the state, and state behavior, although inconceivable in isolation from one another, are nevertheless not linearly or causally linked or strictly coextensive. Such work locates "the specificity of the political" in a immediate "region"[13] between the state as its own ground of power (which alone, as in the liberal conception, would set the state above or apart from class) and the state as possessing no special supremacy or priority in terms of power, as in the more orthodox marxist view.

The idea that the state is relatively autonomous, a kind of first among equals of social institutions, has the genius of appearing to take a stand on the issue of reciprocal constitution of state and society while straddling it. Is the state essentially autonomous of class but partly determined by it, or is it essentially determined by class but not exclusively so? Is it relatively constrained within a context of freedom or relatively free within a context of constraint?[14] As to who or what fundamentally moves and shapes the realities and instrumentalities of domination, and where to go to do something about it, what qualifies what is as ambiguous as it is crucial. Whatever it has not accomplished, however, this literature has at least relieved the compulsion to find all law—directly or convolutedly, nakedly or clothed in unconscious or devious rationalia—to be simply bourgeois, without undercutting the notion that it is determinately driven by interest.

A methodologically post-marxist feminism must confront, on our own terms, the issue of the relation between the state and society, within a theory of social determination adequate to the specificity of sex. Lacking even a tacit theory of the state of its own, feminist practice has instead oscillated between a liberal theory of the state on the one hand and a left theory of the state on the other. Both treat law as the mind of society: disembodied reason in liberal theory, reflection of material interest in left theory. In liberal moments the state is accepted on its own terms as a neutral arbiter among conflicting interests. The law is actually or potentially principled, meaning predisposed to no substantive outcome, thus available as a tool that is not fatally twisted. Women implicitly become an interest group within pluralism, with specific problems of mobilization and representation, exit and voice, sustaining incremental gains and losses. In left moments, the state becomes a tool of dominance and repression, the law legitimizing ideology, use of the legal system a form of utopian idealism or gradualist reform, each apparent gain deceptive or cooptive, and each loss inevitable.

Applied to women, liberalism has supported state intervention on behalf of women as abstract persons with abstract rights, without scrutinizing the content of these notions in gendered terms. Marxism applied to women is always on the edge of counseling abdication of the state as an arena altogether—and with it those women whom the state does not ignore or who are, as yet, in no position to ignore it. Feminism has so far accepted these constraints upon its alternatives: either the state, as primary tool of women's betterment and status transformation, without analysis (hence strategy) for it as male; or civil society, which for women has more closely resembled a state of nature. The state, with it the law, has been either omnipotent or impotent: everything or nothing.

The feminist posture toward the state has therefore been schizoid on issues central to women's survival: rape, battery, pornography, prostitution, sexual harassment, sex discrimination, abortion, the Equal Rights Amendment, to name a few. Attempts to reform and enforce rape laws, for example, have tended to build on the model of the deviant perpetrator and the violent act, as if the fact that rape is a crime means that the society is against it, so law enforcement would reduce or delegitimize it. Initiatives are accordingly directed toward making the police more sensitive, prosecutors more responsive, judges more receptive, and the law, in words, less sexist. This may be progressive in the liberal or the left senses, but how is it empowering in the feminist sense? Even if it were effective in jailing men who do little different from what nondeviant men do regularly, how would such an approach alter women's rapability? Unconfronted are *why* women are raped and the role of the state in that. Similarly, applying laws against battery to husbands, although it can mean life itself, has largely failed to address, as part of the strategy for state intervention, the conditions that produce men who systematically express themselves violently toward women, women whose resistance is disabled, and the role of the state in this dynamic. Criminal enforcement in these areas, while suggesting that rape and battery are deviant, punishes men for expressing the images of masculinity that mean their identity, for which they are otherwise trained, elevated, venerated, and paid. These men must be stopped. But how does that change them or reduce the chances that there will be more like them? Liberal strategies entrust women to the state. Left theory abandons us to the rapists and batterers. The question for feminism is not only whether there is a meaningful difference between the two, but whether either is adequate to the feminist critique of rape and battery as systemic and to the role of the state and the law within that system.

Feminism has descriptions of the state's treatment of the gender difference, but no analysis of the state as gender hierarchy. We need to know. What, in gender terms, are the state's norms of accountability, sources of power, real constituency? Is the state to some degree autonomous of the interests of men or an integral expression of them? Does the state embody and serve male interests in its form, dynamics, relation to society, and specific policies? Is the state constructed upon the subordination of women? If so, how does male power become state power? Can such a state be made to serve the interests of those upon whose powerlessness its power is erected? Would a different relation between state and society, such as may pertain under socialism, make a difference? If not, is masculinity inherent in the state form as such, or is some other form of state, or some other way of governing, distinguishable or imaginable? In the absence of answers to such questions, feminism has been caught between giving more power to the state in each attempt to claim it for women and leaving unchecked power in the society to men. Undisturbed, meanwhile, like the assumption that women generally consent to sex, is the assumption that we consent to this government. The question for feminism, for the first time on its own terms, is: what is this state, from women's point of view?

As a beginning, I propose that the state is male in the feminist sense.[15] The law sees and treats women the way men see and treat women. The liberal state coercively and authoritatively constitutes the social order in the interest of men as a gender, through its legitimizing norms, relation to society, and substantive policies. It achieves this through embodying and ensuring male control over women's sexuality at every level, occasionally cushioning, qualifying, or de jure prohibiting its excesses when necessary to its normalization. Substantively, the way the male point of view frames an experience is the way it is framed by state policy. To the extent possession is the point of sex, rape is sex with a woman who is not yours, unless the act is so as to make her yours. If part of the kick of pornography involves eroticizing the putatively prohibited, obscenity law will putatively prohibit pornography enough to maintain its desirability without ever making it unavailable or truly illegitimate. The same with prostitution. As male is the implicit reference for human, maleness will be the measure of equality in sex discrimination law. To the extent that the point of abortion is to control the reproductive sequelae of intercourse, so as to facilitate male sexual access to women, access to abortion will be controlled by "a man or The Man."[16] Gender, elaborated and sustained by behavioral patterns of application and administration, is maintained as a division of power.

Formally, the state is male in that objectivity is its norm. Objectivity is liberal legalism's conception of itself. It legitimizes itself by reflecting its view of existing society, a society it made and makes by so seeing it, and calling that view, and that relation, practical rationality. If rationality is measured by point-of-viewlessness, what counts as reason will be that which corresponds to the way things are, practical will mean that which can be done without changing anything. In this framework, the task of legal interpretation becomes "to perfect the state as mirror of the society."[17] Objectivist epistemology is the law of law. It ensures that the law will most reinforce existing distributions of power when it most closely adheres to its own highest ideal of fairness. Like the science it emulates, this epistemological stance can not see the social specificity of reflection as Method or its choice to embrace that which it reflects. Such law not only reflects a society in which men rule women; it rules in a male way: "The phallus means everything that sets itself up as a mirror."[18] The rule form, which unites scientific knowledge with state control in its conception of what law is, institutionalizes the objective stance as jurisprudence. A closer look at the substantive law of rape[19] in light of such an argument suggests that the relation between objectification (understood as the primary process of the subordination of women) and the power of the state is the relation between the personal and the political at the level of government. This is not because the state is presumptively the sphere of politics. It is because the state, in part through law, institutionalizes male power. If male power is systemic, it *is* the regime.

II

Feminists have reconceived rape as central to women's condition in two ways. Some see rape as an act of violence, not sexuality, the threat of which intimidates all women.[20] Others see rape, including its violence, as an expression of male sexuality, the social imperatives of which define all women.[21] The first, formally in the liberal tradition, comprehends rape as a displacement of power based on physical force onto sexuality, a preexisting natural sphere to which domination is alien. Thus, Susan Brownmiller examines rape in riots, wars, pogroms, and revolutions; rape by police, parents, prison guards; and rape motivated by racism—seldom rape in normal circumstances, in everyday life, in ordinary relationships, by men as men.[22] Women are raped by guns, age, white supremacy, the state—only derivatively by the penis. The more feminist view to me, one which derives from victims' experiences, sees sexuality as a social sphere of male power of which forced sex is paradigmatic. Rape is not less sexual for being violent; to the extent that coercion has become integral to male sexuality, rape may be sexual to the degree that, and because, it is violent.

The point of defining rape as "violence not sex" or "violence against women" has been to separate sexuality from gender in order to affirm sex (heterosexuality) while rejecting violence (rape). The problem remains what it has always been: telling the difference. The convergence of sexuality with violence, long used at law to deny the reality of women's violation, is recognized by rape survivors, with a difference: where the legal system has seen the intercourse in rape, victims see the rape in intercourse. The uncoerced context for sexual expression becomes as elusive as the physical acts come to feel indistinguishable.[23] Instead of asking, what is the violation of rape, what if we ask, what is the non-violation of intercourse? To tell what is wrong with rape, explain what is right about sex. If this, in turn, is difficult, the difficulty is as instructive as the difficulty men have in telling the difference when women see one. Perhaps the wrong of rape has proven so difficult to articulate[24] because the unquestionable starting point has been that rape is definable as distinct from intercourse, when for women it is difficult to distinguish them under conditions of male dominance.[25]

Like heterosexuality, the crime of rape centers on penetration.[26] The law to protect women's sexuality from forcible violation/expropriation defines the protected in male genital terms. Women do resent forced penetration. But penile invasion of the vagina may be less pivotal to women's sexuality, pleasure or violation, than it is to male sexuality. This definitive element of rape centers upon a male-defined loss, not coincidentally also upon the way men define loss of exclusive access. In this light, rape, as legally defined, appears more a crime against female monogamy than against female sexuality. Property concepts fail fully to comprehend this[27], however, not because women's sexuality is not, finally, a thing, but because it is never ours. The moment we "have" it—"have sex" in the dual sexuality/gender sense—it is lost as ours. This may explain the male incomprehension that, once a woman has had sex, she loses anything when raped. To them we *have nothing* to lose. Dignitary harms, because nonmaterial, are remote to the legal mind. But women's loss through rape is not only less tangible, it is less existent. It is difficult to avoid the conclusion that penetration itself is known to be a violation and that women's sexuality, our gender definition, is itself stigmatic. If this is so, the pressing question for explanation is not why some of us accept rape but why any of us resent it.

The law of rape divides the world of women into spheres of consent according to how much say we are legally presumed to have over sexual access to us by various categories of men. Little girls may not consent; wives must. If rape laws existed to enforce women's control over our own sexuality, as the consent defense implies, marital rape would not be a widespread exception[28], nor would statutory rape proscribe all sexual intercourse with underage girls regardless of their wishes. The rest of us fall into parallel provinces: good girls, like children, are unconsenting, virginal, rapable; bad girls, like wives, are consenting, whores, unrapable. The age line under which girls are presumed disabled from withholding consent to sex rationalizes a condition of sexual coercion women never outgrow. As with protective labor laws for women only, dividing and protecting the most vulnerable becomes a device for not protecting everyone. Risking loss of even so little cannot be afforded. Yet the protection is denigrating and limiting (girls may not choose to be sexual) as well as perverse (girls are eroticized as untouchable; now reconsider the data on incest).

If the accused knows us, consent is inferred. The exemption for rape in marriage is consistent with the assumption underlying most adjudications of forcible rape: to the extent the parties relate, it was not really rape, it was personal.[29] As the marital exemptions erode, preclusions for cohabitants and voluntary social companions may expand. In this light, the partial erosion of the marital rape exemption looks less like a change in the equation between women's experience of sexual violation and men's experience of intimacy, and more like a legal adjustment to the social fact that acceptable heterosexual sex is increasingly not limited to the legal family. So although the rape law may not now always assume that the woman consented simply because the parties are legally one, indices of closeness, of relationship ranging from nodding acquaintance to living together, still contraindicate rape. Perhaps this reflects men's experience that women they know meaningfully consent to sex with them. That cannot be rape; rape must be by someone else, someone unknown. But *women* experience rape most often by men we know.[30] Men believe that it is less awful to be raped by someone one is close to: "The emotional trauma suffered by a person victimized by an individual with whom sexual intimacy is shared as a normal part of an ongoing marital relationship is not nearly as severe as that suffered by a person who is victimized by one with whom that intimacy is not shared."[31] But women feel as much, if not more, traumatized by being raped by someone we have known or trusted, someone we have shared at least an illusion of mutuality with, than by some stranger. In whose interest is it to believe that it is not so bad to be raped by someone who has fucked you before as by someone who has not? Disallowing charges of rape in marriage may also "remove a substantial obstacle to the resumption of normal marital relations."[32] Depending upon your view of normal. Note that the obstacle to normalcy here is not the rape but the law against it. Apparently someone besides feminists finds sexual victimization and sexual intimacy not all that contradictory. Sometimes I think women and men live in different cultures.

Having defined rape in male sexual terms, the law's problem, which becomes the victim's problem, is distinguishing rape from sex in specific cases. The law does this by adjudicating the level of acceptable force starting just above the level set by what is seen as normal male sexual behavior, rather than at the victim's, or women's, point of violation. Rape cases finding insufficient force reveal that acceptable sex, in the legal perspective, can entail a lot of force. This is not only because of the way specific facts are perceived and interpreted, but because of the way the injury itself is defined as illegal. Rape is a sex crime that is not a crime when it looks like sex. To seek to define rape as violent, not sexual, is understandable in this context, and often seems strategic. But assault that is consented to is still assault; rape consented to is intercourse. The substantive reference point implicit in existing legal standards is the sexually normative level of force. Until this norm is confronted as such, no distinction between violence and sexuality will prohibit more instances of women's experienced violation than does the existing definition. The question is what is *seen as* force, hence as violence, in the sexual arena. Most rapes, as women live them, will not be seen to violate women until sex and violence are confronted as mutually definitive. It is not only men convicted of rape who believe that the only thing they did different from what men do all the time is get caught.

The line between rape and intercourse commonly centers on some measure of the woman's "will." But from what should the law know woman's will? Like much existing law, Brownmiller tends to treat will as a question of consent and consent as a factual issue of the presence of force.[33] Proof problems aside, force and desire are not mutually exclusive. So long as dominance is eroticized, they never will be. Women are socialized to passive receptivity; may have or perceive no alternative to acquiescence; may prefer it to the escalated risk of injury and the humiliation of a lost fight; submit to survive. Some eroticize dominance and submission; it beats feeling forced. Sexual intercourse may be deeply unwanted—the woman would never have initiated it—yet no force may be present. Too, force may be used, yet the woman may want the sex—to avoid more force or because she, too, eroticizes dominance. Women and men know this. Calling rape violence, not sex, thus evades, at the moment it most seems to confront, the issue of who controls women's sexuality and the dominance/submission dynamic that has defined it. When sex is violent, women may have lost control over what is done to us, but absence of force does not ensure the presence of that control. Nor, under conditions of male dominance, does the presence of force make an interaction nonsexual. If sex is normally something men do to women, the issue is less whether there was force and more whether consent is a meaningful concept.[34]

To explain women's gender status as a function of rape, Brownmiller argues that the threat of rape benefits all men.[35] She does not specify in what way. Perhaps it benefits them sexually, hence as a gender: male initiatives toward women carry the fear of rape as support for persuading compliance, the resulting appearance of which has been called consent. Here the victims' perspective grasps what liberalism applied to women denies: that forced sex as sexuality is not exceptional in relations between the sexes but constitutes the social meaning of gender: "Rape is a man's act, whether it is male or a female man and whether it is a man relatively permanently or relatively temporarily; and being raped is a woman's experience, whether it is a female or a male woman and whether it is a woman relatively permanently or relatively temporarily."[36] To be rap*able*, a position which is social, not biological, defines what a woman *is*.

Most women get the message that the law against rape is virtually unenforceable as applied to them. Our own experience is more often delegitimized by this than the law is. Women radically distinguish between rape and experiences of sexual violation, concluding that we have not "really" been raped if we have ever seen or dated or slept with or been married to the man, if we were fashionably dressed or are not provably virgin, if we are prostitutes, if we put up with it or tried to get it over with, if we were force-fucked over a period of years. If we probably couldn't prove it in court, it wasn't rape. The distance between most sexual violations of women and the legally perfect rape measures the imposition of someone else's definition upon women's experiences. Rape, from women's point of view, is not prohibited; it is regulated. Even women who know we have been raped do not believe that the legal system will see it the way we do. We are often not wrong. Rather than deterring or avenging rape, the state, in many victims' experiences, perpetuates it. Women who charge rape say they were raped twice, the second time in court. If the state is male, this is more than a figure of speech.

The law distinguishes rape from intercourse by the woman's lack of consent coupled with a man's (usually) knowing disregard of it. A feminist distinction between rape and intercourse, to hazard a beginning approach, lies instead in the *meaning* of the act from women's point of view. What is wrong with rape is that it is an act of the subordination of women to men. Seen this way, the issue is not so much what rape "is" as the way its social conception is shaped to interpret particular encounters. Under conditions of sex inequality, with perspective bound up with situation, whether a contested interaction is rape comes down to whose meaning wins. If sexuality is relational, specifically if it is a power relation of gender, consent is a communication under conditions of inequality. It transpires somewhere between what the woman actually wanted and what the man comprehended she wanted. Instead of capturing this dynamic, the law gives us linear statics face to face. Nonconsent in law becomes a question of the man's force or the woman's resistance or both.[37] Rape, like many crimes and torts, requires that the accused possess a criminal mind (mens rea) for his acts to be criminal. The man's mental state refers to what he actually understood at the time or to what a reasonable man should have understood under the circumstances. The problem is this: the injury of rape lies in the meaning of the act to its victims, but the standard for its criminality lies in the meaning of the same act to the assailants. Rape is only an injury from women's point of view. It is only a crime from the male point of view, explicitly including that of the accused.

Thus is the crime of rape defined and adjudicated from the male standpoint, that is, presuming that (what feminists see as) forced sex is sex. Under male supremacy, of course, it is. What this means doctrinally is that the man's perceptions of the woman's desires often determine whether she is deemed violated. This might be like other crimes of subjective intent if rape were like other crimes. But with rape, because sexuality defines gender, the only difference between assault and (what is socially considered) noninjury is the meaning of the encounter to the woman. Interpreted this way, the legal problem has been to determine whose view of that meaning constitutes what really happened, as if what happened objectively exists to be objectively determined, thus as if this task of determination is separable from the gender of the participants and the gendered nature of their exchange. Thus, even though the rape law oscillates between subjective tests and more objective standards invoking social reasonableness, it uniformly presumes a single underlying reality, not a reality split by divergent meanings, such as those inequality produces. Many women are raped by men who know the meaning of their acts to women and proceed anyway.[38] But women are also violated every day by men who have no idea of the meaning of their acts to women. To them, it is sex. Therefore, to the law, it is sex. That is the single reality of what happened. When a rape prosecution is lost on a consent defense, the woman has not only failed to prove lack of consent, she is not considered to have been injured at all. Hermeneutically unpacked, read: because he did not perceive she did not want him, she was not violated. She had sex. Sex itself cannot be an injury. Women consent to sex every day. Sex makes a woman a woman. Sex is what women are *for*.

To a feminist analysis, men set sexual mores ideologically and behaviorally, define rape as they imagine the sexual violation of women through distinguishing it from their image of what they normally do, and sit in judgment in most accusations of sex crimes. So rape comes to mean a strange (read Black) man knowing a woman does not want sex and going ahead anyway. But men are systematically conditioned not even to notice what women want. They may have not a glimmer of women's indifference or revulsion. Rapists typically believe the woman loved it.[39] Women, as a survival strategy, must ignore or devalue or mute our desires (particularly lack of them) to convey the impression that the man will get what he wants regardless of what we want. In this context, consider measuring the genuineness of consent from the individual assailant's (or even the socially reasonable, i.e., objective, man's) point of view.

Men's pervasive belief that women fabricate rape charges after consenting to sex makes sense in this light. To them, the accusations *are* false because, to them, the facts describe sex. To interpret such events as rapes distorts their experience. Since they seldom consider that their experience of the real is anything other than reality, they can only explain the woman's version as maliciously invented. Similarly, the male anxiety that rape is easy to charge and difficult to disprove (also widely believed in the face of overwhelming evidence to the contrary) arises because rape accusations express one thing men cannot seem to control: the meaning to women of sexual encounters.

Thus do legal doctrines, incoherent or puzzling as syllogistic logic, become coherent as ideology. For example, when an accused wrongly but sincerely believes that a woman he sexually forced consented, he may have a defense of mistaken belief or fail to satisfy the mental requirement of knowingly proceeding against her will.[40] One commentator notes, discussing the conceptually similar issue of revocation of prior consent (i.e., on the issue of the conditions under which women are allowed to control access to their sexuality from one time to the next): "Even where a woman revokes prior consent, such is the male ego that, seized of an exaggerated assessment of his sexual prowess, a man might genuinely believe her still to be consenting; resistance may be misinterpreted as enthusiastic cooperation; protestations of pain or disinclination, a spur to more sophisticated or more ardent love-making; a clear statement to stop, taken as referring to a particular intimacy rather than the entire performance."[41] This equally vividly captures common male readings of women's indications of disinclination under all kinds of circumstances.[42] Now reconsider to what extent the man's perceptions should determine whether a rape occurred. From whose standpoint, and in whose interest, is a law that allows one person's conditioned unconsciousness to contraindicate another's experienced violation? This aspect of the rape law reflects the sex inequality of the society not only in conceiving a cognizable injury from the viewpoint of the reasonable rapist, but in affirmatively rewarding men with acquittals for not comprehending women's point of view on sexual encounters.

Whether the law calls this coerced consent or mistake of fact, the more the sexual violation of women is routine, the more beliefs equating sexuality with violation become reasonable, and the more honestly women can be defined in terms of our fuckability. It would be comparatively simple if the legal problem were limited to avoiding retroactive falsification of the accused's state of mind. Surely there are incentives to lie. But the deeper problem is the rape law's assumption that a single, objective state of affairs existed, one which merely needs to be determined by evidence, where many (maybe even most) rapes involve honest men and violated women. When the reality is split—a woman is raped but not by a rapist?—the law tends to conclude that a rape *did not happen.* To attempt to solve this by adopting the standard of reasonable belief without asking, on a substantive social basis, to whom the belief is reasonable and why—meaning, what conditions make it reasonable—is one-sided: male-sided. What is it reasonable for a man to believe concerning a woman's desire for sex when heterosexuality is compulsory? Whose subjectivity becomes the objectivity of "what happened" is a matter of social meaning, that is, it has been a matter of sexual politics. One-sidedly erasing women's violation or dissolving the presumptions into the subjectivity of either side are alternatives dictated by the terms of the object/subject split, respectively. These are alternatives that will only retrace that split until its terms are confronted as gendered to the ground.

Desirability to men is commonly supposed to be a woman's form of power. This echoes the view that consent is women's form of control over intercourse, different but equal to the custom of male initiative. Look at it: man initiates, woman chooses. Even the ideal is not mutual. Apart from the disparate consequences of refusal, or openness of original options, this model does not envision a situation the woman controls being placed in, or choices she frames, yet the consequences are attributed to her as if the sexes began at arms length, on equal terrain, as in the contract fiction. Ambiguous cases of consent are often archetypically referred to as "half won arguments in parked cars."[43] Why not half lost? Why isn't half enough? Why is it an argument? Why do men still want "it," feel entitled to "it," when women don't want them? That sexual expression is even framed as a matter of woman's consent, without exposing these presuppositions, is integral to gender inequality. Woman's so-called power presupposes her more fundamental powerlessness.[44]

III

The state's formal norms recapitulate the male point of view on the level of design. In Anglo-American jurisprudence, morals (value judgments) are deemed separable and separated from politics (power contests), and both from adjudication (interpretation). Neutrality, including judicial decision making that is dispassionate, impersonal, disinterested, and precedential, is considered desirable and descriptive. Courts, forums without predisposition among parties and with no interest of their own, reflect society back to itself resolved. Government of laws not men limits partiality with written constraints and tempers force with reasonable rule following. This law aspires to science: to the immanent generalization subsuming the emergent particularity, to prediction and control of social regularities and regulations, preferably codified. The formulaic "tests" of "doctrine" aspire to mechanism, classification to taxonomy. Courts intervene only in properly "factualized" disputes,[45] cognizing social conflicts as if collecting empirical data. But the demarcations between morals and politics, the personality of the judge and the judicial role, bare coercion and the rule of law,[46] tend to merge in women's experience. Relatively seamlessly they promote a dominance of men as a social group through privileging the form of power—the perspective on social life—feminist consciousness reveals as socially male. The separation of form from substance, process from policy, role from theory and practice, echoes and reechoes at each level of the regime its basic norm: objectivity.

Consider a central example. The separation of public from private is as crucial to the liberal state's claim to objectivity as its inseparability is to women's claim to subordination. Legally, it has both formal and substantive dimensions. The state considers formal, not substantive, the allocation of public matters to itself to be treated objectively, of private matters to civil society to be treated subjectively. Substantively, the private is defined as a right to "an inviolable personality,"[47] which is guaranteed by ensuring "autonomy or control over the intimacies of personal identity."[48] It is hermetic. It means that which is inaccessible to, unaccountable to, and unconstructed by anything beyond itself. Intimacy occurs in private; this is supposed to guarantee original symmetry of power. Injuries arise in violating the private sphere, not within and by and because of it. Private means consent can be presumed unless disproven. To contain a systematic inequality contradicts the notion itself. But feminist consciousness has exploded the private. For women, the measure of the intimacy has been the measure of the oppression. To see the personal as political means to see the private as public. On this level, women have no privacy to lose or to guarantee. We are not inviolable. Our sexuality, meaning gender identity, is not only violable, it *is* (hence we are) our violation. Privacy is everything women as women have never been allowed to be or to have; at the same time the private is everything women have been equated with and defined in terms of *men's* ability to have. To confront the fact that we have no privacy is to confront our private degradation as the public order. To fail to recognize this place of the private in women's subordination by seeking protection behind a right to that privacy is thus to be cut off from collective verification and state support in the same act.[49] The very place (home, body), relations (sexual), activities (intercourse and reproduction), and feelings (intimacy, selfhood) that feminism finds central to women's subjection form the core of privacy doctrine. But when women are segregated in private, one at a time, a law of privacy will tend to protect the right of men "to be let alone,"[50] to oppress us one at a time. A law of the private, in a state that mirrors such a society, will translate the traditional values of the private sphere into individual women's right to privacy, subordinating women's collective needs to the imperatives of male supremacy.[51] It will keep some men out of the bedrooms of other men.

Liberalism converges with the left at this edge of the feminist critique of male power. Herbert Marcuse speaks of "philosophies which are 'political' in the widest sense—affecting society as a whole, demonstrably transcending the sphere of privacy."[52] This does and does not describe the feminist political: "Women both have and have not had a common world."[53] Isolation in the home and intimate degradation, women share. The private sphere, which confines and separates us, is therefore a political sphere, a common ground of our inequality. In feminist translation, the private is a sphere of battery, marital rape, and women's exploited labor; of the central social institutions whereby women are deprived of (as men are granted) identity, autonomy, control, and self-determination; and of the primary activity through which male supremacy is expressed and enforced. Rather than transcending the private as a predicate to politics, feminism politicizes it. For women, the private necessarily transcends the private. If the most private also most "affects society as a whole," the separation between public and private collapses as anything other than potent ideology. The failure of marxism adequately to address intimacy on the one hand, government on the other, is the same failure as the indistinguishability between marxism and liberalism on questions of sexual politics.

Interpreting further areas of law, a feminist theory of the state will reveal that the idealism of liberalism and the materialism of the left have come to much the same for women. Liberal jurisprudence that the law should reflect society and left jurisprudence that all law does or can do is reflect existing social relations will emerge as two guises of objectivist epistemology. If objectivity is the epistemological stance of which women's sexual objectification is the social process, its imposition the paradigm of power in the male form, then the state will appear most relentless in imposing the male point of view when it comes closest to achieving its highest formal criterion of distanced aperspectivity. When it is most ruthlessly neutral, it will be most male; when it is most sex blind, it will be most blind to the sex of the standard being applied. When it most closely conforms to precedent, to "facts," to legislative intent, it will most closely enforce socially male norms and most thoroughly preclude questioning their content as having a point of view at all. Abstract rights will authorize the male experience of the world. The liberal view that law is society's text, its rational mind, expresses this in a normative mode; the traditional left view that the state, and with it the law, is superstructural or epiphenomenal expresses it in an empirical mode. Both rationalize male power by presuming that it does not exist, that equality between the sexes (room for marginal corrections conceded) is society's basic norm and fundamental description. Only feminism grasps the extent to which the opposite is true: that antifeminism is as normative as it is empirical. Once masculinity appears as a specific position, not just as the way things are, its judgments will be revealed in process and procedure, as well as adjudication and legislation. Perhaps the objectivity of the liberal state has made it appear "autonomous of class." Including, but beyond, the bourgeois in liberal legalism, lies what is male about it. However autonomous of class the liberal state may appear, it is not autonomous of sex. Justice will require change, not reflection—a new jurisprudence, a new relation between life and law.

EDITOR'S NOTE

1. *Sexual Harassment of Working Women: A Case of Sex Discrimination* (New Haven: Yale University Press, 1979).

NOTES

For A. D. and D. K. H. In addition to all those whose help is acknowledged in the first part of this article, "Feminism, Marxism, Method, and the State: An Agenda for Theory," *Signs: Journal of Women in Culture and Society* 7, no. 3 (Spring 1982): 515–44 (hereafter cited as part 1), my students and colleagues at Yale, Harvard, and Stanford contributed profoundly to the larger project of which both articles are parts. Among them, Sonia E. Alvarez, Jeanne M. Barkey, Paul Brest, Ruth Colker, Karen E. Davis, Sharon Dyer, Tom Emerson, Daniel Gunther, Patricia Kliendienst Joplin, Mark Kelman, Duncan Kennedy, John Kaplan, Lyn Lemaire, Mira Marshall, Rebecca Mark, Martha Minow, Helen M. A. Neally, Lisa Rofel, Sharon Silverstein, Dean Spencer, Laurence Tribe, and Mary Whisner stand out vividly in retrospect. None of it would have happened without Lu Ann Carter and David Rayson. And thank you, Meg Baldwin, Annie McCombs, and Janet Spector.

Marxism appears in lower case, Black in upper case, for reasons explained in part 1.

1. Much has been made of the distinction between sex and gender. Sex is thought the more biological, gender the more social. The relation of each to sexuality varies. Since I believe sexuality is fundamental to gender and fundamentally social, and that biology is its social meaning in the system of sex inequality, which is a social and political system that does not rest independently on biological differences in any respect, the sex/gender distinction looks like a nature/culture distinction. I use sex and gender relatively interchangeably.

2. This analysis is developed in part 1. I assume here your acquaintance with the arguments there.

3. Male is a social and political concept, not a biological attribute. As I use it, it has *nothing whatever* to do with inherency, preexistence, nature, inevitability, or body as such. It is more epistemological than ontological, undercutting the distinction itself, given male power to conform being with perspective. The perspective from the male standpoint is not always each man's opinion, although most men adhere to it, nonconsciously and without considering it a point of view, as much because it makes sense of their experience (the male experience) as because it is in their interest. It is rational for them. A few men reject it; they pay. Because it is the dominant point of view and defines rationality, women are pushed to see reality in its terms, although this denies their vantage point as women in that it contradicts (at least some of) their lived experience. Women who adopt the male standpoint are passing, epistemologically speaking. This is not uncommon and is rewarded. The intractability of maleness as a form of dominance suggests that social constructs, although they flow from human agency, can be less plastic than nature has proven to be. If experience trying to do so is any guide, it may be easier to change biology than society.

4. In the Bible, to know a woman is to have sex with her. You acquire carnal knowledge. Many scholarly metaphors elaborate the theme of violating boundaries to appropriate from inside to carry off in usable form: "a penetrating observation," "an incisive analysis," "piercing the veil." Mary Ellman writes, "The male mind . . . is assumed to function primarily like a penis. Its fundamental character is seen to be aggression, and this quality is held essential to the highest or best working of the intellect" (*Thinking about Women* [New York: Harcourt Brace Jovanovich, 1968], p. 23). Feminists are beginning to understand that to know has meant to fuck. See Evelyn Fox Keller, "Gender and Science," *Psychoanalysis and Contemporary Thought* 1, no. 3 (1978): 409–33, esp. 413; and Helen Roberts, ed., *Doing Feminist Research* (London: Routledge & Kegan Paul, 1981). The term "to fuck" uniquely captures my meaning because it refers to sexual activity without distinguishing rape from intercourse, At least since Plato's cave, visual metaphors for knowing have been central to Western theories of knowledge, the visual sense prioritized as a mode of verification. The relationship between visual appropriation and objectification is now only beginning to be explored. "The knowledge gained through still photographs will always be . . . a semblance of knowledge, a semblance of wisdom, as the act of taking pictures is a semblance of wisdom, a semblance of rape. The very muteness of what is, hypothetically, comprehensible in photographs is what constitutes their attraction and provocativeness" (Susan Sontag, *On Photography* [New York: Farrar, Straus & Giroux, 1980], p. 24).

5. Feminism aspires to represent the experience of all women as women see it, yet criticizes anti-feminism and misogyny, including when it appears in female form. This tension is compressed in the

epistemic term of art "the standpoint of all women." We are barely beginning to unpack it. Not all women agree with the feminist account of women's situation, nor do all feminists agree with any single rendition of feminism. Authority of interpretation—the claim to speak as a woman—thus becomes methodologically complex and politically crucial for the same reasons. Consider the accounts of their own experience given by right-wing women and lesbian sadomasochists. How can patriarchy be diminishing to women when women embrace and defend their place in it? How can dominance and submission be violating to women when women eroticize it? Now what is the point of view of the experience of all women? Most responses in the name of feminism, stated in terms of method, either (1) simply regard some women's views as "false consciousness," or (2) embrace any version of women's experience that a biological female claims as her own. The first approach treats some women's views as unconscious conditioned reflections of their oppression, complicitous in it. Just as science devalues experience in the process of uncovering its roots, this approach criticizes the substance of a view because it can be accounted for by its determinants. But if both feminism and antifeminism are responses to the condition of women, how is feminism exempt from devalidation by the same account? That feminism is critical, and antifeminism is not, is not enough, because the question is the basis on which we know something is one or the other when women, all of whom share the condition of women, disagree. The false consciousness approach begs this question by taking women's self-reflections as evidence of their stake in their own oppression, when the women whose self-reflections are at issue question whether their condition is oppressed at all. The second response proceeds as if women are free. Or, at least, as if we have considerable latitude to make, or to choose, the meanings if not the determinants of our situation. Or, that the least feminism can do, since it claims to see the world through women's eyes, is to validate the interpretations women choose. Both responses arise because of the unwillingness, central to feminism, to dismiss some women as simply deluded while granting other women the ability to see the truth. These two resolutions echo the object/subject split: objectivity (my consciousness is true, yours false, never mind why) or subjectivity (I know I am right because it feels right to me, never mind why). Thus is determinism answered with transcendence, traditional marxism with traditional liberalism, dogmatism with tolerance. The first approach claims authority on the basis of its lack of involvement, asserting its view independent of whether the described concurs—sometimes because it does not. It also has no account, other than its alleged lack of involvement, of its own ability to provide such an account. How can some women see the truth and other women not? The second approach claims authority on the basis of its involvement. It has no account for different interpretations of the same experience or any way of choosing among conflicting ones, including those between women and men. It tends to assume that women, as we are, have power and are free in exactly the ways feminism, substantively, has found we are not. Thus, the first approach is one-sidedly outside when there is no outside, the second one-sidedly inside when someone (probably a woman) is inside everything, including every facet of sexism, racism, and so on. So our problem is this: the false consciousness approach cannot explain experience as it is experienced by those who experience it. The alternative can only reiterate the terms of that experience. This is only one way in which the object/subject split is fatal to the feminist enterprise.

6. To stress: the feminist criticism is not that the objective stance fails to be truly objective because it has social content, all the better to exorcise that content in the pursuit of the more truly point-of-viewless viewpoint. The criticism is that objectivity is largely accurate to its/the/a world, which world is criticized; and that it becomes more accurate as the power it represents and extends becomes more total. Analogous criticisms have arisen in the natural sciences, without being seen as threatening to the "science of society" project, or calling into question that project's tacit equation between natural and social objects of knowledge. What if we extend Heisenberg's uncertainty principle to social theory? (Werner Heisenberg, *The Physical Principles of the Quantum Theory* [Chicago: University of Chicago Press, 1930], pp. 4, 20, 62–65). What of the axiomatic method after Gödel's proof? (See Ernest Nagel and James R. Newman, *Gödel's Proof* [New York: New York University Press, 1958].)

7. Andrea Dworkin helped me express this.

8. I mean to imply that contemporary feminism that is not methodologically post-marxist is not radical, hence not feminist on this level. For example, to the extent Mary Daly's *Gyn/Ecology: The Metaethics of Radical Feminism* (Boston: Beacon Press, 1978) is idealist in method—meaning that the subordination of women is an idea such that to think it differently is to change it—it is formally liberal no

matter how extreme or insightful. To the extent Shulamith Firestone's analysis (*The Dialectic of Sex.: The Case for Feminist Revolution* [New York: William Morrow & Co., 1972]) rests on a naturalist definition of gender, holding that women are oppressed by our bodies rather than their social meaning, her radicalism, hence her feminism, is qualified. Susan Griffin's *Pornography and Silence: Culture's Revolt against Nature* (San Francisco: Harper & Row, 1982) is classically liberal in all formal respects including, for instance, the treatment of pornography and eros as a distinction that is fundamentally psychological rather than interested, more deeply a matter of good and bad (morality) than of power and powerlessness (politics). Andrea Dworkin's work, esp. *Pornography: Men Possessing Women* (New York: Perigee Books, 1981), and Adrienne Rich's poetry and essays, exemplify feminism as a methodological departure. This feminism seeks to define and pursue women's interest as the fate of all women bound together. It seeks to extract the truth of women's commonalities out of the lie that all women are the same. If whatever a given society defines as sexual defines gender, and if gender means the subordination of women to men, woman means—is not qualified or undercut by—the uniqueness of each woman and the specificity of race, class, time, and place. In this sense, lesbian feminism, the feminism of women of color, and socialist feminism are converging in a feminist politics of sexuality, race, and class, with a left to right spectrum of its own. This politics is struggling for a practice of unity that does not depend upon sameness without dissolving into empty tolerance, including tolerance of all it exists to change whenever that appears embodied in one of us. A new community begins here. As critique, women's communality describes a fact of male supremacy, of sex "in itself" no woman escapes the meaning of being a woman within a gendered social system, and sex inequality is not only pervasive but may be universal (in the sense of never having not been in some form) although "intelligible only in . . . locally specific forms" (M. Z. Rosaldo, "The Use and Abuse of Anthropology: Reflections on Feminism and Cross-cultural Understanding," *Signs: Journal of Women in Culture and Society* 5, no. 3 [Spring 1980]: 389–417, 417). For women to become a sex"for ourselves" moves community to the level of vision.

9. See Karl Klare, "Law-Making as Praxis," *Telos* 12, no. 2 (Summer 1979): 123–35; Judith Shklar, *Legalism* (Cambridge, Mass.: Harvard University Press, 1964). To examine law as state is not to decide that all relevant state behavior occurs in legal texts. I do think that legal decisions expose power on the level of legitimizing rationale, and that law, as words in power, is central in the social erection of the liberal state.

10. Karl Marx, *Capital, Selected Works*, 3 vols. (Moscow: Progress Publishers, 1969), 2:120, 139–40; *The German Ideology* (New York: International Publishers, 1972), pp. 48–52; *Introduction to Critique of Hegel's Philosophy of Right*, ed. Joseph O'Malley, trans. Annette Jolin (Cambridge: Cambridge University Press, 1970), p. 139; Marx to P. V. Annenkov, 1846, in *The Poverty of Philosophy* (New York: International Publishers, 1963), pp. 179–93, 181.

11. I am criticizing Engel's assumptions about sexuality and women's place, and his empiricist method, and suggesting that the two are linked. Friedrich Engels, *Origin of the Family, Private Property and the State* (New York: International Publishers, 1942).

12. Representative works include Fred Block, "The Ruling Class Does Not Rule: Notes on the Marxist Theory of the State," *Socialist Revolution* 33 (May–June 1977): 6–28; Ralph Miliband, *The State in Capitalist Society* (New York: Basic Books, 1969); Nicos Poulantzas, *Classes in Contemporary Capitalism* (London: New Left Books, 1975), and *Political Power and Social Classes* (London: New Left Books, 1975); Goran Therborn, *What Does the Ruling Class Do When It Rules?* (London: New Left Books, 1978); Norberto Bobbio, "Is There a Marxist Theory of the State?" *Telos* 35 (Spring 1978): 5–16. Theda Skocpol, *States and Social Revolution: A Comparative Analysis of France, Russia and China* (Cambridge: Cambridge University Press, 1979), pp. 24–33, ably reviews much of this literature. Applications to law include Isaac Balbus, "Commodity Form and Legal Form: An Essay on the 'Relative Autonomy' of the Law," *Law and Society Review* 11, no. 3 (Winter 1977): 571–88; Mark Tushnet, "A Marxist Analysis of American Law," *Marxist Perspectives* 1, no. 1 (Spring 1978): 96–116; and Klare (n. 9 above).

13. Poulantzas's formulation follows Althusser. Louis Althusser and Etienne Balibar, *Reading Capital*, trans. Ben Brewster (London: New Left Books, 1968). For Poulantzas, the "specific autonomy which is characteristic of the function of the state . . . is the basis of the specificity of the political" (*Political Power and Social Classes* [n. 12 above], pp. 14, 46). Whatever that means. On structural causality between class and state, see p. 14.

14. See Ernesto Laclau's similar criticism of Miliband in *Politics and Ideology in Marxist Theory* (London: New Left Books, 1977), p. 65.

15. See Susan Rae Peterson, "Coercion and Rape: The State as a Male Protection Racket," in *Feminism and Philosophy*, ed. Mary Vetterling-Braggin, Frederick A. Elliston, and Jane English (Totowa, N.J.: Littlefield, Adams & Co., 1977), pp. 360–71; Janet Rifkin, "Toward a Theory of Law Patriarchy," *Harvard Women's Law Journal* 3 (Spring 1980): 83–92.

16 .Johnnie Tillmon, "Welfare Is a Women's Issue," *Liberation News Service* (February 26, 1972), in *America's Working Women: A Documentary History, 1600 to the Present*, ed. Rosalyn Baxandall, Linda Gordon, and Susan Reverby (New York: Vintage Books, 1976), pp. 357–58.

17. Laurence Tribe, "Constitution as Point of View" (Harvard Law School, Cambridge, Mass., 1982, mimeographed), p. 13.

18. Madeleine Gagnon, "Body I," in *New French Feminisms*, ed. Elaine Marks and Isabelle de Courtivron (Amherst: University of Massachusetts Press, 1980), p. 180. Turns on the mirroring trope, which I see as metaphoric analyses of the epistemological/political dimension of objectification, are ubiquitous in feminist writing: "Into the room of the dressing where the walls are covered with mirrors. Where mirrors are like eyes of men, and the women reflect the judgments of mirrors" (Susan Griffin, *Woman and Nature: The Roaring Inside Her* [New York: Harper & Row, 1979] p. 155). See also Mary Daly, *Beyond God the Father: Toward a Philosophy of Women's Liberation* (Boston: Beacon Press, 1975), pp. 195, 197; Sheila Rowbotham, *Women's Consciousness, Man's World* (Harmondsworth: Pelican Books, 1973), pp. 26–29. "She did suffer, the witch/trying to peer round the looking/glass, she forgot/someone was in the way" (Michelene, "Reflexion," quoted in Rowbotham, p. 2). Virginia Woolf wrote the figure around ("So I reflected . . ."), noticing "the necessity that women so often are to men" of serving as a looking glass in which a man can "see himself at breakfast and at dinner at least twice the size he really is." Notice the doubled sexual/gender meaning: "Whatever may be their use in civilized societies, mirrors are essential to all violent and heroic action. That is why Napoleon and Mussolini both insist so emphatically upon the inferiority of women, for if they were not inferior, they would cease to enlarge" (*A Room of One's Own* [New York: Harcourt, Brace & World, 1969], p. 36).

19. Space limitations made it necessary to eliminate sections on pornography, sex discrimination, and abortion. For the same reason, most supporting references, including those to case law, have been cut. The final section accordingly states the systemic implications of the analysis more tentatively than I think them, but as strongly as I felt I could, on the basis of the single substantive examination that appears here.

20. Susan Brownmiller, *Against Our Will: Men, Women and Rape* (New York: Simon & Schuster, 1976), p. 15.

21. Diana E. H. Russell, *The Politics of Rape: The Victim's Perspective* (New York: Stein & Day, 1977); Andrea Medea and Kathleen Thompson, *Against Rape* (New York: Farrar, Straus & Giroux, 1974); Lorenne M. G. Clark and Debra Lewis, *Rape: The Price of Coercive Sexuality* (Toronto: The Women's Press, 1977), Susan Griffen, "Rape: The All-American Crime," *Ramparts* (September 1971), pp. 26–35; Ti-Grace Atkinson connects rape with "the institutions of sexual intercourse" (*Amazon Odyssey: The First Collection of Writings by the Political Pioneer of the Women's Movement* [New York: Links Books, 1974], pp. 13–23). Kalamu ya Salaam, "Rape: A Radical Analysis from the African-American Perspective," in *Our Women Keep Our Skies from Falling* (New Orleans: Nkombo, 1980), pp. 25–40.

22. Racism, clearly, is everyday life. Racism in the United States, by singling out Black men for allegations of rape of white women, has helped obscure the fact that it is men who rape women, disproportionately women of color.

23. "Like other victims, I had problems with sex, after the rape. There was no way that Arthur could touch me that it didn't remind me of having been raped by this guy I never saw" (Carolyn Craven, "No More Victims: Carolyn Craven Talks about Rape, and about What Women and Men Can Do to Stop It," ed. Alison Wells [Berkeley, Calif., 1978, mimeographed]), p. 2.

24. Pamela Foa, "What's Wrong with Rape?" in Vetterling-Braggin, Elliston, and English (n. 15 above), pp. 347–59; Michael Davis, "What's So Bad about Rape?" (paper presented at Annual Meeting of the Academy of Criminal Justice Sciences, Louisville, Ky., March 1982).

25. "Since we would not want to say that there is anything morally wrong with sexual intercourse per se, we conclude that the wrongness of rape rests with the matter of the woman's consent" (Carolyn M. Shafer and Marilyn Frye, "Rape and Respect," in Vetterling-Braggin, Elliston, and English [n. 15 above], p. 334). "Sexual contact is not inherently harmful, insulting or provoking. Indeed, ordinarily it

is something of which we are quite fond. The difference between ordinary sexual intercourse and rape is that ordinary sexual intercourse is more or less consented to while rape is not" (Davis [n. 24 above], p. 12).

26. Sec. 213.0 of the *Model Penal Code* (Official Draft and Revised Comments 1980), like most states, defines rape as sexual intercourse with a female who is not the wife of the perpetrater "with some penetration however slight." Impotency is sometimes a defense. Michigan's gender-neutral sexual assault statute includes penetration by objects (sec. 520a[h]; 520[b]). See *Model Penal Code*, annotation to sec. 213.1(d) (Official Draft and Revised Comments 1980).

27. Although it is true that men possess women and that bodies are, socially, men's things, I have not analyzed rape as men treating women like property. In the manner of many socialist-feminist adaptations of marxian categories to women's situation, that analysis short-circuits analysis of rape as male sexuality and presumes rather than develops links between sex and class. We need to rethink sexual dimensions of property as well as property dimensions of sexuality.

28. For an excellent summary of the current state of the marital exemption, see Joanne Schulman, "State-by-State Information on Marital Rape Exemption Laws," in *Rape in Marriage*, Diana E. H. Russell (New York: Macmillan, 1982), pp. 375–81.

29. On "social interaction as an element of consent," in a voluntary social companion context, see *Model Penal Code*, sec. 213.1. "The prior *social* interaction is an indicator of consent in addition to actor's and victim's *behavioral* interaction during the commission of the offense" (Wallace Loh, "Q: What Has Reform of Rape Legislation Wrought? A: Truth in Criminal Labeling," *Journal of Social Issues* 37, no. 4 [1981] : 28–52, 47). Perhaps consent should be an affirmative defense, pleaded and proven by the defendant.

30. Pauline Bart found that women were more likely to be raped—that is, less able to stop a rape in progress—when they knew their assailant, particularly when they had a prior or current sexual relationship ("A Study of Women Who Both Were Raped and Avoided Rape," *Journal of Social Issues* 37, no. 4 [1981]: 123–37, 132). See also Linda Belden,"Why Women Do Not Report Sexual Assault" (City of Portland Public Service Employment Program, Portland Women's Crisis Line, Portland, Ore., March 1979, mimeographed); Diana E. H. Russell and Nancy Howell, "The Prevalence of Rape in the United States Revisited," *Signs: Journal of Women in Culture and Society*, vol. 8, no. 4 (1983); and Menachem Amir, *Patterns in Forcible Rape* (Chicago: University of Chicago Press, 1971), pp. 229–52.

31. Answer Brief for Plaintiff-Appellee at 10, People v. Brown, 632 P.2d 1025 (Colo. 1981).

32. Brown, 632 P.2d at 1027 (citing Comment, "Rape and Battery between Husband and Wife,"*Stanford Law Review* 6 [1954]: 719–28, 719, 725).

33. Brownmiller (n. 20 above), pp. 8, 196, 400–407, 427–36.

34. See Carol Pateman, "Women and Consent," *Political Theory* 8, no. 2 (May 1980): 149–68.

35. Brownmiller (n. 20 above), p. 5.

36. Shafer and Frye (n. 25 above), p. 334. Battery of wives has been legally separated from marital rape not because assault by a man's fist is so different from assault by a penis. Both seem clearly violent. I am suggesting that both are also sexual. Assaults are often precipitated by women's noncompliance with gender requirements. See R. Emerson Dobash and Russell Dobash, *Violence against Wives: A Case against the Patriarchy* (New York: Free Press, 1979), pp. 14–20. Nearly all incidents occur in the home, most in the kitchen or bedroom. Most murdered women are killed by their husbands, most in the bedroom. The battery cycle accords with the rhythm of heterosexual sex (see Leonore Walker, *The Battered Woman* [New York: Harper & Row Publishers, 1979], pp. 19–20). The rhythm of lesbian S/M appears similar (Samois, eds. *Coming to Power* [Palo Alto, Calif.: Up Press, 1981]). Perhaps most interchange between genders, but especially violent ones, make sense in sexual terms. However, the larger issue for the relation between sexuality and gender, hence sexuality and violence generally, including both war and violence against women, is: What *is* heterosexuality? If it is the erotization of dominance and submission, altering the participants' gender is comparatively incidental. If it is males over females, gender matters independently. Since I see heterosexuality as the fusion of the two, but with gender a social outcome (such that the acted upon is feminized, is the "girl" regardless of sex, the actor correspondingly masculinized), battery appears sexual on a deeper level. In baldest terms, sexuality is violent, so violence is sexual, violence against women doubly so. If this is so, wives are beaten as well as raped, *as women*—as the acted upon, as gender, meaning sexual, objects. It further follows that all acts *by anyone*

which treat a woman according to her object label "woman" are *sexual* acts. The extent to which sexual acts are acts of objectification remains a question of our account of our freedom to make our own meanings. It is clear, at least, that it is centering sexuality upon genitality that distinguishes battery from rape at exaclty the juncture that both the law, and seeing rape as violence not sex, does.

37. Even when nonconsent is not a legal element of the offense (as in Michigan), juries tend to infer rape from evidence of force or resistance.

38. This is apparently true of undetected as well as convicted rapists. Samuel David Smithyman's sample, composed largely of the former, contained self-selected respondents to his ad, which read: "Are you a rapist? Researchers Interviewing Anonymously by Phone to Protect Your Identity. Call. . . . " Presumably those who chose to call defined their acts as rapes, at least at the time of responding ("The Undetected Rapist" [Ph.D. diss., Claremont Graduate School, 1978], pp. 54–60, 63–76, 80–90, 97–107).

39. "Probably the single most used cry of rapist to victim is 'You bitch . . . slut . . . you know you want it. You *all* want it' and afterward, 'there now, you really enjoyed it, didn't you?' " (Nancy Gager and Cathleen Schurr, *Sexual Assualt: Confronting Rape in America* [New York: Grosset & Dunlap, 1976], p. 244).

40. See Director of Public Prosecutions v. Morgan, 2411 E.R.H.L. 347 (1975); Pappajohn v. The Queen, 11 D.L.R. 3d 1 (1980); People v. Mayberry, 15 Cal. 3d 143, 542 P.2d 1337 (1975).

41. Richard H. S. Tur, "Rape: Reasonableness and Time," *Oxford Journal of Legal Studies* 3 (Winter 1981): 432–41, 441. Tur, in the context of the Morgan and Pappajohn cases, says the "law ought not to be astute to equate wickedness and wishful, albeit mistaken, thinking" (p. 437). In feminist analysis, a rape is not an isolated or individual or moral transgression but a terrorist act within a systematic context of group subjection, like lynching.

42. See Silke Volgelmann-Sine et al., "Sex Differences in Feelings Attributed to a Woman in Situations Involving Coercion and Sexual Advances," *Journal of Personality* 47, no. 3 (September 1979): 420–31, esp. 429–30.

43. Note, "Forcible and Statutory Rape: An Exploration of the Operation and Objectives of the Consent Standard," *Yale Law Journal* 62 (1952): 55–56.

44. A similar analysis of sexual harassment suggests that women have such "power" only so long as we behave according to male definitions of female desirability, that is, only so long as we accede the definition of our sexuality (hence, ourselves, as gender female) to male terms. We have this power only so long as we remain powerless.

45. Peter Gabel, "Reification in Legal Reasoning" (New College Law School, San Francisco, 1980, mimeographed), p.3.

46. Rawls's "original position," for instance, is a version of my objective standpoint (John Rawls, *A Theory of Justice* [Cambridge, Mass.: Harvard University Press, 1971]). Not only apologists for the liberal state, but also some of its most trenchant critics, see a real distinction between the rule of law and absolute arbitrary force. E. P. Thompson, *Whigs and Hunters: The Origin of the Black Act* (New York: Pantheon Books, 1975), pp. 258–69. Douglas Hay argues that making and enforcing certain acts as illegal reinforces a structure of subordination ("Property, Authority, and the Criminal Law," in *Albion's Fatal Tree: Crime and Society in Eighteenth Century England*, ed. D. Hay et al. [New York: Pantheon Books, 1975], pp. 17–31). Michael D. A. Freeman ("Violence against Women: Does the Legal System Provide Solutions or Itself Constitute the Problem?" [Madison, Wis., 1980, mimeographed], p. 12, n. 161) applies this argument to domestic battery of women. Here I extend it to women's situation as a whole, without suggesting that the analysis can *end* there.

47. S. D. Warren and L. D. Brandeis, "The Right to Privacy," *Harvard Law Review* 4 (1890): 193–205.

48. Tom Gerety, "Redefining Privacy," *Harvard Civil Right—Civil Liberties Law Review* 12, no. 2 (Spring 1977): 236.

49. Harris v. McRae, 448 U. S. 287 (1980), which holds that withholding public funds for abortions does not violate the federal constitutional right to privacy, illustrates. See Zillah Eisenstein, *The Radical Future of Liberal Feminism* (New York: Longman, 1981), p. 240.

50. Robeson v. Rochester Folding Box Co., 171 NY 538 (1902); Cooley, *Torts*, sec. 135, 4th ed. (Chicago: Callaghan & Co., 1932).

51. This argument learned a lot from Tom Grey's article, "Eros, Civilization and the Burger Court," *Law and Contemporary Problems* 43, no. 3 (Summer 1980): 83–99.

52. Herbert Marcuse, "Repressive Tolerance," in *A Critique of Pure Tolerance*, ed. Robert Paul Wolff, Barrington Moore, Jr., and Herbert Marcuse (Boston: Beacon Press, 1965), pp. 81–117, esp. p. 91.

53. Adrienne Rich, "Conditions for Work: The Common World of Women," in *Working It Out: Twenty-three Women Writers, Artists, Scientists, and Scholars Talk about Their Lives and Work*, ed. Sara Ruddick and Pamela Daniels (New York: Pantheon Books, 1977), esp. pp. xiv-xxiv, p. xiv.

XI.

THE FEMINIST STANDPOINT
DEVELOPING THE GROUND FOR A SPECIFICALLY FEMINIST HISTORICAL MATERIALISM

Nancy C. M. Hartsock

In this essay, political theorist Nancy Hartsock explains the grounds for a distinctive materialist and feminist theory of knowledge.[1] Hartsock's theory of knowledge shares affinities with Dorothy Smith's "standpoint of women"; it contrasts with the explanation Marcia Millman and Rosabeth Moss Kanter gave of how research inspired by the women's movement increases our knowledge of social life.

Hartsock argues that the "sexual division of labor" uniquely makes available to women a vision of the real social relations that is unavailable to men insofar as they (intentionally or unintentionally) benefit from the exploitation of women. She stresses the importance of political activism not just for moral/political reasons, but also for *scientific* reasons. It is only through struggle against an exploitative system, such as male domination, that one can come to understand its strength and resilience. After all, it is only because we can see how relatively little has been accomplished by eliminating formal laws and principles that are sexist (though it certainly has been worthwhile to do so) that we can understand what else must be changed—the division of labor in housework, in childcare, in wage labor, men's and women's psychological makeups, and so forth—if women are to be emancipated. It was political struggles to change the laws that revealed the tentacles of patriarchy deep in the economy, our psyches, and so forth. Are feminist politics part of feminist research "methods"?

Hartsock's analysis borrows heavily from Marxist epistemology. While some readers will think she transforms the Marxist framework so deeply that it is not clearly Marxist at all, others will find it far too Marxist! As usual, we discover that we cannot "add women" to the existing categories of Western thought without deeply challenging the categories themselves—in this case, Marxist categories.

The clarity of Hartsock's powerful analysis enables us to formulate some questions feminism should be asking. Shouldn't there be an "excolonial" epistemological standpoint for reasons analogous to those advanced for a feminist standpoint? What should be the relationship between the two? (After all, most of the world's women are not white.) Should we feel completely comfortable with claims that feminists (or any other group) can discover the one, true story about the "real relations among human beings?"[2]

The power of the Marxian critique of class domination stands as an implicit suggestion that feminists should consider the advantages of adopting a historical materialist approach to understanding phallocratic domination. A specifically feminist historical materialism might enable us to lay bare the laws of tendency which constitute the structure of patriarchy over time and to follow its development in and through the Western class societies on which Marx's interest centered. A feminist materialism might in addition enable us to expand the Marxian account to include all human activity rather than focussing on activity more characteristic of males in capitalism. The development of such a historical and materialist account is a very large task, one which requires the political and theoretical contributions of many feminists. Here I will address only the question of the epistemological underpinnings such a materialism would require. Most specifically, I will attempt to develop, on the methodological base provided by Marxian theory, an important epistemological tool for understanding and opposing all forms of domination—a feminist standpoint.

Despite the difficulties feminists have correctly pointed to in Marxian theory, there are several reasons to take over much of Marx's approach. First, I have argued elsewhere that Marx's method and the method developed by the contemporary women's movement recapitulate each other in important ways.[1] This makes it possible for feminists to take over a number of aspects of Marx's method. Here, I will adopt his distinction between appearance and essence, circulation and production, abstract and concrete, and use these distinctions between dual levels of reality to work out the theoretical forms appropriate to each level when viewed not from the standpoint of the proletariat but from a specifically feminist standpoint. In this process I will explore and expand the Marxian argument that socially mediated interaction with nature in the process of production shapes both human beings and theories of knowledge. The Marxian category of labor, including as it does both interaction with other humans and with the natural world, can help to cut through the dichotomy of nature and culture, and, for feminists, can help to avoid the false choice of characterizing the situation of women as either "purely natural" or "purely social." As embodied humans we are of course inextricably both natural and social, though feminist theory to date has, for important strategic reasons, concentrated attention on the social aspect.

I set off from Marx's proposal that a correct vision of class society is available from only one of the two major class positions in capitalist society. On the basis of this metatheoretical claim, he was able to develop a powerful critique of class domination. The power of Marx's critique depended on the epistemology and ontology supporting this metatheoretical claim. Feminist Marxists and materialist feminists more generally have argued that the position of women is structurally different from that of men, and that the lived realities of women's lives are profoundly different from those of men.[2] They have not yet, however, given sustained attention to the epistemological consequences of such a claim. Faced with the depth of Marx's critique of capitalism, feminist analysis, as Iris Young has correctly pointed out, often

accepts the traditional Marxian theory of production relations, historical change, and analysis of the structure of capitalism in basically unchanged form. It rightly criticizes that theory for being essentially gender-blind, and hence seeks to supplement Marxist theory of capitalism with feminist theory of a system of male domination. Taking this route, however, tacitly endorses the traditional Marxian position that "the woman question" is auxiliary to the central questions of a Marxian theory of society.[3]

By setting off from the Marxian metatheory I am implicitly suggesting that this, rather than his critique of capitalism, can be most helpful to feminists. I will explore some of the epistemological consequences of claiming that women's lives differ structurally from those of men. In particular, I will suggest that like the lives of proletarians according to Marxian theory, women's lives make available a particular and privileged vantage point on male supremacy, a vantage point which can ground a powerful critique of the phallocratic institutions and ideology which constitute the capitalist form of patriarchy. After a summary of the nature of a standpoint as an epistemological device, I will address the question of whether one can discover a feminist standpoint on which to ground a specifically feminist historical materialism. I will suggest that the sexual division of labor forms the basis for such a standpoint and will argue that on the basis of the structures which define women's activity as contributors to subsistence and as mothers one could begin, though not complete, the construction of such an epistemological tool. I hope to show how just as Marx's understanding of the world from the standpoint of the proletariat enabled him to go beneath bourgeois ideology, so a feminist standpoint can allow us to understand patriarchal institutions and ideologies as perverse inversions of more humane social relations.

The Nature of a Standpoint

A standpoint is not simply an interested position (interpreted as bias) but is interested in the sense of being engaged. It is true that a desire to conceal real social relations can contribute to an obscurantist account, and it is also true that the ruling gender and class have material interests in deception. A standpoint, however, carries with it the contention that there are some perspectives on society from which, however well-intentioned one may be, the real relations of humans with each other and with the natural world are not visible. This contention should be sorted into a number of distinct epistemological and political claims: (1) Material life (class position in Marxist theory) not only structures but sets limits on the understanding of social relations. (2) If material life is structured in fundamentally opposing ways for two different groups, one can expect that the vision of each will represent an inversion of the other, and in systems of domination the vision available to the rulers will be both partial and perverse. (3) The vision of the ruling class (or gender) structures the material relations in which all parties are forced to participate, and therefore cannot be dismissed as simply false. (4) In consequence, the vision available to the oppressed group must be struggled for and represents an achievement which requires both science to see beneath the surface of the social relations in which all are forced to participate, and the education which can only grow from struggle to change those relations. (5) As an engaged vision, the understanding of the oppressed, the adoption of a standpoint exposes the real relations among human beings as inhuman, points beyond the present, and carries a historically liberatory role.

The concept of a standpoint structures epistemology in a particular way. Rather than a simple dualism, it posits a duality of levels of reality, of which the deeper level or essence both includes and explains the "surface" or appearance, and indicates the logic by means of which the appearance inverts and distorts the deeper reality. In addition, the concept of a standpoint depends on the assumption that epistemology grows in a complex and contradictory way from material life. Any effort to develop a standpoint must take seriously Marx's injunction that "all mysteries which lead theory to mysticism find their rational solution in human practice and in the comprehension of this practice."[4] Marx held that the source both for the proletarian standpoint and the critique of capitalism it makes possible is to be found in practical activity itself. The epistemological (and even ontological) significance of human activity is made clear in Marx's argument not only that persons are active but that reality itself consists of "sensuous human activity, practice."[5] Thus Marx can speak of products as crystallized or congealed human activity or work, of products as conscious human activity in another form. He can state that even plants, animals, light, etc. constitute theoretically a part of human consciousness, and a part of human life and activity.[6] As Marx and Engels summarize their position,

> As individuals express their life, so they are. What they are, therefore, coincides with their production, both with *what* they produce and with *how* they produce. The nature of individuals thus depends on the material conditions determining their production.[7]

This starting point has definite consequences for Marx's theory of knowledge. If humans are not what they eat but what they do, especially what they do in the course of production of subsistence, each means of producing subsistence should be expected to carry with it *both* social relations *and* relations to the world of nature which express the social under-standing contained in that mode of production. And in any society with systematically divergent practical activities, one should expect the growth of logically divergent world views. That is, each division of labor, whether by gender or class, can be expected to have consequences for knowledge. Class society, according to Marx, does produce this dual vision in the form of the ruling class vision and the understanding available to the ruled.

On the basis of Marx's description of the activity of commodity exchange in capitalism, the ways in which the dominant categories of thought simply express the mystery of the commodity form have been pointed out. These include a dependence on quantity, duality, and opposition of nature to culture, a rigid separation of mind and body, intention and behavior.[8] From the perspective of exchange, where commodities differ from each other only quantitatively, it seems absurd to suggest that labor power differs from all other commodities. The sale and purchase of labor power from the perspective of capital is simply a contract between free agents, in which "the agreement [the parties] come to is but the form in which they give legal expression of their common will." It is a relation of equality,

> because each enters into relation with the other, as with a simple owner of commodities, and they exchange equivalent for equivalent. . . . The only force that brings them together and puts them in relation with each other, is the selfishness, the gain and the private interests of each. Each looks to himself only, and no one troubles himself about the rest, and just because they do so, do they all, in accordance with the pre-established harmony of things, or under the auspices of an all shrewd providence, work together to their mutual advantage, for the common weal and in the interest of all.

This is the only description available within the sphere of circulation or exchange of commodities, or as Marx might put it, at the level of appearance. But at the level of production, the world looks far different. As Marx puts it,

> On leaving this sphere of simple circulation or of exchange of commodities . . . we can perceive a change in the physiognomy of our *dramatis personae*. He who before was the money-owner, now strides in front as capitalist; the possessor of labor-power follows as his laborer. The one with an air of importance, smirking, intent on business; the other timid and holding back, like one who is bringing his own hide to market and has nothing to expect but—a hiding.

This is a vastly different account of the social relations of the buyer and seller of labor power.[9] Only by following the two into the realm of production and adopting the point of view available to the worker could Marx uncover what is really involved in the purchase and sale of labor power—i.e., uncover the process by which surplus value is produced and appropriated by the capitalist, and the means by which the worker is systematically disadvantaged.[10]

If one examines Marx's account of the production and extraction of surplus value, one can see in it the elaboration of each of the claims contained in the concept of a standpoint. First, the contention that material life structures understanding points to the importance of the epistemological consequences of the opposed models of exchange and production. It is apparent that the former results in a dualism based on both the separation of exchange from use, and on the positing of exchange as the only important side of the dichotomy. The epistemological result, if one follows through the implications of exchange, is a series of opposed and hierarchical dualities—mind/body, ideal/material, social/natural, self/other—even a kind of solipsism—replicating the devaluation of use relative to exchange. The proletarian and Marxian valuation of use over exchange on the basis of involvement in production, in labor, results in a dialectical rather than dualist epistemology: the dialectical and interactive unity (distinction within a unity) of human and natural worlds, mind and body, ideal and material, and the cooperation of self and other (community).

As to the second claim of a standpoint, a Marxian account of exchange vs. production indicates that the epistemology growing from exchange not only inverts that present in the process of production but in addition is both partial and fundamentally perverse. The real point of the production of goods and services is, after all, the continuation of the species, a possibility dependent on their use. The epistemology embodied in exchange then, along with the social relations it expresses, not only occupies only one side of the dualities it constructs, but also reverses the proper ordering of any hierarchy in the dualisms: use is primary, not exchange.

The third claim for a standpoint indicates a recognition of the power realities operative in a community, and points to the ways the ruling group's vision may be *both* perverse *and* made real by means of that group's power to define the terms for the community as a whole. In the Marxian analysis, this power is exercised in both control of ideological production, and in the real participation of the worker in exchange. The dichotomous epistemology which grows from exchange cannot be dismissed either as simply false or as an epistemology relevant to only a few: the worker as well as the capitalist engages in the purchase and sale of commodities, and if material life structures consciousness, this cannot fail to have an effect. This leads into the fourth claim for a standpoint—that it is achieved rather than obvious, a mediated rather than immediate understanding. Because the ruling group controls the means of mental as well is physical production, the production of ideals as well as goods, the standpoint of the oppressed represents an achievement both of science (analysis) and of political struggle on the basis of which this analysis can be conducted.

Finally, because it provides the basis for revealing the perversion of both life and thought, the inhumanity of human relations, a standpoint can be the basis for moving beyond these relations. In the historical context of Marx's theory, the engaged vision available to the producers, by drawing out the potentiality available in the actuality, that is, by following up the possibility of abundance capitalism creates, leads towards transcendence. Thus the proletariat is the only class which has the possibility of creating a classless society. It can do this simply (!) by generalizing its own condition, that is, by making society itself a propertyless producer.[11]

These are the general characteristics of the standpoint of the proletariat. What guidance can feminists take from this discussion? I hold that the powerful vision of both the perverseness and reality of class domination made possible by Marx's adoption of the standpoint of the proletariat suggests that a specifically feminist standpoint could allow for a much more profound critique of phallocratic ideologies and institutions than has yet been achieved. The effectiveness of Marx's critique grew from its uncompromising focus on material life activity, and I propose here to set out from the Marxian contention that not only are persons active, but that reality itself consists of "sensuous human activity, practice." But rather than beginning with men's labor, I will focus on women's life activity and on the institutions which structure that activity in order to raise the question of whether this activity can form the ground for a distinctive standpoint, that is, to determine whether it meets the requirements for a feminist standpoint. (I use the term, "feminist" rather than "female" here to indicate both the achieved character of a standpoint and that a standpoint by definition carries a liberatory potential.)

Women's work in every society differs systematically from men's. I intend to pursue the suggestion that this division of labor is the first and in some societies the only division of labor, and moreover, that it is central to the organization of social labor more generally. On the basis of an account of the sexual division of labor, one should be able to begin to explore the oppositions and differences between women's and men's activity and their consequences for epistemology. While I cannot attempt a complete account, I will put forward a schematic and simplified account of the sexual division of labor and its consequences for epistemology. I will sketch out a kind of ideal type of the social relations and world view characteristic of male and female activity in order to explore the epistemology contained in the institutionalized sexual division of labor. In so doing, I do not mean to attribute this vision to individual women or men any more than Marx (or Lukacs) meant their theory of class consciousness to apply to any particular worker or group of workers. My focus is instead on institutionalized social practices and on the specific epistemology and ontology manifested by the institutionalized sexual division of labor. Individuals, as individuals, may change their activity in ways which move them outside the outlook embodied in these institutions, but such a move can be significant only when it occurs at the level of society as a whole.

I will discuss the "sexual division of labor" rather than the "gender division of labor" to stress, first my belief that the division of labor between women and men cannot be reduced to purely social dimensions. One must distinguish between what Sara Ruddick has termed "invariant and *nearly* unchangeable" features of human life, and those which despite being "*nearly* universal" are "certainly changeable."[12] Thus, the fact that women and not men *bear* children is not (yet) a social choice, but that women and not men rear children in a society structured by compulsory heterosexuality and male dominance is clearly a societal choice. A second reason to use the term "sexual division of labor" is to keep hold of the bodily aspect of existence—perhaps to grasp it over-firmly in an effort to keep it from evaporating altogether. There is some biological, bodily component to human existence. But its size and substantive content will remain unknown until at least the certainly changeable aspects of the sexual division of labor are altered.

On a strict reading of Marx, of course, my enterprise here is illegitimate. While on the one hand, Marx remarked that the very first division of labor occurred in sexual intercourse, he argues that the division of labor only becomes "truly such" when the division of mental and manual labor appears. Thus, he dismisses the sexual division of labor as of no analytic importance. At the same time, a reading of other remarks—such as his claim that the mental/manual division of labor is based on the "natural" division of labor in the family—would seem to support the legitimacy of my attention to the sexual division of labor and even add weight to the radical feminist argument that capitalism is an outgrowth of male dominance, rather than vice versa.

On the basis of a schematic account of the sexual division of labor, I will begin to fill in the specific content of the feminist standpoint and begin to specify how women's lives structure an understanding of social relations, that is, begin to follow out the epistemological consequences of the sexual division of labor. In addressing the institutionalized sexual division of labor, I propose to lay aside the important differences among women across race and class boundaries and instead search for central commonalities. I take some justification from the fruitfulness of Marx's similar strategy in constructing a simplified, two class, two man model in which everything was exchanged at its value. Marx's schematic account in Volume 1 of *Capital* left out of account such factors as imperialism, the differential wages, work, and working conditions of the Irish, the differences between women, men, and children, and so on. While all of these factors are important to the analysis of contemporary capitalism, none changes either Marx's theories of surplus value or alienation, two of the most fundamental features of the Marxian analysis of capitalism. My effort here takes a similiar form in an attempt to move toward a theory of the extraction and appropriation of women's activity and women themselves. Still, I adopt this strategy with some reluctance, since it contains the danger of making invisible the experience of lesbians or women of color.[13] At the same time, I recognize that the effort to uncover a feminist standpoint assumes that there are some things common to all women's lives in Western class societies.

The feminist standpoint which emerges through an examination of women's activities is related to the proletarian standpoint, but deeper going. Women and workers inhabit a world in which the emphasis is on change rather than stasis, a world characterized by interaction with natural substances rather than separation from nature, a world in which quality is more important than quantity, a world in which the unification of mind and body is inherent in the activities performed. Yet, there are some important differences, differences marked by the fact that the proletarian (if male) is immersed in this world only during the time his labor power is being used by the capitalist. If, to paraphrase Marx, we follow the worker home from the factory, we can once again perceive a change in the *dramatis personae*. He who before followed behind as the worker, timid and holding back, with nothing to expect but a hiding, now strides in front while a third person, not specifically present in Marx's account of the transaction between capitalist and worker (both of whom are male) follows timidly behind, carrying groceries, baby, and diapers.

The Sexual Division of Labor

Women's activity as institutionalized has a double aspect—their contribution to subsistence, and their contribution to childrearing. Whether or not all of us do both, women as a sex are institutionally responsible for producing both goods and human beings and all women are forced to become the kinds of people who can do both. Although the nature of women's contribution to subsistence varies immensely over time and space, my primary focus here is on capitalism, with a secondary focus on the Western class societies which preceded it.[14] In capitalism, women contribute both production for wages and production of goods in the home, that is, they like men sell their labor power and produce both commodities and surplus value, and produce use-values in the home. Unlike men, however, women's lives are institutionally defined by their production of use-values in the home.[15] And here we begin to encounter the narrowness of the Marxian concept of production. Women's production of use-values in the home has not been well understood by socialists. It is no surprise to feminists that Engels, for example, simply asks how women can continue to do the work in the home and also work in production outside the home. Marx too takes for granted women's responsibility for household labor. He repeats, as if it were his own, the question of a Belgian factory inspector: If a mother works for wages, "how will [the household's] internal economy be cared for; who will look after the young children; who will get ready the meals, do the washing and mending?"[16]

Let us trace both the outlines and the consequences of woman's dual contribution to subsistence in capitalism. Women's labor, like that of the male worker, is contact with material necessity. Their contribution to subsistence, like that of the male worker, involves them in a world in which the relation to nature and to concrete human requirements is central, both in the form of interaction with natural substances whose quality, rather than quantity, is important to the production of meals, clothing, etc., and in the form of close attention to the natural changes in these substances. Women's labor both for wages and even more in household production involves a unification of mind and body for the purpose of transforming natural substances into socially defined goods. This too is true of the labor of the male worker.

There are, however, important differences. First, women as a group work more than men. We are all familiar with the phenomenon of the "double day," and with indications that women work many more hours per week than men.[17] Second, a larger proportion of women's labor time is devoted to the production of use values than men's. Only some of the goods women produce are commodities (however much they live in a society structured by commodity production and exchange). Third, women's production is structured by repetition in a different way than men's. While repetition for both the woman and the male worker may take the form of production of the same object, over and over—whether apple pies or brake linings—women's work in housekeeping involves a repetitious cleaning.[18]

Thus, the male worker in the process of production, is involved in contact with necessity, and interchange with nature as well as with other human beings but the process of production or work does not consume his whole life. The activity of a woman in the home as well as the work she does for wages keeps her continually in contact with a world of qualities and change. Her immersion in the world of use—in concrete, many-qualitied, changing material processes—is more complete than his. And if life itself consists of sensuous activity, the vantage point available to women on the basis of their contribution to subsistence represents an intensification and deepening of the materialist world view and consciousness available to the producers of commodities in capitalism, an intensification of class consciousness. The availability of this outlook to even non-working-class women has been strikingly formulated by Marilyn French in *The Women's Room*.

Washing the toilet used by three males, and the floor and walls around it, is, Mira thought, coming face to face with necessity. And that is why women were saner than men, did not come up with the mad, absurd schemes men developed; they were in touch with necessity, they had to wash the toilet bowl and floor.[19]

The focus on women's subsistence activity rather than men's leads to a model in which the capitalist (male) lives a life structured completely by commodity exchange and not at all by production, and at the furthest distance from contact with concrete material life. The male worker marks a way station on the path to the other extreme of the constant contact with material necessity in women's contribution to subsistence. There are, of course important differences along the lines of race and class. For example, working class men seem to do more domestic labor than men higher up in the class structure—car repairs, carpentry, etc. And until very recently, the wage work done by most women of color replicated the housework required by their own households. Still, there are commonalities present in the institutionalized sexual division of labor which make women responsible for both housework and wage work.

The female contribution to subsistence, however, represents only a part of women's labor. Women also produce/reproduce men (and other women) on both a daily and a long-term basis. This aspect of women's "production" exposes the deep inadequacies of the concept of production as a description of women's activity. One does not (cannot) produce another human being in anything like the way one produces an object such as a chair. Much more is involved, activity which cannot easily be dichotomized into play or work. Helping another to develop, the gradual relinquishing of control, the experience of the human limits of one's action—all these are important features of women's activity as mothers. Women as mothers even more than as workers, are institutionally involved in processes of change and growth, and more than workers, must understand the importance of avoiding excessive control in order to help others grow.[20] The activity involved is far more complex than the instrumental working with others to transform objects. (Interestingly, much of women's wage work—nursing, social work, and some secretarial jobs in particular—requires and depends on the relational and interpersonal skills women learned by being mothered by someone of the same sex.)

This aspect of women's activity too is not without consequences. Indeed, it is in the production of men by women and the appropriation of this labor and women themselves by men that the opposition between feminist and masculinist experience and outlook is rooted, and it is here that features of the proletarian vision are enhanced and modified for the woman and diluted for the man. The female experience in reproduction represents a unity with nature which goes beyond the proletarian experience of interchange with nature. As another theorist has put it, "reproductive labor might be said to combine the functions of the architect and the bee: like the architect, parturitive woman knows what she is doing; like the bee, she cannot help what she is doing." And just as the worker's acting on the external world changes both the world and the worker's nature, so too "a new life changes the world and the consciousness of the woman."[21] In addition, in the process of producing human beings, relations with others may take a variety of forms with deeper significance than simple cooperation with others for common goals—forms which range from a deep unity with another through the many-leveled and changing connections mothers experience with growing children. Finally, the female experience in bearing and rearing children involves a unity of mind and body more profound than is possible in the worker's instrumental activity.

Motherhood in the large sense, i.e., motherhood as an institution rather than experience, including pregnancy and the preparation for motherhood almost all female children receive as socialization, results in the construction of female existence as centered with a complex relational nexus.[22] One aspect of this relational existence is centered on the experience of living in a female rather than male body. There are a series of boundary challenges inherent in the female physiology—challenges which make it impossible to maintain rigid separation from the object world. Menstruation, coitus, pregnancy, childbirth, lactation—all represent challenges to bodily boundaries.[23] Adrienne Rich has described the experience of pregnancy as one in which the embryo was both inside and

> daily more separate, on its way to becoming separate from me and of-itself. In early pregnancy the stirring of the fetus felt like ghostly tremors of my own body, later like the movements of a being imprisoned in me; but both sensations were *my* sensations, contributing to my own sense of physical and psychic space.[24]

In turn, the fact that women but not men are primarily responsible for young children means that the infant first experiences itself as not fully differentiated from the mother, and then as an I in relation to an It that it later comes to know as female.[25]

Jane Flax and Nancy Chodorow have argued that the object relations school of psychoanalytic theory puts forward a materialist psychology, one which I propose to treat as a kind of empirical hypothesis. If the account of human development provided by object relations is correct, one ought to expect to find consequences—both psychic, and social. According to object relations theory, the process of differentiation from a woman by both male and female children reinforces boundary confusion in female egos and boundary strengthening in males. Individuation is far more conflictual for male than for female children, in part because both mother and son experience the other as a definite "other." The experience of oneness on the part of both mother and infant seems to last longer with girls.[26]

The complex relational world inhabited by women has its start in the experience and resolution of the oedipal crisis, cleanly resolved for the boy, whereas the girl is much more likely to retain both parents as love objects. The nature of the crisis itself differs by sex: the boy's love for the mother is an extension of mother-infant unity and thus essentially threatening to his ego and independence. Male ego-formation necessarily requires repressing this first relation and negating the mother.[27] In contrast, the girls' love for the father is less threatening both because it occurs outside this unity and because it occurs at a later stage of development. For boys, the central issue to be resolved concerns gender identification; for girls the issue is psychosexual development.[28] Chodorow concludes that girls' gradual emergence from the oedipal period takes place in such a way that empathy is built into their primary definition of self, and they have a variety of capacities for experiencing another's needs or feelings as their own. Put another way girls, because of female parenting, are less differentiated from others than boys, more continuous with and related to the external object world. They are differently oriented to their inner object world as well.[29]

The more complex female relational world is reinforced by the process of socialization. Girls learn roles from watching their mothers; boys must learn roles from rules which structure the life of an absent male figure. Girls can identify with a concrete example present in daily life; boys must identify with an abstract set of maxims only occasionally concretely present in the form of the father. Thus, not only do girls learn roles with more interpersonal and relational skills, but the process of role learning itself is embodied in the concrete relation with the mother. The male, in contrast, must identify with an abstract, cultural stereotype and learn abstract behaviors not attached to a well-known person. Masculinity is idealized by boys whereas femininity is concrete for girls.[30]

Women and men, then, grow up with personalities affected by different boundary experiences, differently constructed and experienced inner and outer worlds, and preoccupations with different relational issues. This early experience forms an important ground for the female sense of self as connected to the world and the male sense of self as separate, distinct, and even disconnected. By retaining the preoedipal attachment to the mother, girls come to define and experience themselves as continuous with others. In sum, girls enter adulthood with a more complex layering of affective ties and a rich, ongoing inner set of object relations. Boys, with a simpler oedipal situation and a clear and early resolution, have repressed ties to another. As a result, women define and experience themselves relationally and men do not.[31]

Abstract Masculinity and the Feminist Standpoint

This excursion into psychoanalytic theory has served to point to the differences in the male and female experience of self due to the sexual division of labor in childrearing. These different (psychic) experiences both structure and are reinforced by the differing patterns of male and female activity required by the sexual division of labor, and are thereby replicated as epistemology and ontology. The differential male and female life activity in class society leads on the one hand toward a feminist standpoint and on the other toward an abstract masculinity.

Because the problem for the boy is to distinguish himself from the mother and to protect himself against the real threat she poses for his identity, his conflictual and oppositional efforts lead to the formation of rigid ego boundaries. The way Freud takes for granted the rigid distinction between the "me and not-me" makes the point well: "Normally, there is nothing of which we are more certain than the feeling of ourself, of our own ego. This ego appears to us as something autonomous and unitary, marked off distinctly from everything else." At least toward the outside, "the ego seems to maintain clear and sharp lines of demarcation."[32] Thus, the boy's construction of self in opposition to unity with the mother, his construction of identity as differentiation from the other, sets a hostile and combative dualism at the heart of both the community men construct and the masculinist world view by means of which they understand their lives.

I do not mean to suggest that the totality of human relations can be explained by psychoanalysis. Rather I want to point to the ways male rather than female experience and activity replicates itself in both the hierarchical and dualist institutions of class society and in the frameworks of thought generated by this experience. It is interesting to read Hegel's account of the relation of self and other as a statement of male experience: the relation of the two consciousnesses takes the form of a trial by death. As Hegel describes it, "each seeks the death of the other."

> Thus, the relation of the two self-conscious individuals is such that they provide themselves and each other through a life-and-death struggle. They must engage in this struggle, for they must raise their certainty *for themselves* to truth, both in the case of the other and in their own case.[33]

The construction of the self in opposition to another who threatens one's very being reverberates throughout the construction of both class society and the masculinist world view and results in a deepgoing and hierarchical dualism. First, the male experience is characterized by the duality of concrete versus abstract. Material reality as experienced by the boy in the family provides no model and is unimportant in the attainment of masculinity. Nothing of value to the boy occurs with the family, and masculinity becomes an abstract ideal to be achieved over the opposition of daily life.[34] Masculinity must be attained by means of opposition to the concrete world of daily life, by escaping from contact with the female world of the household into the masculine world of public life. This experience of two worlds, one valuable, if abstract and deeply unattainable, the other useless and demeaning, if concrete and necessary, lies at the heart of a series of dualisms—abstract/concrete, mind/body, culture/nature, ideal/real, stasis/change. And these dualisms are overlaid by gender: only the first of each pair is associated with the male.

Dualism, along with the dominance of one side of the dichotomy over the other, marks phallocentric society and social theory. These dualisms appear in a variety of forms—in philosophy, technology, political theory, and the organization of class society itself. One can, for example, see them very clearly worked out in Plato, although they appear in many other forms.[35] There, the concrete/abstract duality takes the form of an opposition of material to ideal, and a denial of the relevance of the material world to the attainment of what is of fundamental importance: love of knowledge, or philosophy (masculinity). The duality between nature and culture takes the form of a devaluation of work or necessity, and the primacy instead of purely social interaction for the attainment of undying fame. Philosophy itself is separate from nature, and indeed, exists only on the basis of the domination of (at least some) of the philosopher's own nature.[36] Abstract masculinity, then, can be seen to have structured Western social relations and the modes of thought to which these relations give rise at least since the founding of the *polis*.

The oedipal roots of these hierarchical dualisms are memorialized in the overlay of female and male connotations: it is not accidental that women are associated with quasi-human and nonhuman nature, that the female is associated with the body and material life, that the lives of women are systematically used as examples to characterize the lives of those ruled by their bodies rather than their minds.[37]

Both the fragility and fundamental falseness of the masculinist ideology and the deeply problematic nature of the social relations from which it grows are apparent in its reliance on a series of counterfactual assumptions and contentions. Consider how the following contentions are contrary to lived experience: the body is both irrelevant and in opposition to the (real) self, an impediment to be overcome by the mind; the female mind either does not exist (Do women have souls?) or works in such incomprehensible ways as to be un-intelligible (the "enigma of woman"); what is real and primary is imperceptible to the senses and impervious to nature and natural change. What is remarkable is not only that these contentions have absorbed a great deal of philosophical energy, but, along with a series of other counterfactuals, have structured social relations for centuries.

Interestingly enough the epistemology and society constructed by men suffering from the effects of abstract masculinity have a great deal in common with that imposed by commodity exchange. The separation and opposition of social and natural worlds, of abstract and concrete, of permanence and change, the effort to define only the former of each pair as important, the reliance on a series of counter factual assumptions—all this is shared with the exchange abstraction. Abstract masculinity shares still another of its aspects with the exchange abstraction: it forms the basis for an even more problematic social synthesis. Hegel's analysis makes clear the problematic social relations available to the self which maintains itself by opposition: each of the two subjects struggling for recognition risks its own death in the struggle to kill the other, but if the other is killed the subject is once again alone.[38] In sum, then, the male experience when replicated as epistemology leads to a world conceived as, and (in fact) inhabited by, a number of fundamentally hostile others whom one comes to know by means of opposition (even death struggle) and yet with whom one must construct a social relation in order to survive.

The female construction of self in relation to others leads in an opposite direction—toward opposition to dualisms of any sort, valuation of concrete, everyday life, sense of a variety of connectednesses and continuities both with other persons and with the natural world. If material life structures consciousness, women's relationally defined existence, bodily experience of boundary challenges, and activity of transforming both physical objects and human beings must be expected to result in a world view to which dichotomies are foreign. Women experience others and themselves along a continuum whose dimensions are evidenced in Adrienne Rich's argument that the child carried for nine months can be defined "*neither* as me or as not-me," and she argues that inner and outer are not polar opposites but a continuum.[39] What the sexual division of labor defines as women's work turns on issues of change rather than stasis, the changes involved in producing both use-values and commodities, but more profoundly in the activity of rearing human beings who change in both more subtle and more autonomous ways than any inanimate object. Not only the qualities of things but also the qualities of people are important in women's work; quantity becomes peripheral. In addition, far more than the instrumental cooperation of the workplace is required; the mother-child relation and the maintenance of the family, while it has instrumental aspects, is not defined by them. Finally, the unity of mental and manual labor, and the directly sensuous nature of much of women's work leads to a more profound unity of mental and manual labor, social and natural worlds, than is experienced by the male worker in capitalism. The unity grows from the fact that women's bodies, unlike men's, can be themselves instruments of production: in pregnancy, giving birth, or lactation, arguments about a division of mental from manual labor are fundamentally foreign.

That this is indeed women's experience is documented in both the theory and practice of the contemporary women's movement and needs no further development here.[40] The more important question here is whether female experience and the world view constructed by female activity can meet the criteria for a standpoint. If we return to the five claims carried by the concept of a standpoint, it seems clear that women's material life activity has important epistemological and ontological consequences for both the understanding and construction of social relations. Women's activity, then, does satisfy the first requirement of a standpoint.

I can now take up the second claim made by a standpoint: that the female experience not only inverts that of the male, but forms a basis on which to expose abstract masculinity as both partial and fundamentally perverse, as not only occupying only one side of the dualities it has constructed, but reversing the proper valuation of human activity. The partiality of the masculinist vision and of the societies which support this understanding is evidenced by its confinement of activity proper to the male to only one side of the dualisms. Its perverseness, however, lies elsewhere. Perhaps the most dramatic (though not the only) reversal of the proper order of things characteristic of the male experience is the substitution of death for life.

The substitution of death for life results at least in part from the sexual division of labor in childrearing. The self surrounded by rigid ego-boundaries, certain of what is inner and what is outer, the self experienced as walled city, is discontinuous with others. Georges Bataille has made brilliantly clear the ways in which death emerges as the only possible solution to this discontinuity and has followed the logic through to argue that reproduction itself must be understood not as the creation of life, but as death. The core experience to be understood is that of discontinuity and its consequences. As a consequence of this experience of discontinuity and aloneness, penetration of ego-boundaries, or fusion with another is experienced as violent. Thus, the desire for fusion with another can take the form of domination of the other. In this form, it leads to the only possible fusion with a threatening other: when the other ceases to exist as a separate, and for that reason, threatening being. Insisting that another submit to one's will is simply a milder form of the destruction of discontinuity in the death of the other since in this case one is no longer confronting a discontinuous and opposed will, despite its discontinuous embodiment. This is perhaps one source of the links between sexual activity, domination, and death.

Bataille suggests that killing and sexual activity share both prohibitions and religious significance. Their unity is demonstrated by religious sacrifice since the latter:

> is intentional like the act of the man who lays bare, desires and wants to penetrate his victim. The lover strips the beloved of her identity no less than the bloodstained priest his human or animal victim. The woman in the hands of her assailant is despoiled of her being . . . loses the firm barrier that once separated her from others . . . is brusquely laid open to the violence of the sexual urges set loose in the organs of reproduction; she is laid open to the impersonal violence that overwhelms her from without.[41]

Note the use of the term "lover" and "assailant" as synonyms and the presence of the female as victim.

The importance of Bataille's analysis lies in the fact that it can help to make clear the links between violence, death, and sexual fusion with another, links which are not simply theoretical but actualized in rape and pornography. Images of women in chains, being beaten, or threatened with attack carry clear social messages, among them that "the normal male is sexually aggressive in a brutal and demeaning way."[42] Bataille's analysis can help to understand why "men advertise, even brag, that their movie is the 'bloodiest thing that ever happened in front of a camera'."[43] The analysis is supported by the psychoanalyst who suggested that although one of the important dynamics of pornography is hostility, "one can raise the possibly controversial question whether in humans (especially males) powerful sexual excitement can ever exist without brutality also being present."[44]

Bataille's analysis can help to explain what is erotic about "snuff" films, which not only depict the torture and dismemberment of a woman, but claim that the actress is *in fact* killed. His analysis suggests that perhaps she is a sacrificial victim whose discontinuous existence has been succeeded in her death by "the organic continuity of life drawn into the common life of the beholders."[45] Thus, the pair "lover-assailant" is not accidental. Nor is the connection of reproduction and death.

"Reproduction," Bataille argues, "implies the existence of *discontinuous* beings." This is so because, "Beings which reproduce themselves are distinct from one another, and those reproduced are likewise distinct from each other, just as they are distinct from their parents. Each being is distinct from all others. His birth, his death, the events of his life may have an interest for others, but he alone is directly concerned in them. He is born alone. He dies alone. Between one being and another, there is a *gulf*, a discontinuity."[46] (Clearly it is not just a gulf, but is better understood as a chasm.) In reproduction sperm and ovum unite to form a new entity, but they do so from the death and disappearance of two separate beings. Thus, the new entity bears within itself "the transition to continuity, the fusion, fatal to both, of two separate beings."[47] Thus, death and reproduction are intimately linked, yet Bataille stresses that "it is only death which is to be identified with continuity." Thus, despite the unity of birth and death in this analysis, Bataille gives greater weight to a "tormenting fact: the urge towards love, pushed to its limit, is an urge toward death."[48] Bataille holds to this position despite his recognition that reproduction is a form of growth. The growth, however, he dismisses as not being "ours," as being only "impersonal."[49] This is not the female experience, in which reproduction is hardly impersonal, nor experienced as death. It is, of course, in a literal sense, the sperm which is cut off from its source, and lost. No wonder, then, at the masculinist occupation with death, and the feeling that growth is "impersonal," not of fundamental concern to oneself. But this complete dismissal of the experience of another bespeaks a profound lack of empathy and refusal to recognize the very being of another. It is a manifestation of the chasm which separates each man from every other being and from the natural world, the chasm which both marks and defines the problem of community.

The preoccupation with death instead of life appears as well in the argument that it is the ability to kill (and for centuries, the practice) which sets humans above animals. Even Simone de Beauvoir has accepted that "it is not in giving life but in risking life that man is raised above the animal; that is why superiority has been accorded in humanity not to the sex that brings forth but to that which kills."[50] That superiority has been accorded to the sex which kills is beyond doubt. But what kind of experience and vision can take reproduction, the creation of new life, and the force of life in sexuality, and turn it into death—not just in theory but in the practice of rape, pornography, and sexual murder? Any why give pride of place to killing? This is not only an inversion of the proper order of things, but also a refusal to recognize the real activities in which men as well as women are engaged. The producing of goods and the reproducing of human beings are certainly life-sustaining activities. And even the deaths of the ancient heroes in search of undying fame were pursuits of life, and represented the attempt to avoid death by attaining immortality. The search for life, then, represents the deeper reality which lies beneath the glorification of death and destruction.

Yet one cannot dismiss the substitution of death for life as simply false. Men's power to structure social relations in their own image means that women too must participate in social relations which manifest and express abstract masculinity. The most important life activities have consistently been held by the powers that be to be unworthy of those who are fully human most centrally because of their close connections with necessity and life: motherwork (the rearing of children), housework, and until the rise of capitalism in the West, any work necessary to subsistence. In addition, these activities in contemporary capitalism are all constructed in ways which systematically degrade and destroy the minds and bodies of those who perform them.[51] The organization of motherhood as an institution in which a woman is alone with her children, the isolation of women from each other in domestic labor, the female pathology of loss of self in service to others—all mark the transformation of life into death, the distortion of what could have been creative and communal activity into oppressive toil, and the destruction of the possibility of community present in women's relational self-definition. The ruling gender's and class's interest in maintaining social relations such as these is evidenced by the fact that when women set up other structures in which the mother is not alone with her children, isolated from others—as is frequently the case in working class communities or communities of people of color—these arrangements are categorized as pathological deviations.

The real destructiveness of the social relations characteristic of abstract masculinity, however, is now concealed beneath layers of ideology. Marxian theory needed to go beneath the surface to discover the different levels of determination which defined the relation of capitalist and (male) worker. These levels of determination and laws of motion or tendency of phallocratic society must be worked out on the basis of female experience. This brings me to the fourth claim for a standpoint—its character as an achievement of both analysis and political struggle occurring in a particular historical space. The fact that class divisions should have proven so resistant to analysis and required such a prolonged political struggle before Marx was able to formulate the theory of surplus value indicates the difficulty of this accomplishment. And the rational control of production has certainly not been achieved.

Feminists have only begun the process of revaluing female experience, searching for common threads which connect the diverse experiences of women, and searching for the structural determinants of the experiences. The difficulty of the problem faced by feminist theory can be illustrated by the fact that it required a struggle even to define household labor, if not done for wages, as work, to argue that what are held to be acts of love instead must be recognized as work whether or not wages are paid.[52] Both the valuation of women's experience, and the use of this experience as a ground for critique are required. A feminist standpoint may be present on the basis of the common threads of female experience, but it is neither self-evident nor obvious.

Finally, because it provides a way to reveal the perverseness and inhumanity of human relations, a standpoint forms the basis for moving beyond these relations. Just as the proletarian standpoint emerges out of the contradiction between appearance and essence in capitalism, understood as essentially historical and constituted by the relation of capitalist and worker, the feminist standpoint emerges both out of the contradiction between the systematically differing structure of male and female life activity in Western cultures. It expresses female experience at a particular time and place, located within a particular set of social relations. Capitalism, Marx noted, could not develop fully until the notion of human equality achieved the status of universal truth.[53] Despite women's exploitation both as unpaid reproducers of the labor force and as a sex-segregated labor force available for low wages, then, capitalism poses problems for the continued oppression of women. Just as capitalism enables the proletariat to raise the possibility of a society free from class domination, so too, it provides space to raise the possibility of a society free from all forms of domination. The articulation of a feminist standpoint based on women's relational self-definition and activity exposes the world men have constructed and the self-understanding which manifests these relations as partial and perverse. More importantly, by drawing out the potentiality available in the actuality and thereby exposing the inhumanity of human relations, it embodies a distress which requires a solution. The experience of continuity and relation—with others, with the natural world, of mind with body—provides an ontological base for developing a nonproblematic social synthesis, a social synthesis which need not operate through the denial of the body, the attack on nature, or the death struggle between the self and other, a social synthesis which does not depend on any of the forms taken by abstract masculinity.

What is necessary is the generalization of the potentiality made available by the activity of women—the defining of society as a whole as propertyless producer both of use-values and of human beings. To understand what such a transformation would require we should consider what is involved in the partial transformation represented by making the whole of society into propertyless producers of use-values—i.e., socialist revolution. The abolition of the division between mental and manual labor cannot take place simply by means of adopting worker-self-management techniques, but instead requires the abolition of private property, the seizure of state power, and lengthy post-revolutionary class struggle. Thus, I am not suggesting that shared parenting arrangements can abolish the sexual division of labor. Doing away with this division of labor would of course require institutionalizing the participation of both women and men in childrearing; but just as the rational and conscious control of the production of goods and services requires a vast and far-reaching social transformation, so the rational and conscious organization of reproduction would entail the transformation both of *every* human relation, and of human relations to the natural world. The magnitude of the task is apparent if one asks what a society without institutionalized gender differences might look like.

Conclusion

An analysis which begins from the sexual division of labor—understood not as taboo, but as the real, material activity of concrete human beings—could form the basis for an analysis of the real structures of women's oppression, an analysis which would not require that one sever biology from society, nature from culture, an analysis which would expose the ways women both participate in and oppose their own subordination. The elaboration of such an analysis cannot but be difficult. Women's lives, like men's, are structured by social relations which manifest the experience of the dominant gender and class. The ability to go beneath the surface of appearances to reveal the real but concealed social relations requires both theoretical and political activity. Feminist theorists must demand that feminist theorizing be grounded in women's material activity and must as well be a part of the political struggle necessary to develop areas of social life modeled on this activity. The outcome could be the development of a political economy which included women's activity as well as men's, and could as well be a step toward the redefining and restructuring of society as a whole on the basis of women's activity.

Generalizing the activity of women to the social system as a whole would raise, for the first time in human history, the possibility of a fully human community, a community structured by connection rather than separation and opposition. One can conclude then that women's life activity does form the basis of a specifically feminist materialism, a materialism which can provide a point from which both to critique and to work against phallocratic ideology and institutions.

My argument here opens a number of avenues for future work. Clearly, a systematic critique of Marx on the basis of a more fully developed understanding of the sexual division of labor is in order. And this is indeed being undertaken by a number of feminists. A second avenue for further investigation is the relation between exchange and abstract masculinity. An exploration of Mauss's *The Gift* would play an important part in this project, since he presents the solipsism of exchange as an overlay on and substitution for a deeper going hostility, the exchange of gifts as an alternative to war. We have seen that the necessity for recognizing and receiving recognition from another to take the form of a death struggle memorializes the male rather than female experience of emerging as a person in opposition to a woman in the context of a deeply phallocratic world. If the community of exchangers (capitalists) rests on the more overtly and directly hostile death struggle of self and other, one might be able to argue that what underlies the exchange abstraction is abstract masculinity. One might then turn to the question of whether capitalism rests on and is a consequence of patriarchy. Perhaps then feminists can produce the analysis which could amend Marx to read: "Though class society appears to be the source, the cause of the oppression of women, it is rather its consequence." Thus, it is "only at the last culmination of the development of class society [that] this, its secret, appear[s] again, namely, that on the one hand it is the *product* of the oppression of women, and that on the other it is the *means* by which women participate in and create their own oppression."[54]

EDITOR'S NOTES

1. Another version of this essay appears in Hartsock's *Money, Sex and Power* (Boston: Northeastern University Press, 1984).

2. These issues are discussed in the concluding essay. See, also, the more extended analysis in Sandra Harding, ed., *The Science Question in Feminism* (Ithaca, N.Y.: Cornell University Press, 1986).

NOTES

I take my title from Iris Young's call for the development of a specifically feminist historical materialism. See "Socialist Feminism and the Limits of Dual Systems Theory," in *Socialist Review* 10, 2/3 (March–June, 1980). My work on this paper is deeply indebted to a number of women whose ideas are incorporated here, although not always used in the ways they might wish. My discussions with Donna Haraway and Sandra Harding have been intense and ongoing over a period of years. I have also had a number of important and useful conversations with Jane Flax, and my project here has benefited both from these contacts, and from the opportunity to read her paper, "Political Philosophy and the Patriarchal Unconscious: A Psychoanalytic Perspective on Epistemology and Metaphysics." In addition I have been helped immensely by collective discussions with Annette Bickel, Sarah Begus, and Alexa Freeman. All of these people (along with Iris Young and Irene Diamond) have read and commented on drafts of this paper. I would also like to thank Alison Jaggar for continuing to question me about the basis on which one could claim the superiority of a feminist standpoint and for giving me the opportunity to deliver the paper at the University of Cincinnati Philosophy Department Colloquium; and Stephen Rose for taking the time to read and comment on a rough draft of the paper at a critical point in its development.

1. See my "Feminist Theory and the Development of Revolutionary Strategy," in Zillah Eisenstein, ed., *Capitalist Patriarchy and the Case for Socialist Feminism* (New York: Monthly Review, 1978).

2. The recent literature on mothering is perhaps the most detailed on this point. See Dorothy Dinnerstein, *The Mermaid and the Minotaur* (New York: Harper and Row, 1976); Nancy Chodorow, *The Reproduction of Mothering* (Berkeley: University of California Press, 1978).

3. Iris Young, "Socialist Feminism and the Limits of Dual Systems Theory," *in Socialist Review* 10, 2/3 (March–June, 1980), p. 180.

4. Eighth Thesis on Feuerbach, in Karl Marx, "Theses on Feuerbach," in *The German Ideology*, C. J. Arthur, ed. (New York: International Publishers, 1970), p. 121.

5. Ibid. Conscious human practice, then, is at once both an epistemological category and the basis for Marx's conception of the nature of humanity itself. To put the case even more strongly, Marx argues that human activity has both an ontological and epistemological status, that human feelings are not "merely anthropological phenomena," but are "truly ontological affirmations of being." See Karl Marx, *Economic and Philosophic Manuscripts of 1844*, Dirk Struik, ed. (New York: International Publishers, 1964), pp. 113, 165, 188.

6. Marx, *1844*, p. 112. Nature itself, for Marx, appears as a form of human work, since he argues that humans duplicate themselves actively and come to contemplate themselves in a world of their own making. (Ibid., p. 114). On the more general issue of the relation of natural to human worlds see the very interesting account by Alfred Schmidt, *The Concept of Nature in Marx*, tr. Ben Foukes (London: New Left Books, 1971).

7. Marx and Engels, *The German Ideology*, pp. 42.

8. See Alfred Sohn-Rethel, *Intellectual and Manual Labor: A Critique of Epistemology* (London: Macmillan, 1978). I should note that my analysis both depends on and is in tension with Sohn-Rethel's. Sohn-Rethel argues that commodity exchange is a characteristic of all class societies—one which comes to a head in capitalism or takes its most advanced form in capitalism. His project, which is not mine, is to argue that (a) commodity exchange, a characteristic of all class societies, is an original source of abstraction, (b) that this abstraction contains the formal element essential for the cognitive faculty of conceptual thinking, and (c) that the abstraction operating in exchange, an abstraction in practice, is the source of the ideal abstraction basic to Greek philosophy and to modern science. (See Ibid., p. 28). In addition to a different purpose, I should indicate several major differences with Sohn-Rethel. First, he treats the productive forces as separate from the productive relations of society and ascribes far too much autonomy to them. (See, for example, his discussions on pp. 84–86, 95.) I take the position that the distinction between the two is simply a device used for purposes of analysis rather than a feature of the real world. Second, Sohn-Rethel characterizes the period preceding generalized commodity production as primitive communism. (See p. 98.) This is however an inadequate characterization of tribal societies.

9. Karl Marx, *Capital*, I (New York: International Publishers, 1967), p. 176.

10. I have done this elsewhere in a systematic way. For the analysis, see my discussion of the exchange abstraction in *Money, Sex, and Power: An Essay on Domination and Community* (New York: Longman, 1983).

11. This is Iris Young's point. I am indebted to her persuasive arguments for taking what she terms the "gender differentiation of labor" as a central category of analysis (Young, "Dual Systems Theory," p. 185). My use of this category, however, differs to some extent from hers. Young's analysis of women in capitalism does not seem to include marriage as a part of the division of labor. She is more concerned with the division of labor in the productive sector.

12. See Sara Ruddick, "Maternal Thinking," *Feminist Studies* 6, 2 (Summer, 1980): 364.

13. See, for discussions of this danger, "Disloyal to Civilization: Feminism, Racism, Gynephobia," in Adrienne Rich, *On Lies, Secrets, and Silence* (New York: W. W. Norton & Co., 1979), pp. 275–310; Elly Bulkin, "Racism and Writing: Some Implications for White Lesbian Critics," in *Sinister Wisdom*, No. 6 (Spring, 1980).

14. Some cross-cultural evidence indicates that the status of women varies with the work they do. To the extent that women and men contribute equally to subsistence, women's status is higher than it would be if their subsistence-work differed profoundly from that of men; that is, if they do none or

almost all of the work of subsistence, their status remains low. See Peggy Sanday, "Female Status in the Public Domain," in Michelle Rosaldo and Louise Lamphere, eds., *Women, Culture, and Society* (Stanford: Stanford University Press, 1974), p. 199. See also Iris Young's account of the sexual division of labor in capitalism, mentioned above.

15. It is irrelevant to my argument here that women's wage labor takes place under different circumstances than men's—that is, their lower wages, their confinement to only a few occupational categories, etc. I am concentrating instead on the formal, structural features of women's work. There has been much effort to argue that women's domestic labor is a source of surplus value, that is, to include it within the scope of Marx's value theory as productive labor, or to argue that since it does not produce surplus value it belongs to an entirely different mode of production, variously characterized as domestic or patriarchal. My strategy here is quite different from this. See, for the British debate, Mariarosa Dalla Costa and Selma James, *The Power of Women and the Subversion of the Community* (Bristol: Falling Wall Press, 1975); Wally Secombe, "The Housewife and Her Labor Under Capitalism," *New Left Review* 83 (January–February, 1974); Jean Gardiner, "Women's Domestic Labour," *New Left Review* 89 (March, 1975); and Paul Smith, "Domestic Labour and Marx's Theory of Value," in Annette Kuhn and Ann Marie Wolpe, eds., *Feminism and Materialism* (Boston: Routledge and Kegan Paul, 1978). A portion of the American debate can be found in Ira Gerstein, "Domestic Work and Capitalism," and Lisa Vogel, "The Earthly Family," *Radical America* 7, 4/5 (July–October, 1973); Ann Ferguson, "Women as a New Revolutionary Class," in Pat Walker, ed., *Between Labor and Capital* (Boston: South End Press, 1979).

16. Frederick Engels, *Origins of the Family, Private Property and the State* (New York: International Publishers, 1942); Karl Marx, *Capital*, Vol. I, p. 671. Marx and Engels have also described the sexual division of labor as natural or spontaneous. See Mary O'Brien, "Reproducing Marxist Man," in Lorenne Clark and Lynda Lange, eds., *The Sexism of Social and Political Theory: Women and Reproduction from Plato to Nietzsche* (Toronto: University of Toronto Press, 1979).

17. For a discussion of women's work. see Elise Boulding, "Familial Constraints on Women's Work Roles," in Martha Blaxall and B. Reagan, eds., *Women and the Workplace* (Chicago: University of Chicago Press, 1976), esp. the charts on pp. 111, 113.

An interesting historical note is provided by the fact that even Nausicaa, the daughter of a Homeric king, did the household laundry. (See M. I. Finley, *The World of Odysseus* [Middlesex, England: Penguin, 1979], p. 73.) While aristocratic women were less involved in actual labor, the difference was one of degree. And as Aristotle remarked in *The Politics*, supervising slaves is not a particularly uplifting activity. The life of leisure and philosophy, so much the goal for aristocratic Athenian men, then, was almost unthinkable for any woman.

18. Simone de Beauvoir holds that repetition has a deeper significance and that women's biological destiny itself is repetition. (See *The Second Sex*, tr. H. M. Parshley [New York: Knopf, 1953,] p. 59.) But see also her discussion of housework in Ibid., pp. 434ff. There her treatment of housework is strikingly negative. For de Beauvoir, transcendence is provided in the historical struggle of self with other and with the natural world. The oppositions she sees are not really stasis vs. change, but rather transcendence, escape from the muddy concreteness of daily life, from the static, biological, concrete repetition of "placid femininity."

19. Marilyn French, *The Women's Room* (New York: Jove, 1978), p. 214.

20. Sara Ruddick, "Maternal Thinking," presents an interesting discussion of these and other aspects of the thought which emerges from the activity of mothering. Although I find it difficult to speak the language of interests and demands she uses, she brings out several valuable points. Her distinction between maternal and scientific thought is very intriguing and potentially useful (see esp. pp. 350–353).

21. O'Brien, "Reproducing Marxist Man," p. 115, n. 11.

22. It should be understood that I am concentrating here on the experience of women in Western culture. There are a number of crosscultural differences which can be expected to have some effect. See, for example, the differences which emerge from a comparison of childrearing in ancient Greek society with that of the contemporary Mbuti in central Africa. See Phillip Slater, *The Glory of Hera* (Boston: Beacon, 1968) and Colin Turnbull, "The Politics of Non-Aggression," in Ashley Montagu, ed., *Learning Non-Aggression* (New York: Oxford University Press, 1978).

23. See Nancy Chodorow, "Family Structure and Feminine Personality," in Rosaldo and Lamphere, *Woman, Culture and Society*, p. 59.

24. Adrienne Rich, *Of Woman Born* (New York: Norton, 1976), p. 63.

25. See Chodorow, *The Reproduction of Mothering*, and Flax, "The Conflict Between Nurturance and Autonomy in Mother-Daughter Relations and in Feminism," *Feminist Studies* 4, 2 (June, 1978). I rely on the analyses of Dinnerstein and Chodorow but there are difficulties in that they are attempting to explain why humans, both male and female, fear and hate the female. My purpose here is to invert their arguments and to attempt to put forward a positive account of the epistemological consequences of this situation. What follows is a summary of Chodorow, *The Reproduction of Mothering*.

26. Chodorow, *Reproduction*, pp. 105–109.

27. This is Jane Flax's point.

28. Chodorow, *Reproduction*, pp. 127–131, 163.

29. Ibid., p. 166.

30. Ibid., pp. 174–178. Chodorow suggest a correlation between father absence and fear of women (p. 213), and one should, treating this as an empirical hypotheses, expect a series of cultural differences based on the degree of father absence. Here the ancient Greeks and the Mbuti provide a fascinating contrast. (See n. 22 above.)

31. Ibid., p. 198. The flexible and diffuse female ego boundaries can of course result in the pathology of loss of self in responsibility for and dependence on others. (The obverse of the male pathology of experiencing the self as walled city.)

32. Sigmund Freud, *Civilization and Its Discontents* (New York: Norton, 1961), pp. 12–13.

33. Hegel, *Phenomenology of Spirit* (New York: Oxford University Press, 1979), trans. A. V. Miller, p. 114. See also Jessica Benjamin's very interesting use of this discussion in "The Bonds of Love: Rational Violence and Erotic Domination," *Feminist Studies* 6, 1 (June 1980).

34. Alvin Gouldner has made a similar argument in his contention that the Platonic stress on hierarchy and order resulted from a similarly learned opposition to daily life which was rooted in the young aristocrat's experience of being taught proper behavior by slaves who could not themselves engage in this behavior. See *Enter Plato* (New York: Basic Books, 1965), pp. 351–355.

35. One can argue, as Chodorow's analysis suggests, that their extreme form in his philosophy represents an extreme father-absent (father-deprived?) situation. A more general critique of phallocentric dualism occurs in Susan Griffin, *Woman and Nature* (New York: Harper & Row, 1978).

36. More recently, of course, the opposition to the natural world has taken the form of destructive technology. See Evelyn Fox Keller, "Gender and Science," *Psychoanalysis and Contemporary Thought* 1, 3 (1978), reprinted in Sandra Harding and Merrill Hintikka, eds., *Discovering Reality: Feminist Perspectives on Epistemology, Metaphysics, Methodology and Philosophy of Science* (Dordrecht, Holland: D. Reidel Publishing Co., 1983).

37. See Elizabeth Spelman, "Metaphysics and Misogyny: The Soul and Body in Plato's Dialogues," mimeo. One analyst has argued that its basis lies in the fact that "the early mother, monolithic representative of nature, is a source, like nature, of ultimate distress as well as ultimate joy. Like nature, she is both nourishing and disappointing, both alluring and threatening . . . The infant loves her . . . and it hates her because, like nature, she does not perfectly protect and provide for it . . . The mother, then—like nature, which sends blizzards and locusts as well as sunshine and strawberries—is perceived as capricious, sometimes actively malevolent." Dinnerstein, *Mermaid and the Minotaur*, p. 95.

38. See Benjamin, (n. 33 above), p. 152. The rest of her analysis goes in a different direction than mine, though her account of *The Story of O* can be read as making clear the problems for any social synthesis based on the Hegelian model.

39. Rich, *Of Woman Born*, p. 64, p. 167. For a similar descriptive account, but a dissimilar analysis, see David Bakan, *The Duality of Human Existence* (Boston: Beacon, 1966).

40. My arguments are supported with remarkable force by both the theory and practice of the contemporary women's movement. In theory, this appears in different forms in the work of Dorothy Riddle, "New Visions of Spiritual Power," *Quest: a Feminist Quarterly* 1, 3 (Spring, 1975); Susan Griffin, *Woman and Nature*, esp. Book IV: 'The Separate Rejoined'; Adrienne Rich, *Of Woman Born*, esp. pp. 62–68; Linda Thurston, "On Male and Female Principle," *The Second Wave* 1, 2 (Summer, 1971). In feminist political organizing, this vision has been expressed as an opposition of leadership and hierarchy, as an effort to prevent the development of organizations divided into leaders and followers. It has also taken the form of an insistence on the unity of the personal and the political, a stress on the concrete rather than on

abstract principles (an opposition to theory), and a stress on the politics of everyday life. For a fascinating and early example, see Pat Mainardi, "The Politics of Housework," in Leslie Tanner, ed., *Voices of Women's Liberation* (New York: New American Library, 1970).

41. George Bataille, *Death and Sensuality* (New York: Arno Press, 1977), p. 90.

42. Women Against Violence Against Women Newsletter, June, 1976, p. 1.

43. *Aegis: A Magazine on Ending Violence Against Women*, November/December, 1978, p. 3.

44. Robert Stoller, *Perversion: The Erotic Form of Hatred* (New York: Pantheon, 1975), p. 88.

45. Bataille, *Death and Sensuality*, p. 91. See pp. 91ff for a more complete account of the commonalities of sexual activity and ritual sacrifice.

46. Bataille, *Death and Sensuality*, p. 12 (italics mine). See also de Beauvoir's discussion in *The Second Sex*, pp. 135, 151.

47. Bataille, *Death and Sensuality*, p. 14.

48. Ibid., p. 42. While Adrienne Rich acknowledges the violent feelings between mothers and children, she quite clearly does not put these at the heart of the relation *(Of Woman Born)*.

49. Bataille, *Death and Sensuality*, pp. 95–96.

50. de Beauvoir, *The Second Sex*, p. 58. It should be noted that killing and risking life are ways of indicating one's contempt for one's body, and as such are of a piece with the Platonic search for disembodiment.

51. Consider, for example, Rich's discussion of pregnancy and childbirth, Ch. VI and VII, *Of Woman Born*. And see also Charlotte Perkins Gilman's discussion of domestic labor in *The Home* (Urbana, Ill.: The University of Illinois Press, 1972).

52. The Marxist-feminist efforts to determine whether housework produces surplus value and the feminist political strategy of demanding wages for housework represent two (mistaken) efforts to recognize women's non-wage activity as work. Perhaps domestic labor's non-status as work is one of the reasons why its wages—disproportionately paid to women of color—are so low, and working conditions so poor.

53. *Capital*, Vol. I, p. 60.

54. See Marx, *1844*, p. 117.

XII.

CONCLUSION
EPISTEMOLOGICAL QUESTIONS

Sandra Harding

How should the analyses produced by feminist research in the social sciences be justified? In one sense, we do not need to ask this question since every researcher provides evidence that is intended to justify the results of her or his research. However, the kind of evidence presented often would not be acceptable to people who assess men's experiences, values, and judgments as the paradigm of human experience and women's as only an immature, partial, or deviant form of men's. In some respects, the epistemologies assumed in the new analyses of women and gender directly conflict with traditional ones, and they do so in ways that are not always recognized. Therefore, questions about how to justify the analyses do frequently arise. Moreover, in certain respects the feminist epistemologies also directly conflict with each other. These conflicts *between* the feminist justificatory strategies also have been overlooked.

Once we undertake to use women's experience as a resource to generate scientific problems, hypotheses, and evidence, to design research for women, and to place the researcher in the same critical plane as the research subject, traditional epistemological assumptions can no longer be made. These agendas have led feminist social scientists to ask questions about who can be a knower (only men?); what tests beliefs must pass in order to be legitimated as knowledge (only tests against men's experiences and observations?); what kinds of things can be known (can "subjective truths," ones that only women—or only some women—tend to arrive at, count as knowledge?); the nature of objectivity (does it require "point-of-viewlessness"?); the appropriate relationship between the researcher and her/his research subjects (must the researcher be disinterested, dispassionate, and socially invisible to the subject?); what should be the purposes of the pursuit of knowledge (to produce information *for* men?).

Each of the above issues could be the topic of a lengthy discussion. Instead, I want to provide an overview of some important tensions between the feminist analyses of such issues and the traditional theories of knowledge from which these feminists borrow, and between the feminist epistemologies themselves. I shall look at these tensions as they have emerged in response to two problems. First, I outline contrasting attempts to account for the fact that it is politically value-laden research processes that are producing the more complete and less distorted social analyses. We can see here the tension between "feminist empiricist" and "the feminist standpoint" epistemologies, and between each of these and the traditional theory of knowledge from which it borrows. Then, I turn to examine briefly the tension between both of these epistemologies, on the one hand, and postmodernist skepticisms about just such attempts to tell "true stories"—or at least less false ones—about ourselves and the world around us, on the other hand.[1]

Can Politicized Inquiry Produce More Complete and Less Distorted Research Results?

A major source of feminist challenge to traditional epistemologies arises from the following problem. Feminism is a political movement for social change. Looked at from the perspective of science's self-understanding, "feminist knowledge," "feminist science," "feminist sociology"—or psychology or economics—should be a contradiction in terms. Scientific knowledge-seeking is supposed to be value-neutral, objective, dispassionate, disinterested, and so forth. It is supposed to be protected from political interests, goals, and desires (such as feminist ones) by the norms of science. In particular, science's "method" is supposed to protect the results of research from the social values of the researchers. And yet it is obvious to all that many claims which clearly have been generated through research guided by feminist concerns, nevertheless appear more plausible (better supported, more reliable, less false, more likely to be confirmed by evidence, etc.) than the beliefs they replace. How can politicized inquiry be increasing the objectivity of inquiry?

Feminist Empiricism

The main response to this problem by social researchers has been feminist empiricism. In research reports one frequently finds the argument that the sexist and androcentric claims to which the researcher objects are caused by social biases. Social biases are conceptualized as prejudices that are based on false beliefs (due to superstition, custom, ignorance, or miseducation) and hostile attitudes. These prejudices enter research particularly at the stage when scientific problems are being identified and defined, but they also can appear in the design of research and in the collection and interpretation of data. Feminist empiricists argue that sexist and androcentric biases are eliminable by stricter adherence to the existing methodological norms of scientific inquiry; it is "bad science" or "bad sociology," etc, which is responsible for these biases in the results of research.

But how can the scientific community (the sociological one, psychological one, etc.) come to see that more than individual biases are the problem here—that its work *has* been shaped by culture-wide androcentric prejudices? Here is where we can see the importance of movements for social liberation, such as the women's movement. As Marcia Millman and Rosabeth Moss Kanter have pointed out, movements for social liberation "make it possible for people to see the world in an enlarged perspective because they remove the covers and blinders that obscure knowledge and observation." The women's movement has generated just such possibilities. Furthermore, feminist empiricists often point out that the women's movement creates the opportunity for more women researchers, and for more feminist researchers (male and female), who are more likely than sexist men to notice androcentric biases.

This justificatory strategy is by no means uncontroversial. Nevertheless, it is often thought to be the least threatening of the feminist epistemologies for two reasons. Most importantly, it appears to leave intact much of science's self-understanding of the principles of adequate scientific research as they are taught to students, quoted to Congress, and viewed on television (regardless of whether scientists actually believe them). This justificatory strategy appears to challenge mainly the incomplete way empiricism has been practiced, not the norms of empiricism themselves: mainstream inquiry has not rigorously enough adhered to its own norms. To say this in other words, it is thought that social values and political agendas can raise new issues that enlarge the scope of inquiry and reveal cause for greater care in the conduct of inquiry, but that the logic of explanation and research still conforms to standard empiricist rules.

Moreover, one can appeal to the forces responsible for the origins of modern science itself, as well as to later widely recognized moments of scientific growth, to increase the plausibility of this kind of claim. After all, wasn't it the bourgeois revolution of the fifteenth to seventeenth centuries which made it possible for early modern thinkers to see the world in an enlarged perspective? Wasn't it this great social revolution from feudalism to modernism which removed the covers and blinders that obscured earlier knowledge-seeking and observation? Furthermore, wasn't the proletarian revolution of the late nineteenth century responsible for yet one more leap in the objectivity of knowledge claims as it permitted an understanding of the effects of class struggles on social relations? Finally, doesn't the twentieth-century deconstruction of European and American colonialism have obvious positive effects on the growth of scientific knowledge? From these historical perspectives, the contemporary women's revolution is just the most recent of these revolutions, each of which moves us yet closer to the goals of the creators of modern science.

Though feminist empiricism appears in these ways to be consistent with empiricist tendencies, further consideration reveals that the feminist component deeply undercuts the assumptions of traditional empiricism in three ways: feminist empiricism has a radical future.[2] In the first place, feminist empiricism argues that the "context of discovery" is just as important as the "context of justification" for eliminating social biases that contribute to partial and distorted explanations and understandings. Traditional empiricism insists that the social identity of the observer is irrelevant to the "goodness" of the results of research. It is not supposed to make a difference to the explanatory power, objectivity, and so on of the research's results if the researcher or the community of scientists are white or black, Chinese or British, rich or poor in social origin. But feminist empiricism argues that women (or feminists, male and female) as a group are more likely than men (nonfeminists) as a group to produce claims unbiased by androcentrism, and in that sense objective results of inquiry. It argues that the authors of the favored social theories are not anonymous at all: they are clearly men, and usually men of the dominant classes, races, and cultures. The people who identify and define scientific problems leave their social fingerprints on the problems and their favored solutions to them.

Second, feminist empiricism makes the related claim that scientific method is not effective at eliminating social biases that are as wide-spread as androcentrism. This is especially the case when androcentrism arrives in the inquiry process through the identification and definition of research problems. Traditional empiricism holds that scientific method will eliminate any social biases as a hypothesis goes through its rigorous tests. But feminist empiricism argues that an androcentric picture of nature and social life emerges from the testing by men only of hypotheses generated by what men find problematic in the world around them. The problem here is not only that the hypotheses which would most deeply challenge androcentric beliefs are missing from those alternatives sexists consider when testing their favored hypotheses. It is also that traditional empiricism does not direct researchers to locate themselves in the same critical plane as their subject matters. Consequently, when nonfeminist researchers gather evidence for or against hypotheses, "scientific method"—bereft of such a directive—is impotent to locate and eradicate the androcentrism that shapes the research process.

Finally, feminist empiricists often exhort social scientists to follow the existing research norms more rigorously. On the other hand, they also can be understood to be arguing that it is precisely following these norms that contributes to androcentric research results.[3] The norms themselves have been constructed primarily to produce answers to the kinds of questions men ask about nature and social life and to prevent scrutiny of the way beliefs which are nearly or completely culture-wide in fact cannot be eliminated from the results of research by these norms. A reliable picture of women's worlds and of social relations between the sexes often requires alternative approaches to inquiry that challenge traditional research habits and raise profound questions which are no longer marginalized as deviant.

Thus feminist empiricism intensifies recent tendencies in the philosophy and social studies of science to problematize empiricist epistemological assumptions.[4] There is a tension between the feminist uses of empiricist justificatory strategies and the parental empiricist epistemology. However, empiricism is not the only resource that has been used to justify the intimate relationship between the politics of the women's movement and the new research on women and gender.

The Feminist Standpoint

A second response to the question about how to justify the results of feminist research is provided by the feminist standpoint theorists. Knowledge is supposed to be based on experience, and the reason the feminist claims can turn out to be scientifically preferable is that they originate in, and are tested against, a more complete and less distorting kind of social experience. Women's experiences, informed by feminist theory, provide a potential grounding for more complete and less distorted knowledge claims than do men's. Thus the standpoint theorists offer a different explanation than do feminist empiricists of how research that is directed by social values and political agendas can nevertheless produce empirically preferable results of research.[5]

This justificatory approach originates in Hegel's insight into the relationship between the master and the slave, and the development of Hegel's perceptions into the "proletarian standpoint" by Marx, Engels, and Lukacs.[6] The argument here is that human activity, or "material life," not only structures but also sets limits on human understanding: what we do shapes and constrains what we can know. As Nancy Hartsock argues, if human activity is structured in fundamentally opposing ways for two different groups (such as men and women), "one can expect that the vision of each will represent an inversion of the other, and in systems of domination the vision available to the rulers will be both partial and perverse." Men in the ruling classes and races reserve for themselves the right to perform only certain kinds of human activity, assigning the balance to women and men in other subjugated groups. What they assign to others they rationalize as merely natural activity—whether this be manual labor, emotional labor, or reproduction and child care—in contrast to what they regard as the distinctively cultural activity that they reserve for themselves. Of course, their "ruling" activities (in our society, management and administration) could not occur unless others were assigned to perform the social labors they disdain.

For these theorists, knowledge emerges for the oppressed only through the struggles they wage against their oppressors. It is through feminist struggles against male domination that women's experience can be made to yield up a truer (or less false) image of social reality than that available only from the perspective of the social experience of men of the ruling classes and races. Thus a feminist standpoint is not something anyone can have by claiming it, but an achievement. (A standpoint differs in this respect from a perspective.) To achieve a feminist standpoint one must engage in the intellectual and political struggle necessary to see nature and social life from the point of view of that disdained activity which produces women's social experiences instead of from the partial and perverse perspective available from the "ruling gender" experience of men.

Like feminist empiricism, the feminist standpoint reveals key problems in its paternal discourse. Where Marxism suggests that sexism is entirely a consequence of class relations, a problem within only the superstructural social institutions and bourgeois ideology, the feminist version sees sexual relations as at least as causal as economic relations in creating forms of social life and belief. Like feminist empiricism, the standpoint approach takes women and men to be fundamentally sex classes. In contrast to Marxist assumptions, they are not merely or perhaps even primarily members of economic classes, though class, like race and culture, also mediates women's opportunities to gain empirically adequate understandings of nature and social life. Just as feminist empiricism's radical future pointed toward epistemological assumptions that empiricism could not accommodate, so, too, the feminist standpoint's radicalism points toward epistemological assumptions that Marxism cannot contain.

The reader needs to remember at this point that standpoint theorists are not defending any form of relativism. I argued in the introductory essay that feminist researchers are never proposing that women's and men's characteristic social experiences provide *equal* grounds for reliable knowledge claims. This kind of relativist claim is not being advanced at the level of these epistemologies or justificatory strategies, as I noted earlier. For instance, it is not *equally true* that men's experiences provide the only legitimate origin of scientific problems, as traditional social science has assumed, and also that women's experiences provide a legitimate origin of scientific problems, let alone *the best* origin, as the standpoint theorists argue. For the standpoint theorists, this inequality is due to the fact that the activities of men shape the horizons of their knowledge and support interests in ignorance of the misery generated by the domination of women.

Should one have to choose between feminist empiricism and the feminist standpoint as justificatory strategies? I think not. A justificatory strategy is intended to convince, and it is important to notice that these two are likely to appeal to quite different audiences. Feminist empiricism is useful precisely because it stresses the continuities between traditional justifications of scientific research and feminist ones, as these would be understood by social scientists. In contrast, the feminist standpoint stresses the continuities between the radical upheavals in social understanding created by nineteenth-century class struggles and those created by feminist inquiry. These can be appreciated by political economists and those familiar with the post-Kuhnian histories and sociologies of science. The two epistemologies also appear locked into dialogue with each other. The relationship they have to each other reflects the struggles in mainstream discourses between liberal and Marxist theories of human nature and politics. Perhaps choosing one over the other insures choosing more than feminism should want of those paternal discourses; we are shaped by what we reject as well as by what we accept.

The tensions between the two feminist epistemologies and the tensions within each one suggest their transitional natures. They are *transitional epistemologies*, and there are good reasons to see that as a virtue. Let us see what these are before turning to the second question that has elicited contradictory feminist epistemological responses.

Transitional Epistemologies

Transitional epistemologies are appropriate for transitional cultures. In one sense or another every modern culture (as opposed to a traditional one) is undergoing changes and thus is transitional. Perhaps every legitimate modern epistemology is transitional. But some moments in history are more transitional than others, and we live in one of those moments.

In transitional cultures, epistemologies and sciences are frequently in tension with each other. We can look back in history and see that scientists have often used justificatory strategies which their own substantive scientific claims have undermined (sometimes inadvertently). For example, the early modern scientists routinely appealed to religious beliefs as a justification for their scientific claims; one important reason their claims should be accepted, they said, was because science "increased piety and learning" as it revealed in detail the goodness of God's designs. Some may have thought the appeal to religious authority merely an expedient move in light of the history of church censorship of scientific claims. But many scientists apparently believed what they said. Evidently, they didn't notice that their scientific claims were in the process of creating a world in which appeals to God would no longer provide satisfactory explanations of natural phenomena for many people.

We can see the tension between epistemologies and the sciences in the feminist epistemological discussions. We, too, live in a transitional culture: feminism is both a product and a cause of the changes underway. Perhaps sciences and epistemologies should always be in tension with each other: if the grounds for accepting knowledge claims are in perfect fit with the claims advanced, we should worry about what kinds of knowledge are being suppressed, subjugated, sent underground. After all, it is just such a hegemenous science/epistemology to which feminist scholars object. Androcentric biology and social sciences "proved" that women were biologically and socially inferior to men in myriad ways, and androcentric epistemology insisted that only men could be "knowers" and, therefore, legitimately question biological and social science claims. No wonder it had been so difficult to gather support for feminist social analyses.[7]

There are, thus, good reasons to regard the tensions within and between feminist empiricism and the feminist standpoint as valuable ones. Each paternal epistemology implicitly appeals to kinds of authority (of the individual, asocial observer; of the male wage-worker) that inquiry based on women's distinctive experiences is in the process of challenging. But in our transitional world, it is liberal and Marxist understandings that are still regarded as the legitimate ones in the social sciences. If women's authority in matters of knowledge were already recognized, that would be because we no longer needed a distinctively feminist social science. The tensions within the feminist epistemologies show that we are in no different a situation than were the early modern astronomers who appealed in one breath to the "increase in piety and learning" which the use of the telescope could advance. Perhaps the tensions between them point to, but do not themselves provide, directions toward a world in which piety toward traditional androcentric authorities will not be the most plausible way to justify new learning.[8]

Can There Be Feminist Science?

A second set of epistemological issues has arisen between the feminist empiricists and standpoint theorists, on the one hand, and the feminist critics of Enlightenment assumptions—the feminist postmodernists—on the other hand. The empiricists and standpoint theorists are both attempting to ground accounts of the social world which are less partial and distorted than the prevailing ones. In this sense, they are attempting to produce a feminist science—one that better reflects the world around us than the incomplete and distorting accounts provided by traditional social science. This science would not substitute one gender-loyalty for the others, but, instead, advance the objectivity of science. The feminist postmodernists raise questions about this epistemological project. Can there be a feminist science, or is any *science* doomed to replicate undesirable—and perhaps even androcentric—ways of being in the world?

There appear to be two at least somewhat distinct origins of skepticism about the kind of epistemological project in which both the feminist empiricists and the standpoint theorists are engaged. One emerges from feminists who participate in the agendas of such otherwise disparate discourses as those of semiotics, deconstruction, and psychoanalysis. The other has appeared in the writings of women of color.

The discourses mentioned are all deeply skeptical of universalizing claims for reason, science, language, progress, and the subject/self. Thus both of the feminist epistemological strategies we examined are legitimate targets of such skepticism, since they assume that through reason, observation, and progressive politics, the more authentic "self" produced by feminist struggles can tell "one true story" about "the world": there can be a kind of feminist author of a new "master story," a narrative about social life which feminist inquiry will produce. The critics respond, but "perhaps 'reality' can have 'a' structure only from the falsely universalizing perspective of the master. That is, only to the extent that one person or group can dominate the whole, can 'reality' appear to be governed by one set of rules or be constituted by one privileged set of social relations."[9]

This kind of criticism points to the way science constructs the fiction of the human mind as a glassy mirror which can reflect a world that is out there and ready-made for reflecting.[10] In contrast, we can detect ("in reality"?) that at any moment in history there are many "subjugated knowledges" that conflict with, and are never reflected in, the dominant stories a culture tells about social life. Moreover, some argue that women are a primary location of these subjugated knowledges—in fact, that the female subject is a "site of differences."[11] From this perspective, there can never be *a* feminist science, sociology, anthropology, or epistemology, but only many stories that different women tell about the different knowledge they have.

A second source of criticism of a unitary feminist perspective implied by the two epistemological strategies emerges from women of color. For instance, Bell Hooks insists that what makes feminism possible is not that women share certain kinds of experiences, for women's experiences of patriarchal oppression differ by race, class, and culture. Instead, feminism names the fact that women can federate around their common resistance to all the different forms of male domination.[12] Thus there could not be "a" feminist standpoint as the generator of true stories about social life. There could, presumably, only be feminist oppositions, and criticisms of false stories. There could not be feminist science, because feminism's opposition to domination stories locates feminism in an antagonistic position toward any attempts to do science—androcentric or not. These strains of postmodernism are richer and more complex than these few paragraphs can reveal. But one can already sense the troubles they create for other feminist epistemologies.

Should feminists be willing to give up the political benefits which can accrue from believing that we are producing a new, less biased, more accurate, social science? Social scientists might well want to respond to the postmodernist critics that we do need to federate our feminisms in opposition to all of the ways in which domination is enacted and institutionalized. But it is premature for women to be willing to give up what they have never had. Should women—no matter what their race, class, or culture—find it reasonable to give up the desire to know and understand the world from the standpoint of their experiences *for the first time*? As several feminist literary critics have suggested, perhaps only those who have had access to the benefits of the Enlightenment can "give up" those benefits.[13]

There are good reasons to find valuable the tension between these two epistemological positions. We need to think critically about the fundamental impulses of knowledge-seeking, and especially of science, even as we transform them to feminists' (plural!) ends.

One can easily see that the new feminist analyses unsettle traditional assumptions about knowledge as they challenge familiar beliefs about women, men, and social life. How could it have been otherwise when our ways of knowing are such an important part of our ways of participating in the social world?

NOTES

1. An earlier but fuller discussion of these issues can be found in my *The Science Question in Feminism* (Ithaca, N.Y.: Cornell University Press, 1986).

2. Zillah Eisenstein has made this point about liberal feminism, which is the political theory represented in the epistemological domain by feminist empiricism. See *The Radical Future of Liberal Feminism* (New York: Longman, 1981) and Catharine MacKinnon's discussion of the connections between empiricist "objectivism" and liberalism in the law in her paper in this volume.

3. For example, it is a problem that in most social sciences it is a norm of inquiry to have only male researchers listen to only male informants' reports of both men's and women's beliefs. It is widely recognized that men provide androcentric understandings of both men's and women's beliefs and behaviors.

4. Examples of these other recent sociological critiques of empiricist epistemological assumptions can be found in David Bloor, *Knowledge and Social Imagery* (London: Routledge & Kegan Paul, 1977); Karin Knorr-Cetina, *The Manufacture of Knowledge* (Oxford: Pergamon, 1981); and Bruno Latour and Steve Woolgar, *Laboratory Life: the Social Construction of Scientific Facts* (Beverly Hills, Calif.: Sage, 1979). For critiques of empiricist epistemology owing more direct debts to Marxist perspectives, see, for example, Leszek Kolakowski, *The Alienation of Reason: A History of Positivist Thought*, trans. N. Guterman (Garden City, N. Y.: Anchor Books, 1969); and Alfred Sohn-Rethel, *Intellectual and Manual Labor* (London: Macmillan, 1978).

5. If pressed, social scientists who advance empiricist defenses of their feminist research might well admit that drawing on women's experiences does more than merely enlarge the scope of inquiry. For instance, though Millman and Kanter are reasonably read as advancing an empiricist justification in the opening paragraphs of their essay, in the balance of the paper they appear to be fully aware that the insistent partiality of traditional sociology results in perverse views of women and social life. If feminists were merely arguing that men's experiences provide only a partial grounding for knowledge claims, then relativism would be an appropriate epistemological stance—contrary to the arguments I made in the introductory essay. Instead, it is precisely because we cannot "add women" and gender to the existing bodies of social scientific belief that relativism is inappropriate. Existing bodies of belief do not just ignore women and gender; they distort our understanding of all of social life by ignoring the ways women and gender shape social life and by advancing false claims about both women and gender.

6. In this volume, the feminist standpoint epistemologies are developed in the papers by Dorothy

Smith and Nancy Hartsock. See the citations in their essays. Other influential papers exploring this epistemology are Jane Flax's "Political Philosophy and the Patriarchal Unconscious: A Psychoanalytic Perspective on Epistemology and Metaphysics," in *Discovering Reality: Feminist Perspectives on Epistemology, Metaphysics, Methodology and Philosophy of Science*, ed. S. Harding and M. Hintikka (Dordrecht, Holland: Reidel Publishing Co., 1983); Hilary Rose, "Hand, Brain and Heart: A Feminist Epistemology for the Natural Sciences," in *Signs: Journal of Women in Culture and Society*, vol. 9, no. 1 (1983). See also my "Why Has the Sex-Gender System Become Visible Only Now?," in Harding and Hintikka, *Discovering Reality*. Is MacKinnon also proposing a standpoint epistemology?

7. This is a good place for the reader to test her/his ability to explain why it is that feminist inquiry *does not* fall into this epistemological trap.

8. See the discussion of the "New Science Movement" in England in W. Van den Daele, "The Social Construction of Science", in *The Social Production of Scientific Knowledge*, ed. E. Mendelsohn, P. Weingart, and R. Whitley (Dordrecht, Holland: Reidel Publishing Co., 1977). In chap. 9 of *The Science Question in Feminism*, I point to the interesting similarities between the goals of these 17th-century political and scientific radicals and those of the contemporary women's movement.

9. Jane Flax, "Gender as a Social Problem: In and For Feminist Theory," *American Studies/Amerika Studien*, Journal of the German Association for American Studies (1986): 17. It is interesting that one of the theorists responsible for contributing to the development of the standpoint epistemology here voices skepticism toward it. I think that postmodernist skepticisms of the sort indicated can be found in all of the feminist standpoint theorists—another good reason to see both as transitional epistemologies.

10. Richard Rorty's *Philosophy and the Mirror of Nature* (Princeton: Princeton University Press, 1979) provides a powerful criticism of the philosophical groundings of these assumptions.

11. Teresa de Lauretis's phrase, in *Feminist Studies/Critical Studies*, ed. T. de Lauretis (Bloomington: Indiana University Press, 1986), p. 14.

12. Bell Hooks, *Feminist Theory From Margin to Center* (Boston: South End Press, 1983).

13. See Nancy K. Miller, "Changing the Subject: Authorship, Writing, and the Reader," and Biddy Martin and Chandra Talpade Mohanty, "Feminist Politics: What's Home Got to Do with It?," in *Feminist Studies/Critical Studies*, ed. T. de Lauretis.

INDEX

Aldridge, Delores: black female participation in labor force, 101

Anastasi, Anne: president of American Psychological Association, 41

Anderson, Michael: size of household, 111

Aristotle: supervision of slaves not uplifting activity, 178n

Barkan, David: on "agency" approach to research, 31–32

Bart, Pauline: women and informal power, 32; acquaintance rape, 154n

Bataille, Georges: on violence, death, sexual activity, and reproduction, 171–73

Beard, Mary: women and the Renaissance, 26n

de Beauvoir, Simone: influenced by Engels, 22; women and the Renaissance, 26n; on killing as distinguishing characteristic of humanity, 173; transcendence and repetition, 178n

Bebel, August: influenced by Engels, 22

Becker, Howard: on creation of deviance, 75

Bennett, Lerone: on history and black experience, 77–78

Benston, Margaret: extension of tools of class analysis to women, 18

Bernard, Jessie: on David Barkan, 31; separate worlds of men and women, 33; discussed "tipping points," 53

Bettelheim, B.: sexism and fairy tales, 64

Bierstedt, Robert: sociology and the transcendental, 89, 91

Billingsley, Andrew: relationship of blacks to white society, 100; limitations of model, 101; adopted concept of ethnic subsociety, 103

Blauner, Robert: on black culture as product of discrimination, 104

Blos, P.: adolescence as individuation, 62

Boring, E. G.: on sex bias in psychological research, 39

Briggs, Jean: study of Eskimos and emotion, 92

Brownmiller, Susan: concept of rape in liberal tradition, 141; will and consent, 144; threat of rape as benefit to all men, 144

Burckhardt, Jacob: on place of women in Renaissance, 17, 26n

Cain, Mead: study of time use in Bangladesh, 133n

Calkins, Mary: president of American Psychological Society, 39

Carlson, Rae: on David Barkan, 31

Chekhov, Anton: discrepancy in judgment between women and men, 57–58

Chodorow, Nancy: on environment and sex difference, 59; refuted masculine bias of psychoanalytic theory, 60–61; and Lever's observations, 62; sex difference in social orientation, 66; adult development, 67; object relations theory, 167; sex difference in individuation, 167–68; father absence and fear of women, 179n

Clark, Kenneth B.: president of American Psychological Association, 41; on experience as researcher in Harlem, 78–79

Daniels: effects of informal male networks, 32; traditional roles of women, 33; need for research on women, 35

Davis, Angela: on historical lack of protective barriers for black women, 103

Davis, Natalie Zemon: on study of history of social relations of sexes, 21

DuBois, W. E. B.: "double consciousness" of blacks, 76

Duby, Georges: household as basis of taxation, 116

Duncan, Carol: on modern erotic art and themes of domination and victimization, 21

Ellis, Havelock: criticism of Freud, 43

Ellman, Mary: on the male mind and the penis, 150n

Engels, Friedrich: and history of feminist thought, 11; not member of proletariat, 11; relation of women's to men's history, 17–18; women and transition to patriarchy, 21–22; nuclear family, 111; on concept of production, 113, 114; presumed subordinaton of women, 138; assumptions and method, 152n; significance of human activity, 160; women's labor in home and in production, 165; sexual division of labor natural, 178n; development of the proletarian standpoint, 185

Erikson, E.: sex bias in stages of psychosocial development, 63–64; conventional versus neohumanist identity, 66

Flax, Jane: object relations theory, 167

Fox-Genovese, Elizabeth: nation-state and capitalism, 116

Franklin, Rosalind: and devaluation of women's research in natural sciences, 4

Frazier, E. Franklin: influence on study of black family, 98–99; isolation as source of matriarchy in black family, 100; limitations of model, 101; values of family life, 101

French, Marilyn: women's subsistence activities and class consciousness, 165–66

Freud, Sigmund: sex bias in works of, 40; and Havelock Ellis, 43; as basis of sex bias in psychology, 59; on sex difference in puberty, 62–63; criticized women's sense of justice, 68; on demarcation of the ego, 168–69

Friedan, Betty: criticized sexism of psychology, 38

Galton, Francis: sex bias in research of, 39

Gilligan, Carol: women and moral judgment, 10, 68

Goode, William: nuclear family, 111

Gordon, Milton: concept of ethnic subsociety, 103–104